Corruption and Money Laundering

Palgrave Series on Asian Governance

Series editor:
Michael Wesley, Griffith University, Australia

Books appearing in the series:

Dissident Democrats: The Challenge of Democratic Leadership in Asia
Edited by John Kane, Haig Patapan, and Benjamin Wong

Corruption and Money Laundering: A Symbiotic Relationship
by David Chaikin and J.C. Sharman

Corruption and Money Laundering

A Symbiotic Relationship

David Chaikin and J.C. Sharman

palgrave
macmillan

CORRUPTION AND MONEY LAUNDERING

First published in 2009 by
PALGRAVE MACMILLAN®
in the United States—a division of St. Martin's Press LLC,
175 Fifth Avenue, New York, NY 10010.

Where this book is distributed in the UK, Europe and the rest of the world, this is by Palgrave Macmillan, a division of Macmillan Publishers Limited, registered in England, company number 785998, of Houndmills, Basingstoke, Hampshire RG21 6XS.

Palgrave Macmillan is the global academic imprint of the above companies and has companies and representatives throughout the world.

ISBN: 978–0–230–61360–7

Library of Congress Cataloging-in-Publication Data

Chaikin, David.
Corruption and money laundering : a symbiotic relationship / David Chaikin and J.C. Sharman.
p. cm.—(Palgrave series on Asian governance)
Includes bibliographical references.
ISBN-13: 978–0–230–61360–7
ISBN-10: 0–230–61360–8
1. Corruption—Asia. 2. Corruption—Pacific Area. 3. Money laundering—Asia. 4. Money laundering—Pacific Area. I. Sharman, J. C. (Jason Campbell), 1973– II. Title.

JQ29.5C65 2009
364.1′323—dc22 2008047354

A catalogue record of the book is available from the British Library.

Design by Newgen Imaging Systems (P) Ltd., Chennai, India.

First edition: July 2009

10 9 8 7 6 5 4 3 2 1

Printed in the United States of America.

For Dorothy, Chaikin's late mother.

For Bilyana and Sharman's family.

Contents

Acknowledgments ix

Introduction 1

1 The Corruption-Money Laundering Nexus 7

2 International Responses to Corruption and Money Laundering 31

3 Points of Vulnerability 59

4 Senior Public Officials and Politically Exposed Persons 83

5 Best Practice for International Cooperation 115

6 The Marcos Kleptocracy 153

Conclusion: Solutions and Prospects for the Corruption-Money Laundering Nexus 187

Notes 199

Bibliography 213

Index 227

Acknowledgments

Our biggest debts are to those who were generous enough to give us their time in talking to us (either individually or together) about corruption, money laundering, and the relationship between them, though we emphasize that the book's conclusions should in no way implicate our interviewees. Because of the sensitivity of the topic many of these we do not acknowledge by name, but the institutions included the Asia-Pacific Group on Money Laundering, the Financial Action Task Force, Asia-Pacific Economic Co-operation, the United Nations Office on Drugs and Crime, the Organisation for Economic Co-operation and Development, the Commonwealth Secretariat, the Asian Development Bank, the World Bank, the U.S. Treasury, the Hong Kong Independent Commission Against Corruption, the Australian Federal Police, and the Australian Attorney General's Department. Relating to individuals we would also like to thank Gordon Hook, Rita O'Sullivan, David Shannon, Rick Small, Klaudijo Stroligo, Christine Uriarte, Kevin Vandergrift, Emile van der Does de Willebois, and Bruce Zagaris, though once again the book is not necessarily reflective of their views and the responsibility for any error lies with the authors

Chaikin would like to gratefully acknowledge financial support from the Faculty of Economics and Business at the University of Sydney, while Sharman gratefully acknowledges financial support from the Australian Research Council Discovery Grant DP0771521 and the ARC Centre of Excellence in Policing and Security.

Introduction

The twin problems of corruption and money laundering together have a devastating impact on national economies, international security, and human development. The World Bank and the International Monetary Fund (IMF) consider corruption the greatest obstacle to lifting millions of people out of poverty. Money laundering is vital to all profit-driven crime: the illegal trafficking of drugs, arms, and people, extortion and kidnapping, tax evasion and fraud, and especially corruption. From the spectacular collapse of the Bank of Credit and Commerce International in the early 1990s to current controversy over the British government's cancellation of an investigation into a corruption-tainted $86 billion arms deal, such crimes have attracted the attention of governments and the general public alike. As a result, these closely linked problems are the targets of a panoply of international policy and legal initiatives.

Corruption and money laundering are symbiotic: not only do they tend to co-occur, but more importantly the presence of one tends to create and reciprocally reinforce the incidence of the other. Corruption produces enormous profits to be laundered, estimated at more than $1 trillion of illicit funds annually,[1] funds that are increasingly laundered in the international financial system. At the same time, bribery, trading in influence, and embezzlement can compromise the working of anti-money laundering (AML) systems. This book analyzes the nature of the corruption-money laundering nexus and the various forms it can take. It proposes measures to enhance the effectiveness of AML systems by protecting their integrity, and argues for the potential contribution of AML measures to the fight against corruption.

A crucial concern motivating both the recent surge in policy interest in a corruption-money laundering nexus and this book is the implementation failures experienced in combating each issue in isolation. Why has the enactment by more than 180 countries of apparently comprehensive AML laws, regulations, and organizational structures failed to have a demonstrable impact on the level of money laundering? Similarly, why has the widespread acceptance of global anticorruption standards failed to reduce the level of large-scale international corruption?[2] This book suggests that the current strategies to deal with money laundering and corruption have fallen short of expectations at least in part because these problems have been considered in isolation. Our contention is that by investigating money laundering and corruption in a systematic and above all integrated fashion, the knowledge of both illicit activities and the remedies to address each will be improved. Following the money trail should help to detect and deter corrupt exchanges, while protecting AML agencies from corruption can be expected to boost their future effectiveness. Criminals do not consider financial crimes in isolation; neither should those seeking to attack such practices.

The central proposition of this book can be simply put: that corruption and money laundering, previously researched in isolation from each other, are closely interrelated. The failure to properly understand the corruption–money laundering nexus inhibits our knowledge of each problem, and undermines the success of policy measures to tackle them. Through a policy and legal analysis, the book shows how corruption facilitates money laundering, and vice versa. Furthermore, it demonstrates specifically how the responses developed to combat one type of financial crime can productively be employed in fighting the other. Though detailed definitions are provided in chapter one, money laundering can be understood as the process of obscuring the illegal origins of money derived from crime, corruption as the abuse of entrusted authority for private gain. Money laundering can take many different forms, but corruption covers an even wider range of behavior, from petty bribery to insider trading to wholesale looting by kleptocrat dictators. To prevent the discussion from being pulled in too many directions, coverage is limited to instances of large-scale corruption, often featuring senior political figures (so-called grand corruption), involving the cross-border movements of money or assets. As well as involving the largest dollar amounts, this kind of corruption poses the greatest threat to economic development, political stability, and the exercise of representative government. The occurrence and magnitude of these crimes are difficult to measure with any certainty, but corruption and money laundering are serious problems for most countries all over the world, rich and poor, large and small.

Although both corruption and money laundering have been high on the international governance agenda for some time, calls to analyze the relationship between them are much more recent. In the past few years the World Bank, the United Nations, the Asian Development Bank, and others have called for a more integrated approach to these two problems. For example, in 2007 the World Bank Governance and Corruption strategy noted that "Corruption and money laundering are a related and self-reinforcing phenomenon."[3] Similarly, the United Nations has stated: "There are important links between corruption and money-laundering...A high degree of co-ordination is thus required to combat both problems and to implement measures that impact on both areas."[4] Together with the launch of a joint UN–World Bank Stolen Assets Recovery initiative in September 2007 and its subsequent endorsement by the G7 leaders, these pronouncements underline the prominence of this issue, but also the current lack of detailed studies of the overlap and links between these kinds of crime.

In part this gap in our knowledge is to do with the relative novelty of corruption and money laundering as global policy priorities. Each has only come to prominence from the early 1990s. But more important is the artificial separation whereby agencies tend to focus too narrowly on their missions: anticorruption agencies deal with corruption, but not money laundering; AML bodies deal with money laundering, but not corruption. Furthermore, given the political sensitivity of large-scale or grand corruption and money laundering, diplomatic niceties tend to prevent a forthright consideration of policy and legal problems in confronting these issues.

Evidence for the arguments advanced in this book is drawn from a range of official documents and reports, academic writings, and media coverage. Especially important, however, are a series of discussions and interviews conducted by the authors in 2007 in Washington, London, Vienna, Paris, Strasbourg, Sydney, and Bangkok with key policymakers. Chaikin's earlier hands-on experience working with the Philippines government to recover funds stolen by former president Marcos also features prominently, especially in chapter six. Although the examples and lessons discussed are drawn from all over the globe, there is a particular focus on the corruption–money laundering nexus in the Asia-Pacific region. Despite the drug-related money laundering from the Golden Triangle and Afghanistan, and the grand corruption and crony capitalism in the Philippines, Indonesia, and elsewhere, these sorts of crime are probably no more prominent in the Asia-Pacific than anywhere else. But this region does provide a unique mix of rich, poor, and middle income countries operating under very different legal and political systems, together with an incredible diversity of cultures. Aside from global arrangements, there is a reasonable degree of regional cooperation to combat corruption and money laundering, but not to the atypically high degree found in Europe or the North Atlantic region more generally, where most analysts and scholars have devoted their attention.

Argument and Chapter Overview

Before mapping out the structure of the individual chapters to come, it is important to establish the book's three central aims. The first is to describe and analyze the various ways in which corruption and money laundering are related and often mutually reinforcing. The second aim is to diagnose vulnerabilities and shortcomings in the existing treaties, laws, and policies to combat corruption and money laundering, especially in the way these measures are implemented in practice. Last, the book argues for policy and legal reforms to target these kinds of financial crime more effectively.

With these overall goals in mind, chapter one first defines and explains corruption and money laundering. The second section gives a thumbnail sketch of the historical evolution of international standards to counter each type of crime. The remainder of the chapter explicates the corruption–money laundering nexus, illustrating the symbiotic tendencies at work with a case study from the South Pacific. Finally, it makes the argument (developed in the subsequent chapters) that success requires a more integrated approach to these related crimes. Such an integrated approach is both practical in legal and policy terms, as well as making good economic sense.

Chapter two provides an overview of the current initiatives relevant to the money laundering–corruption nexus. Because of the sprawling and uncoordinated nature of many of the relevant standards and policy developments in this area, often organizations pursuing complementary goals are unaware of the potential for productive intellectual exchange between them. It is still harder for those in private business and outside observers of the policy process to obtain such a synoptic view. This chapter will provide a succinct coverage of the various international initiatives in this area, from the United Nations to the Asian Development Bank. The strengths and weaknesses of these initiatives are then evaluated in subsequent chapters.

There is a presumption among practitioners that few of those engaged in corruption and money laundering are convicted for their activities, and only a very small proportion of the money involved in each is seized. Chapter three discusses the vulnerabilities that have led to such disappointing results. One example is the failure of many countries to criminalize money laundering related to corruption. The next section discusses the deficiencies in applying standard anticorruption techniques (particularly registers of assets and income sources) to AML bodies, but also to judges and prosecutors. The decision on whether or not to prosecute politically sensitive cases should be insulated from the government of the day. In the private sector, the ability of unregulated firms to establish and sell anonymous shell companies represents a significant weakness. Last, the bureaucratic disconnect between anticorruption and AML bodies undermines preventative surveillance and investigations.

Ensuring the integrity of political leaders and other senior public officials is simultaneously the most important and most difficult challenge of good governance. Chapter four explores how the finances of senior public officials (also know as politically exposed persons or PEPs) should be scrutinized to promote honesty and accountability. It is argued that the existing definition of senior public officials is too narrow. This category should include subnational leaders, senior figures in political parties, military and security police leaders, those directing public enterprises, and politically connected religious leaders. The treatment of extended families or clans, and extramarital affairs, are further complications. The most serious omission, however, is the restriction of PEP regulations in a large majority of countries to cover only foreign and not domestic officials. At present just how PEPs are to be identified is underspecified and has largely been delegated by public authorities to private firms, especially banks, who often do not have sufficient expertise and resources to perform this task. At the very least, governments must be prepared to give much more specific guidance to firms on this matter.

Grand corruption and money laundering are inescapably international phenomena. As such, any adequate response is fundamentally premised on international cooperation. Some of the most important issues discussed in chapter five are the exchange of intelligence, evidence, and suspects (extradition) across borders. The chapter surveys the variety of relevant international treaties and conventions to give a brief account of best international practice in these areas.

The recovery of funds stolen by corrupt officials and stashed abroad is one of the most important goals of mutual legal assistance. It is an area of pronounced interest among developing countries in Asia and elsewhere, as in the last few years hundreds of millions of dollars have been repatriated to the Philippines and Nigeria. The chapter demonstrates how policymakers can best use AML intelligence and asset confiscation provisions to recover these funds.

The chapter on Ferdinand Marcos is a practical case study of the money laundering–corruption nexus. It explains how Marcos was able to use his position as president of the Philippines to become reputedly one of the biggest thieves in history. The money laundering methods used by Marcos in hiding his corrupt proceeds were so sophisticated that government officials believe that less than 10 percent (approximately $1 billion at 1986 value) of his illicit assets were recovered after the decision of a Swiss court in 2003. Legal action to recover the Marcos plunder is still ongoing in several countries. Neither Marcos himself, nor his family, nor any of his cronies served even so much as a single day in jail for their crimes.

The Conclusion outlines the future prospects of the struggle against the corruption–money laundering nexus, and draws together the central findings and suggestions for reform made throughout the body of the book. Prominent among these conclusions is the current underutilization of AML laws, regulations, and institutions in fighting corruption. The AML system provides governments with very powerful tools for gathering financial intelligence, enhancing international cooperation and recovering assets laundered and hidden in other countries. Yet too often the potential of these measures to counter corruption is overlooked because of an excessively-rigid bureaucratic separation of roles between different agencies. Thus while a more integrated approach is not a magic bullet solution for either corruption or money laundering, currently there is a near-ironic mismatch: countries in the Asia-Pacific and elsewhere are sorely afflicted by corruption, and yet are failing to capitalize on the investment they have made in AML systems that could assist in countering corruption. Because corruption is the single most important financial crime in many countries, and perhaps even the greatest obstacle to economic development, even modest progress would provide significant benefits to national welfare. In combination the chapters to come indicate how such progress can be achieved.

Chapter 1

The Corruption-Money Laundering Nexus

Introduction and Overview

This first chapter is roughly divided into two halves. The first defines corruption and money laundering in separate sections explaining why each issue moved from the margins to the center of the international policy stage in the 1990s. Currently, corruption receives more attention than any other single factor in discussing economic development and political governance, whereas twenty years ago it was largely a nonissue. Four actors in particular are important in explaining this shift: the United States, the Organization for Economic Cooperation and Development (OECD), the World Bank, and Transparency International. More broadly, a growing conviction among economists that corruption lies behind many development failures, and well-publicized examples of spectacular grand corruption in Africa, Eastern Europe, Asia, and elsewhere changed the climate of opinion among the general public and policymakers alike. Money laundering was first seen as a new way of putting pressure on the international illicit drug trade. Led by the United States, the G7 countries established the Financial Action Task Force (FATF), which subsequently defined and diffused a standard package of anti-money laundering (AML) policies worldwide. In doing so, the FATF has enjoyed support from a constellation of other international institutions, ranging from the United Nations to specialized regional AML bodies.

The second portion of the chapter introduces the contention that corruption and money laundering have been treated as separate issues, whereas the responses can and should be integrated. There is a practical nexus between corruption and money laundering, but also a policy disconnect. This disconnect is a product of the separate historical origins of efforts to counter each kind of crime, and an overly rigid bureaucratic division of labor between anticorruption and

AML bodies. In developing countries, a lack of "ownership" of anti-corruption and AML policy can mean that their effectiveness may be a matter of indifference. A concrete instance of the corruption-money laundering nexus at work is drawn from the South Pacific island state of Vanuatu. This simple example illustrates how corrupt officials can launder illicit gains, and then subvert the mechanisms designed to detect and punish such misconduct. The final section argues that the legal overlap between conventions on corruption and money laundering, and the expense of AML systems, means that an integrated response is both desirable and practicable. At present, the potential contribution of AML regulations to tackle corruption is too rarely exploited.

Corruption

The term corruption covers a vast range of activities, from petty bribery to grand corruption, private sector insider trading to public sector embezzlement. In seeking to communicate the essence of the concept Transparency International initially hit upon the formula that corruption was "the abuse of public office for private gain." Even this expansive rendering was not broad enough, and thus to include private sector corruption this was revised to read "the misuse of entrusted power for private gain." A slew of international organizations including the Asian Development Bank, World Bank, and the IMF agreed in 2006 to settle on a definition of corruption as "the offering, giving, receiving, soliciting, directly or indirectly, of anything of value to influence improperly the actions of another party."[1] The UNCAC is more specific, including all of the following activities: the active and passive bribery of domestic and foreign public officials as well as officials from international organizations; the embezzlement or diversion of public property by an official; trading in influence or illicit enrichment by a public officials; and bribery and embezzlement in the private sector (Articles 15–22). Active bribery refers to the party paying the bribe, while passive bribery is the party receiving the money. According to the various international conventions and agreements, offering and soliciting bribes count as corruption, even if the advances are rejected and no exchange takes place; it is the intention that matters. Offering kickbacks through an intermediary or to a third party related to the target is also included, as is being an accessory or accomplice. Officials that steal public property (embezzlement) or improperly favor family or friends in discharging their duties (nepotism) are engaged in corruption. Corruption generally involves monetary stakes, but does not have to. Companies and other legal persons can be held criminally liable for corruption as well as individuals; the criminal liability of parent companies for the criminal acts of subsidiaries is less clear. There is a growing consensus that corruption can also occur between two private companies, rather than always having to involve a public official.

Given the scope of corruption, the sheer range of conduct covered under the various definitions is daunting. As stated in the introduction, this book deals only with a small but important subset: large-scale or grand corruption involving cross-border financial transfers. No attempt is made here to review the vast and growing literature on corruption by academics and practitioners.[2] It makes sense to focus on international grand corruption because it has been identified as perhaps the most damaging type, not only in the sums of money stolen, but also in the broader societal consequences.[3] The most recent meeting of countries party to the United Nations Convention Against Corruption (UNCAC) in 2008 singled out grand corruption by kleptocratic governments as a key priority. Central documents such as the OECD's Anti-Bribery Convention and the UNCAC emphasize the inherently international nature of corruption,[4] as well as the need for a coordinated multilateral response.

The relatively recent concern with corruption as an international policy issue stands in contrast to its long history in almost every society. It may well be true that for as long as there have been institutions and delegated power, this power has been abused by some for personal gain. Although there is a similarly long history of national efforts to stop domestic corruption, international efforts are of much more recent vintage, dating generally from the 1990s. Why did this issue come to prominence when it did and in the way it did? Four actors in particular have been important for the change whereby the campaign against corruption has achieved a major international policy and media profile: the United States, the OECD, the World Bank, and Transparency International. While details of the specific anticorruption strategies are spelled out in chapters 2 and 5, the role each of these actors played is briefly explained here.

In 1977 the United States passed the Foreign Corrupt Practices Act (FCPA), which outlawed U.S. corporations bribing foreign public officials. The Act came in the wake of the Watergate scandal, revelations of U.S. arms company Lockheed bribing Japanese, Dutch, Italian, and West German government officials, and a general effort to reestablish political and corporate probity. It was in many ways far ahead of its time. Most other OECD states not only had failed to criminalize the bribery of overseas officials, but instead facilitated such conduct through making the bribes tax deductible as a business expense. American multinational firms were put in a difficult position: they could hardly be seen to argue in favor of corruption, and yet to the extent that the law was enforced it put them at a significant commercial disadvantage relative to their overseas competitors. Since turning back the clock to the pre-1977 status quo was impossible, the logical move for U.S. corporations was to try to level the playing field by lobbying for an international agreement that also covered foreign competitors. Early action from Washington on bribing foreign officials thus set in play what Braithwaite and Drahos describe as a "ratcheting up" effect.[5] Just as tight U.S. domestic regulations on the use of ozone-depleting chemicals put U.S. businesses in the forefront of the campaign for strict international environmental standards, so too American firms' self-interested lobbying pushed the government for international action on the anticorruption front.

The UN General Assembly had briefly raised corruption as an issue in 1975,[6] but Washington's efforts to win an international agreement in the UN's Economic and Social Committee had been thwarted by disagreements with developing countries by 1981.[7] The United States then began to look to the OECD as a logical steward for responding to the issue. The OECD provided a much smaller and more homogenous group of nations than the UN, with a correspondingly greater chance of reaching a consensus. Furthermore, the multinational firms that U.S. government and corporate representatives were most worried about were disproportionately from fellow OECD members, rather than from developing countries. The Working Group on Bribery was set up under the Directorate for Financial and Enterprise Affairs, issuing a set of recommendations in 1994, with a further recommendation in 1996 that bribes no longer be tax deductible. After long negotiations with fellow members of the OECD (many of whom were only lukewarm toward the idea) the Convention on Combating the Bribery of Foreign Officials in International Business Transactions (the OECD Anti-Bribery Convention) was agreed upon in November 1997, and came into force in February 1999. Although this was neither a global agreement nor the first international anticorruption convention (the Organization of American States having concluded one in 1996), it did mark the first major formal commitment by the world's largest and most advanced economies that international corruption was unacceptable, and a problem that required a joint response. The Convention specifies that countries must criminalize the bribery of foreign officials. It sets out guidance on what kinds of behavior constitute bribery, appropriate remedies in terms of "effective, proportionate and dissuasive" criminal penalties and asset freezing and confiscation, sets standards for maintaining accurate accounting records, and enjoins members to extend the fullest mutual legal assistance. Significantly, the Convention specifies that those signatories that have made bribery of a domestic official a predicate offence for money laundering must do the same for the bribing of foreign officials also. As detailed in the next chapter, since 1999 the OECD Working Group on Bribery has involved itself in a searching process of peer review to assess signatories' compliance with the provisions of the Convention.

If the OECD Convention disrupted the understanding that corruption was "business as usual" in rich countries, it was the World Bank, supported by the IMF, that did so for poor countries. From the beginning of his presidency in 1995, James Wolfensohn was pivotal in the emphasis placed on "the cancer of corruption," a focus that has not changed since his term ended.[8] The World Bank's move coincided with more and more economists coming to the view that persistent development failures were often caused by weak or predatory corrupt states.[9] The IMF came around to the view that corruption caused significant macroeconomic failures.[10] By 2004 this issue had become so central that the World Bank simply stated: "The Bank has identified corruption as the single greatest obstacle to economic and social development. It undermines development by distorting the rule of law and weakening the institutional foundation on which economic growth depends."[11] Officially governance is broader than just corruption, being "the manner in which public officials and institutions acquire and exercise their authority to shape public policy and provide public goods and services."[12] In practice, though, "governance" is often used as a blander and less direct synonym where the word "corruption" might offend delicate sensibilities.

In keeping with the degree of emphasis placed on corruption, countering this phenomenon was seen to require a range of instruments and approaches. First was ensuring that the World Bank's projects themselves were run in a transparent and accountable fashion. Advice proffered to loan recipients was to protect the integrity of governmental processes (in revenue, expenditure, procurement, auditing, etc.), and to prevent corrupt practices through such means as setting up independent anticorruption bodies, but also involving the media and civil society to keep officials honest.[13] In a few high-profile cases the World Bank either threatened or did in fact cut off loans to those governments that repeatedly failed to hew to the new anticorruption line. Despite the presumption that, given that it held the purse strings, the World Bank should easily have been able to push recalcitrant Third World governments into line through cutting funding, in fact even countries as small and economically vulnerable as Equatorial Guinea and Papua New Guinea generally managed to keep their loans while at best going through the motions of promoting good governance.[14]

Behind the actions of the two Bretton Woods institutions, the OECD, and later the UNCAC was the nongovernmental organization (NGO) Transparency International. Founded in 1993, Transparency International was dedicated to an uncompromising struggle to stamp out corruption worldwide. The founders were critical of the lack of attention devoted to corruption by both governments and international organizations. Its subsequent success can be traced in large part to the fact that Transparency International has been close enough to intergovernmental organizations (especially the World Bank) to gain a hearing for its views and policy advice, yet distant enough to be direct and undiplomatic in criticizing the practice and toleration of corruption. As with most other successful NGOs, Transparency International has been very skilful in garnering media attention to both publicize its aims and apply political pressure in pursuit of these aims.

Perhaps the most coverage has been generated by the annual Corruption Perceptions Index.[15] As an illicit practice dependent on secrecy, the incidence and scale of corruption is obviously difficult to measure. To finesse this problem, from 1995 Transparency International began surveying foreign business people to find out their views on how prevalent corruption is in different countries, with the final result released as a ranking from the least to the most corrupt (for 2007 Denmark, Finland, and New Zealand were rated as least corrupt, and Somalia, Burma, and Iraq as the most). The Index has attracted criticism for being backward looking, tending to lock in initial low rankings, and unfairly suggesting that corruption is a developing country problem only.[16] Nevertheless, whatever its methodological flaws, in pragmatic terms it has been a runaway success, and has also caused some embarrassment for those at the lower end of the table. In 1999 Transparency International released a second ranking to capture the supply side of corruption: the Bribe Payers' Index, a survey of which country's multinational firms are most likely to engage in improper practices. Of the thirty major exporting countries assessed in 2006, firms from Switzerland, Sweden, and Australia were perceived as least likely to engage in corruption (though with reference to the last-mentioned this preceded the discovery that the Australian Wheat Board had been paying massive kickbacks to Saddam Hussein's government). Those from India, China, and Russia were regarded as most likely to offer bribes. Although not always receiving the same high profile, Transparency International as a whole and its various national chapters have been active in researching and publishing on corruption, and attending the international circuit of anticorruption meetings, seminars, and workshops. It has promoted the use of holistic anticorruption strategies involving the executive, legislature, audit institutions, judiciary, media, civil society, international institutions, and dedicated anticorruption bodies as detailed in the Anti-Corruption Handbook and National Integrity Systems studies. Through a combination of its media and behind-the-scenes activities, Transparency International has become perhaps one of the most successful NGOs in achieving policy change.

Thanks to the initiatives and lobbying of the U.S. government, the OECD, the World Bank, Transparency International, and others, the climate of international opinion toward corruption by the late 1990s was completely different from that which prevailed in the 1970s and 1980s. Then, with the exception of the United States, corruption was tacitly accepted by rich and poor country governments, at least in international transactions if not at home. The World Bank and IMF regarded corruption as a political matter for governments and thus outside their remit. Economists and other scholars saw corruption as either irrelevant for economic growth, or perhaps even in a positive light as the grease that made the wheels of government turn.[17]

Instances such as the chaotic and corrupt transition to a market economy in Russia and elsewhere in Eastern Europe, the continuing failure of standard development nostrums in Africa, and later the emerging market crisis of 1997–98, often attributed to crony capitalism, helped to change both elite and mass perceptions. Economists inside and outside the policy world increasingly argued that "institutions matter,"[18] and thus that predatory governments or corrupt officials would stifle economic growth. Through a combination of "seminar diplomacy," donor advice, and occasional prodding through loan conditionality and political pressure, standard tools of corruption prevention policy (codes of conduct, independent anticorruption commissions, etc.) diffused in the developing world. Among the OECD, consistent pressure from the United States and outsiders such as Transparency International led to a compact whereby each member agreed to foreswear the use of bribery in gaining an advantage for its firms abroad. The formal results of this normative shift is the framework of global and regional treaties and agreements designed to fight the international manifestations of corruption and facilitate cooperation between states in addressing this type of crime (detailed in the following chapter). The practical results, however, are much less apparent. The measurement difficulties notwithstanding, even among those most active in pushing the cause of anticorruption, there is a distinct lack of optimism that corruption is in retreat. Despite the undoubted progress in international and domestic law, there are still very few convictions for corruption in developed or developing countries. In general, survey data compiled by Transparency International and the World Bank Institute show that only a few countries have experienced a decline in levels of corruption. Thus the progress in consciousness raising and legislating has yet to be matched by widespread implementation successes.

Money Laundering

Money laundering refers to the process of obscuring the illicit origins of money derived from crime. Aside from the general metaphor of taking illegal "dirty" money and "cleaning" it to look legitimate, the term more directly derives from the (possibly apocryphal) story of Al Capone's strategy of using laundromats and other small businesses to disguise profits from bootlegged alcohol during the prohibition era. The term only became common in the wake of the Watergate investigations in the 1970s. Money laundering occurs after a predicate offence has brought money into the hands of criminals. Predicate offences such as robbing a bank, selling heroin, or people trafficking are motived by criminals' desire for profits, but may leave the offenders with the problem of reintroducing large sums of money into the legitimate financial system without arousing the suspicions of law enforcement authorities. Consider, for example, the problem of those who robbed the Northern Bank in Northern Ireland in 2004 of almost $50 million in cash. It is hardly viable to simply walk into another bank and try to deposit this sum of money. Money provides both the motive for many crimes, but also the means, in terms of working capital. By disrupting this illicit finance, AML measures aim to make the predicate offences less profitable, and thus less attractive, as well as denying criminals working capital. By countering money laundering as an offence distinct from the underlying crime it is hoped that the number of predicate offences will fall.

Hiding the illicit origins of criminal money is probably as old as crime itself. But with the rise of both cross-border crime and the growth in legitimate international finance and trade, money laundering has taken on an increasingly international character. To a greater and greater extent, criminals have faced the problem of returning "dirty money" from foreign markets to their home country. But there are also increased opportunities for obscuring the true source of this money from national law enforcement authorities provided by the complexities of increasingly globalized banking and finance sectors. Those looking to escape the long arm of the law can gain advantage from the relative ease and speed of using the international financial system compared with the difficulties and delays associated with cooperation between different national police and judicial institutions.

More than any other single issue, concerns about the international drug trade put money laundering on the policy agenda in the 1980s as a problem requiring a coordinated response from states. This reflected the huge amounts of money associated with the drug trade (reputed to be the world's second or third most valuable commodity after weapons and oil) running into hundreds of billions of dollars, and increasing recognition of the social and political damage drug crime inflicted on source, transit, and consumer countries. This rise to prominence also reflected the domestic political importance of the drug issue within the United States, which led the way as the first country to criminalize money laundering in 1986. American law enforcement bodies' interest in fighting crime through following the money trail also arose in line with the increased use of the Racketeer-Influenced and Corrupt Organizations (RICO) Act of 1970 against criminal syndicates from the mid-1980s.[19] The RICO Act has some similarities with money laundering laws in targeting the assets of criminal enterprises.

The prominence accorded to the "war on drugs" in U.S. domestic policy goes a long way to explain the energetic support from the United States for an international AML regime. The limited success (at best) of efforts to counter drug trafficking led to increased interest in alternative avenues of attack against this type of crime. Targeting the huge sums of money associated with illegal drugs sales seemed a promising response. The international nature of the drug trade quickly led to domestic measures being internationalized. Although much of Washington's international AML efforts has occurred within the multilateral setting of the FATF, the first response was unilateral. To this day, the United States has retained powerful unilateral options to supplement the actions of the FATF and other similar multilateral institutions. Despite some variations, these unilateral measures have usually been given teeth by the threat to exclude targeted individuals, firms or even states from the U.S. banking market, and from international wire transfer networks dominated by the United States. On the other side of the Atlantic, the Council of Europe, Interpol, and the Commonwealth also assisted the process of placing the issue of money laundering on the international agenda, working out the parameters of the problem, and drafting a response with a series of conferences and working groups. The first major international agreement to counter money laundering was the 1988 UN Vienna Convention Against Illicit Trade in Narcotic Drugs and Psychotropic Substances. The name alone suggests the limited view of money laundering as a facet of the drug trade, but this notwithstanding the Vienna Convention set down many of the main elements of the current AML regime.[20] The first of these was to create the criminal offence of money laundering. The fact that over the last two decades over 180 countries have criminalized money laundering in some form or other is a notable achievement in itself. The Vienna Convention established the principle of confiscating the proceeds of drug crime, which in turn necessitated procedures for tracing and freezing these assets. The Convention also made incremental though important improvements in mutual legal assistance procedures including the international collection of evidence and extradition.

From the early 1990s, international AML efforts experienced a rapid and massive expansion as major international institutions endorsed and diffused AML rules, and new specialized AML international organizations were created. The most important of these was the FATF, created in 1990. Substantively, the coverage of the AML laws expanded both legally (away from the narrow focus on drugs to all other profit-driven crimes) and geographically (beyond the initial core of rich OECD states to include the developing world). As the institutional guardian of the Vienna Convention, the UN Office on Drugs and Crime (UNODC) was increasingly active in playing a supporting role by providing technical assistance to developing states to translate the general obligations of the AML regime into national legislation. The European Union, but even more so the Council of Europe, were also very active in AML policy across the continent in the 1990s. The Strasbourg-based Council of Europe concluded the Convention on the Laundering, Search, Seizure and Confiscation of the Proceeds from Crime in 1990. Aside from being the first to use the term "money laundering," this treaty shifted the focus from drugs to all crimes, and explicitly invited signatories from beyond the membership of the organization itself. Beginning in 1991, the European Commission has passed three directives mandating increasingly strict standards to counter money laundering among the member states.

The most influential body in setting AML standards from its inception to the present day has undoubtedly been the FATF. The FATF is not a formal treaty organization, but rather depends on periodic decisions to renew its existence by member states. Meeting in plenary sessions three times a year, it has only a small permanent secretariat of fifteen staff members housed within the OECD headquarters in Paris. But the FATF's lack of formal treaty status and limited personnel have not restricted its policy influence, both within and beyond its membership. The first international institution founded specifically to counter money laundering, the FATF once again grew out of a concern with the war on drugs. Following the call of the 1989 G7 heads of state summit, the organization took shape in an intensive process of meetings between government officials and regulators in late 1989 and early 1990. Aside from the G7 members, participation was soon extended to the other OECD states. The FATF has since been keen to expand to incorporate "strategically important" developing countries, including Brazil, Argentina, South Africa, India, China, as well as Russia, with a further round of expansion in progress.

The main output of the initial round of meetings was the 40 Recommendations, laying out best international practice in AML. Although the Recommendations have been periodically revised since 1990, with 9 Special Recommendations on the financing of terrorism added in 2001, the basic provisions have remained substantially the same. The FATF echoed the Vienna convention in stressing the importance of criminalizing money laundering and enhancing international cooperation in keeping with the borderless nature of the threat. In a crucial departure from the Vienna Convention, however, the Recommendations held that the criminal justice system was not sufficient to tackle money laundering by itself. Instead, it was necessary to concentrate on preventing money laundering through regulating private financial intermediaries, particularly banks. Subsequently, it has been private financial firms, following FATF-mandated rules legislated by national governments, that have borne most of the burden of fighting money laundering. Furthermore, from 1996 the FATF revised the Recommendations to shift the focus from drug money to illegal profits from all types of crime. Specifically, banks and other financial institutions are enjoined to apply "Know Your Customer" rules, meaning that they must verify the true identity of those opening accounts with reference to passports, driver's licences, and other official identification documents. Banks have further been placed under the obligation to report "suspicious transactions" (for instance, customers depositing large amounts of cash) to the authorities. The coverage of these regulations has progressively been expanded to include other businesses such as insurance companies, bureaux de change, check cashing offices, and casinos.

In tandem with the FATF, the UNODC, the Commonwealth, and others have helped to extend the coverage of the AML regime into the developing world through conferences and technical assistance programs. From 2002 these institutions were joined by the World Bank and the IMF. By 2005 the FATF had fostered the creation of eight new regional international organizations, covering every part of the world, each devoted to propagating the 40 + 9 Recommendations among its member states through self- and peer-assessment. These regional bodies are the Caribbean Financial Action Task Force (founded in 1990), Asia-Pacific Group on Money Laundering (1997), the Council of Europe's MONEYVAL (1997), the Eastern and Southern African Anti-Money Laundering Group (ESAAMLG; 1999), the Inter-Governmental Group against Money Laundering in West Africa (GIABA 1999), the Financial Action Group of South America (GAFISUD 2000), the Middle Eastern and North African Financial Action Task Force (MENAFATF 2004), and the Eurasian Anti-Money Laundering Group (EAG 2004).

The Asia-Pacific Group (APG) has been one of the most active regional bodies and is also the largest, currently comprised of thirty-six countries. The Group includes an incredible amount of diversity and geographical range within its membership: from the tiny South Pacific island nations, to India, Pakistan, and Afghanistan, from Japan and South Korea, through to Southeast Asia, Canada, and the United States. One prominent absentee is China (instead part of the Eurasian Group), which refused to join in a fit of diplomatic pique due to the inclusion of Taiwan within the APG. The secretariat is based in Sydney, and, as with the FATF, it has the same responsibilities of coordinating regular mutual evaluations of its members, holding annual plenaries and more specialized workshops as the other regional bodies, again all in line with the 40 + 9 Recommendations.

A key concern driving this process of the international diffusion of AML regulations has been the fear of a "displacement effect": that because of the mobility of crime and money, tough standards in one country could be out-flanked if criminals could merely redirect financial flows to other countries with lax standards. The defining metaphor holds that the international AML regime "is only as strong as the weakest link in the chain." Ultimately concerns about this displacement effect, and frustration with voluntary, capacity-building approaches in strengthening "weak links" gave rise to the strategy of blacklisting by the FATF. The FATF is, and was always intended as being, a limited membership club that nevertheless is devoted to tackling an inherently global problem. Rather than just seeking to ratchet up its members' AML standards (through self- and peer-assessment), the FATF has from its inception also sought to encourage nonmember states to do the same. The organization has enjoyed substantial success in this aspect of its mission. For the first decade of its existence, the FATF succeeded in diffusing its 40 Recommendations through a program of outreach and a series of regional seminars, often cosponsored by other international organizations. From 2000, however, this consensual approach was eclipsed by a strategy of coordinated blacklisting, represented by the Non-Co-operative Countries and Territories (NCCT) list.

Although the FATF eschewed a blacklist in its formative years, it reserved the option of creating such a list if more consensual methods proved insufficient.[21] The first step in compiling the list was for member states (assisted by the secretariat) to discuss which nonmember jurisdictions had been causing them particular problems. Four geographically delineated review groups were set up to assess twenty-nine jurisdictions against a slate of twenty-five criteria.[22] In June 2000 the NCCT list was formally released featuring fifteen jurisdictions.[23] Recommendation 21, requiring extra scrutiny of transactions from these jurisdictions, was applied, with a further escalation of pressure and perhaps ultimately sanctions reserved for those who did not comply in a timely fashion. To be delisted, the countries in question not only had to accept the FATF Recommendations, but to demonstrate to the satisfaction of the FATF that these principles were being applied in practice. A second and third wave of reviews in 2001 and 2002 saw new countries being added, while other adjudged to have complied were removed.[24] In November 2002 the FATF suspended the process of adding new countries after pressure was exerted by the IMF Board (among others), unhappy with the coercive cast of the NCCT list.[25] In return the IMF agreed to adopt FATF AML standards in performing its assessments of member states' financial systems. Aside from the countries that ended up on the lists, the NCCT list quickly concentrated the attention of many other states, which rushed through legislation to avoid being caught by the FATF in subsequent rounds.[26] After 2001, the association of money laundering and terrorism has produced a massive expansion in the amount of money made available by governments to combat general financial crime.

The response to money laundering has in many ways been a showpiece of international cooperation. Led by the United States, developed states have designed a demanding set of AML regulations. Rather than mere gestures or exhortations, these involve far-reaching and expensive reforms by both governments and private firms. Furthermore, these standards have now been exported to the majority of developing countries, including some tax haven countries that were previously the least willing to drop the veil of financial secrecy. The relevant international organizations have been understandably keen to claim credit for these successes.

Much harder to assess, however, is whether all this treaty-making, legislating, regulating, and technical assistance has actually made a difference in reducing money laundering. There are obvious measurement difficulties in deciding to what extent, if at all, AML policies have been effective. Nevertheless, many of the most prominent experts are skeptical that the exponential increase in resources devoted to AML policies has brought much in the way of a reduction in crime.[27] The relevant international organizations themselves, although more upbeat, are still notably cautious in their claims about the extent to which money laundering has been disrupted. A study in Britain, with some of the world's toughest policies in place, indicated that laundering a sum of money would cost at most 5–15 percent of the principal.[28]

Corruption and Money Laundering: The Disconnect and the Nexus

In earlier discussing the development of corruption and money laundering as separate international policy priorities that happened to come on to the agenda at around the same time, the structure of the chapter so far has mimicked what was until recently the prevailing wisdom. There just didn't seem to be much in common between fighting drug lords and alleviating poverty in Africa. This last section first seeks to explain why these two issues have been considered in isolation, then puts forward an exemplary actual case of the corruption-money laundering nexus, and finally previews the logic of an integrated response to this symbiotic relationship. The empirical example is drawn from the South Pacific, but typifies the common linkages between corruption and money laundering. The last section puts forward the case that combining previously isolated responses to these kinds of financial crime is practical because of the substantial overlap in the requirements of international anticorruption and AML regimes. It is desirable because countries are currently getting poor value for money as they fail to exploit the anticorruption potential of AML regulations.[29]

The main reasons for the failure to appreciate the close relationship between corruption and money laundering are primarily historical and bureaucratic. The policy communities and specific institutions created to fight one or other type of crime arose with separate and unrelated missions. Functional specialization and bureaucratic inertia have tended to freeze this separation in place. Financial intelligence units (FIUs) see corruption as outside their area of responsibility, and anticorruption bodies regard money laundering in the same way. Additionally, in many developing countries there is a belief that AML and anticorruption policies and institutions have been foisted upon them by outsiders.[30] Rather than addressing important local priorities, agencies in each area are often maintained on sufferance to act as window-dressing in impressing powerful outsiders. In this view, the point of AML and anticorruption bodies is not to fight corruption, money laundering, or the links between them, but rather to enable local officials to pay lip service to dominant norms in various international fora.

Evidence for the bureaucratic disconnect between anticorruption and AML policy can be drawn from a statement of the ESAAMLG:

> Another problem within the region is that the issue of money laundering is misunderstood and regarded as a separate, "stand alone" entity. This is evidenced by the fact that some member countries have developed financial sector reform strategies and anti-corruption strategies that have failed to address the FATF recommendations... Country policy makers should be aware that... money laundering is the flip side of corruption and other criminal activity. Corruption is one of the predicate offences for money laundering. Cutting off the means to use the proceeds of crime is a major deterrent... It is therefore of paramount importance that AML/CFT [Countering the Finance of Terrorism] programmes are integrated not only within national development plans but also within financial sector reform and anti-corruption programmes.[31]

Those interviewed from international organizations responsible for providing technical assistance in these areas say it is common for AML and anticorruption bodies from the same country to have never heard of each other, let alone cooperated operationally.

Perhaps another reason why this disconnect persists is because of a lack of ownership (to use the development jargon) among developing countries of anticorruption and AML policies. Interviews with a number of officials from five countries in Africa, Asia, and the Caribbean indicate that money laundering and corruption are not domestic priorities. Instead, the fact that so many developing countries are passing laws and regulations and establishing institutions to combat money laundering is a matter of impressing the international community, particularly aid donors and the Bretton Woods institutions. Further interviews with officials from international organizations and bilateral aid agencies providing technical assistance in this field confirm the picture that although, for example, it may be "an article of faith" among rich countries that poor countries need AML systems,[32] the latter have a much more ambivalent and pragmatic attitude to the subject.

But this disconnect is not limited to developing countries. In its summary of the second round of country surveys, the OECD Working Group on Bribery discusses how financial intelligence gathered by AML agencies is rarely used in corruption investigations.[33] Although conclusive evidence is lacking it seems that both the private sector firms responsible for lodging reports of suspicious transactions and the AML agencies themselves have something of a blind spot when it comes to transactions that may be suspicious on the grounds of corruption. The guidelines and examples provided by AML bodies for private firms on when to make a report discuss crimes such as drug trafficking or fraud, but almost never corruption. In addition, to fully exploit the potential of greater financial intelligence, asset confiscation provisions, and so on in reducing corruption, private sector firms, police, prosecutors, and judges should be aware that money laundering and corruption are related crimes, and that the responses are complementary.[34]

What this disconnect misses is the close affinity between corruption and money laundering, as well as the utility of policy and legal responses developed to fight one type of crime for also dealing with the other. To the extent that AML bodies are corrupt, they will not be effective. For the struggle against money laundering as a whole to be effective, not only must the integrity of FIUs be protected, but so too that of judges, prosecutors, and the private sector reporting entities providing the raw data for law enforcement (as detailed in the next chapter). To the extent that corruption is kept out of the system, more money launderers will tend to be caught and the associated underlying crimes can be expected to fall.

But if corruption can facilitate the laundering of the proceeds of crime, so too can money laundering aid corruption. For example, if a minister or other senior public official is given a large cash bribe in return for selecting a particular foreign contractor, the official in question must hide the illicit origins of these funds. In essence the challenge is no different from those faced by drug-traffickers or any other profit-driven crime: how to distance the money from the original crime (i.e., the predicate offence), and reintroduce it into the financial system without arousing suspicion. Once again, not only are the crimes related, but the responses to corruption and money laundering are potentially complementary. To the extent that it is difficult to launder kickbacks and bribes, the barriers to corruption are raised, there is more likelihood of getting caught, and the amount of corruption in the system should decline. Some examples in the following paragraphs help to establish this proposition.

Although grand corruption is often the stuff of headlines, unlike many of the other examples reviewed in this book the following material on Vanuatu from the 1990s received little outside coverage.

But as is demonstrated later, this lack of international attention in no way diminished the local impact. Furthermore, this instance exemplifies the common elements of the corruption-money laundering nexus at work in countless other nations in a stark manner. Key features include: the use of the international financial system and particularly foreign shell companies to launder bribes; senior officials' efforts to undermine accountability mechanisms to protect their laundered money; the severe and widespread impact of corruption in threatening development and political stability; and finally the tendency of perpetrators to escape unconvicted with the illicit funds, largely as a result of implementation failures rather than bad laws as such. Each of these elements is dealt with at length in the following chapters.

In January 1992, Cyclone Betsy caused extensive damage to the South Pacific archipelago state of Vanuatu. Among others, the French government sent $30,000 to aid recovery efforts. Maxime Carlot Korman, the prime minister of Vanuatu at the time, opened an account "Carlot Maxime Comité Secours [Relief Committee] Cyclone Betsy" with the Banque d'Hawai'i (Vanuatu), citing himself as sole beneficiary, and granting power of attorney over the account to his secretary Gerald Leymang. The French aid money was deposited into the account, which formed the nucleus for a personal and political slush fund. To augment this fund, the prime minister then began contacting Vanuatu's honorary consuls overseas requiring them to provide him with cash or money via wire transfer to retain their positions. The text of a leaked handwritten fax to one such consul, Paul Than, is indicative:

> For my election, I make this request to be put to our Asian Trade Commissioners, I ask them to transfer their contribution as requested to my ASIACITI TRUST Company in Hong Kong and Shanghai Banking Corporation 10 Collyer Quay Ocean Building # 01, Singapore 0104, MASCOT HOLDING INC. # 141 246660 01. Or in Malaysia at the Kuala Lumpur Bank, BUMIPUTRA MALAYSIA BERHAD, No. BRANCH AIRPORT A/C CA 1173–48. A / C CA 1173–48. Paul, the Singapore Honorary Consul has already put 10,000 dollars US in my account. Mr Masumoto promises me to meet me [*sic*] in Tokyo and give me 5,000 dollars on 24 August. Please Paul ask the others to do their part immediately. If I receive negative answers from the others I will personally as PM and Minister for Foreign Affairs cancel their nomination as Vanuatu Government Reps in [*sic*] overseas.[35]

Much of the money received was siphoned from the corporate accounts in Singapore and Malaysia to the Cyclone Betsy Relief Fund account, and some of the remainder to the prime minister's personal account. The receipts totalled $1.1 million, or forty-five times the prime minister's annual salary.[36] In the two days before the November 1995 election the prime minister made 256 cash withdrawals and checks to cash between $150 and $800.[37] Much of the remainder of the money was transferred to the prime minister's personal account, with some used to fund his party's convention. Upon this evidence being made public after an investigation by the ombudsman in 1998, Mr. Korman (then former prime minister) did not contest either that the accounts in Singapore and Malaysia were under his control, or that he had illegally solicited the money for reelection.[38] No charges were laid, and there were no efforts to recover the money.

What light does this relatively obscure example shed on the corruption-money laundering nexus? First, although the efforts to disguise the corrupt payments were certainly crude, they do illustrate some typical features. The prime minister disguised the payments by passing them through overseas bank accounts in the name of a foreign shell company under his control (Mascot Holdings Singapore), the company having been set up earlier by a Corporate Service Provider (Asiaciti Trust). A further effort to break the link between the prime minister and the money was by using an intermediary for the withdrawals, by granting power of attorney over the Cyclone Betsy relief account to his secretary. Second, the relatively small amounts involved in the Cyclone Betsy case should not obscure the significance of this kind of corruption. Another report from the ombudsman in December 1997 found that from 1993 to 1995 almost the entire cabinet, parliament, and leadership cadre of the ruling party had been instructing the directors of the national pension fund to grant them unsecured loans, despite the formal legal independence of the board and in violation of the rules governing the scheme.[39] Once the ombudsman released her report, major riots broke out in the nation's capital, the government appealed for foreign assistance, and a state of emergency was declared. On two separate occasions over the past decade the government of Vanuatu has been bribed by con men to guarantee fraudulent loans that would have emptied the national treasury.

Third, the Vanuatu case shows the tendency of senior public officials to protect their corrupt dealings by undermining accountability mechanisms. In this case, attempts to remove the ombudsman in 1997 by the same ministers accused of corruption were foiled by the strong independence provisions built into the 1995 Act establishing the office. Attempts to cut pay and conditions for the staff were prevented by fact that the office was funded by the Commonwealth and other foreign donors. Staff without permanent residency rights were threatened with expulsion from the country,[40] but the final defeat of the ombudsman was when parliament repealed the authorizing Act in 1998. A new ombudsman act was passed and a new ombudsman appointed, with the new incumbent being a political ally of those in cabinet, despite himself facing charges of embezzlement at the time of appointment from a previous position at the Development Bank of Vanuatu. The new act removed the independence of the ombudsman office, with staff members now brought under the same rules as any other public servants. The ombudsman could no longer go to the Supreme Court if recommendations were not followed, and the office's information gathering powers were truncated.

Fourth, and typically, despite serious criminal conduct alleged and the wealth of detailed evidence presented, no charges were ever laid against senior officials, nor was any corrupt money recovered as a result of the reports. The commissioner of police was unwilling to further investigate the conduct revealed (perhaps because another ombudsman report had revealed his two prior criminal convictions and illegal appointment by Prime Minister Korman; Vanuatu Ombudsman's Office, "Public Report on the Improper Appointment of Mr. Luc Siba as the Commissioner of Police and his Misconduct in Office"). In most instances the director of public prosecutions declined to lay charges; in the few exceptions, either cases failed on technicalities, or were ordered but never took place. Miscreants got away scot-free, thanks largely to implementation failures. Willie Jimmy, the finance minister identified as being at the heart of several of the most serious scandals in the 1990s, including unauthorized loans from the retirement fund, has been regularly reelected and retains his cabinet position.[41] In two ways, however, the Vanuatu example is misleading: it is not common to have so much detail on successful corrupt dealings, and there is no reason to believe that corruption in Vanuatu was or is worse than in most other countries. Indeed, Vanuatu was selected as one of the first countries to receive unconditional aid from the U.S. Government's Millennium Challenge Corporation on the grounds of its exceptionally clean government, scoring in the top 1 percent of countries for control of corruption in 2008.[42] In summary, the main features of the nexus are present in this case. Corrupt officials seek to launder illicit funds in the international financial system. These same officials seek to subvert the institutions responsible for combating corruption and financial crime, although as Vanuatu did not have an FIU until 2000 they were not dedicated AML agencies. And as chapter 2 seeks to demonstrate, the application of AML procedures (e.g., enhanced scrutiny of senior officials, establishing the true ownership of shell companies, reporting suspicious transaction) would have made this kind of corruption much more difficult.

The Case for Using AML Systems in an Anticorruption Role

This final section of the chapter is devoted to outlining two compelling reasons for using AML systems to fight corruption. The first is the degree of overlap whereby meeting international anticorruption standards largely requires fulfilling international AML standards. The second, and more important, factor is the expense and current underutilization of AML systems. Previously limited to rich countries, the spread of the AML regime into the developing world has seen poor countries bearing higher and higher direct and indirect costs to meet best international practice in this area. Because many developing countries have less sophisticated financial crime (with much smaller financial sectors and more locally centered illicit drug economies compared to developed countries), corruption is often the major source of funds to be laundered.[43] But so far, expensive AML regimes have not been deployed against corruption. In this context, the leading work on the cost effectiveness of AML systems notes that for poorer countries "an effective AML regime is essentially a luxury good."[44]

Complying with prevailing international anticorruption standards entails meeting international AML standards. The complementarities in responding to these related types of financial crimes have thus been increasingly recognized in international conventions, even if this has not filtered down to the level of implementation. This legal overlap is most obvious in the 2003 UNCAC (as of January 20, 2009, signed by 140 countries and ratified by 129[45]). But other UN conventions devoted to fighting the drug trade (the 1988 Vienna Convention), organized crime (the 2000 Palermo Convention), and the financing of terrorism (2002) also call upon signatories to adopt the main planks of AML policy. In combination, these three conventions call on state parties to criminalize money laundering; set up systems to apply due diligence to the customers of financial institutions; adopt a reporting regime for suspicious transactions; set up FIUs to gather and collate financial data to pass on to the police; and follow the recommendations of international AML bodies. The UNCAC calls for the same commitments (see especially Articles 14, 23, 52, and 58), and such steps as setting up arrangements to monitor cross-border movements of cash, including sender and receiver information on wire transfers, applying extra scrutiny to the finances of public officials, and ensuring cooperation among judicial, law enforcement, and financial regulatory authorities.[46] Similar provisions are found in the various regional conventions aimed at the same sort of problems, whether by the Organization of American States, the African Union, or the Asian Development Bank (The Inter-American Convention against Corruption, the African Union Convention on Preventing and Combating Corruption, and the Asian Development Bank/Organization for Economic Co-operation and Development Action Plan for the Asia-Pacific). Thus if countries are to meet international standards in combating the illicit drug trade, organized crime, the financing of terrorism, and especially corruption, they must adopt the laws, regulations, and institutions that together constitute the AML system.

Yet probably the more convincing reason for developing countries in particular to employ AML systems in an anticorruption capacity is economic rather than legal. At present AML systems are both expensive and underused, especially in poor countries. Although data are scarce, the costs of AML systems for developing countries have so far probably outweighed the benefits.[47] The centerpiece of any national AML system is the FIU, responsible for receiving and sifting through suspicious transaction reports from private financial institutions and passing significant intelligence on to law enforcement. Those staffing FIUs must combine a knowledge of financial and legal issues, which has meant that suitably qualified personnel command high salaries. The need to communicate and monitor the extensive regulatory requirements imposed on the private sector can require a sizeable FIU. Other public regulatory bodies (such as central banks, insurance supervisors, securities regulators, and company registrars) have also acquired AML responsibilities, generally involving retraining, additional staff, and more money.

The accounting firm KPMG has conducted two rounds of surveys on the costs of the AML system to prominent banks around the world, with results published in 2004 and 2007. In 2007 it was reported that banks' AML compliance costs had increased by an average of 58 percent since 2004, far in excess of expectations.[48] Regionally, the increase was 59 percent in Latin America and the Caribbean, 60 percent in the former Soviet Union, and 70 percent in the Middle East and Africa.[49] The leading factor behind these rising costs was the requirement to monitor for suspicious transactions, and the need to train staff in AML principles and procedures. A study commissioned by the Commonwealth Secretariat found that the direct and indirect costs of the AML system in Vanuatu, Mauritius, and Barbados over the four-year period 2002–05 were $6.25 million, $40 million, and $42.5 million, respectively, a heavy burden for such small economies.[50] As more and more countries join the global AML regime, and as the standards expected of them become more demanding, these costs are likely to increase steeply. KPMG reports that international banks expect compliance costs to increase by "only" another 34 percent by 2010, a figure it suggests is overly optimistic.[51] Furthermore, the Commonwealth survey suggests that such large international banks are perhaps least impacted by rising regulatory standards in this area, and thus the costs are much greater for smaller financial firms.[52] International reviews of developing countries' AML compliance conducted in the past few years almost always identify a long list of deficiencies to be fixed, requiring yet more resources.

The increasing burden of the AML regime on the developing world would be less remarkable if it had resulted in a significant number of convictions, large sums of dirty money confiscated, or a reduction in associated predicate crimes. But there is very little sign of either domestic or international benefits as a result of developing countries being incorporated within the global AML regime. Most developing countries have yet to record a single money laundering conviction or dollar confiscated (excepting the United States, most developed countries have only a handful of convictions[53]). In Niger, for example, one of the poorest and least developed countries in the world, the FIU set up at the beginning of 2006 had eighteen months later only received one suspicious transaction report (which turned out to be sent in error), with no investigations or prosecutions. Explaining why such countries end up with an AML regime, Reuters and Truman note: "It is an article of faith to the authorities in industrial countries that all nations need to have effective AML regimes, but resources are scarce. The global threat posed by weaknesses in poor countries may be quite minor."[54]

More broadly, the bedrock of international AML standards, the FATF's 40 Recommendations on money laundering and 9 Special Recommendations on the financing of terrorism, were drawn up to operate in the context of its members' large and sophisticated financial environments. It is questionable to what extent these standards are applicable to economies (such as Niger and Vanuatu) where cash and barter are the norm, proper identification is lacking, and people do not even have recorded, fixed addresses. The problem is compounded because hitherto FATF studies of money laundering have been based on developed countries' experiences. Even allowing for their relative novelty, the lack of results associated with AML systems in the developing world makes them an expensive distraction from other urgent development needs, and imposes a significant regulatory burden on small, fragile financial sectors. Yet the position could be otherwise; the following chapters spell out the potential for existing AML systems in developing countries to produce major benefits by helping to reduce corruption. Equally, they also explain how anticorruption techniques can safeguard the integrity of the AML system broadly defined.

Chapter 2

International Responses to Corruption and Money Laundering

Introduction and Overview

If the number and variety of global and regional efforts to counter corruption and money laundering were anything to go by, it might be assumed that these problems had been consigned to the past. On the other hand, the fact that corruption and money laundering are still with us, and perhaps even more widespread than a decade ago, may lead to the depressing verdict that all the conventions, treaties, action plans, and so on are little more than ineffectual window dressing, the plenaries, conferences, and seminars just irrelevant talk shops. In fact, however, neither extreme, the heights of dizzying optimism or the depths of crushing pessimism, is warranted. While it is hard to match the growth in international initiatives to combat these financial crimes against any definitive yardsticks of progress, this chapter argues that it is vital to appreciate the nature and scope of international cooperation in this arena. The new frameworks, globally and in the Asia-Pacific region, provide new opportunities to deter, detect, and apprehend corrupt officials and money launderers. These legal and policy innovations are responses to a moving target: as financial deregulation and technological change have advanced, so too have criminals found it easier to use the international financial system to hide and launder their illicit gains. And so while the regulations have become more rigorous, the techniques for financial crime have become more sophisticated. Following on from the historical discussion in the previous chapter about the rise to prominence of corruption and money laundering, this chapter presents a synoptic account of the major international initiatives relevant to tackling the corruption-money laundering nexus, with a particular focus on modes of implementation. This broad-brush coverage is designed to complement the much more selective, in-depth treatment of the best practice in international cooperation in chapter 5. Before hand, the chapter immediately following this one will then lay out the major points of vulnerability under the existing standards.

Despite the independent and distinct origins of global campaigns to counter corruption and money laundering recounted already, current initiatives in each field increasingly call for an integrated approach to dealing with both problems. The key point is that, so far, such an integrated approach remains more of an aspiration than a reality. Yet it is important to summarize the limited progress that has been made in this area, and highlight the potential for much more substantial achievements using arrangements already in place. A common stumbling block for both interested observers and practitioners is the sheer diversity of overlapping, partially complementary anticorruption and anti-money laundering (AML) treaties, projects, and action plans in train. One interviewee suggested that the World Bank alone had eleven separate anticorruption programs, which were not in the habit of talking to one another. Even if this particular claim is exaggerated, the often uncoordinated nature of international action means that effort is often wasted on needless duplication, and the left hand may not know what the right is doing. This ignorance is costly: because corruption and money laundering are often so closely linked, responses that proceed in isolation will often be ineffective. Opportunities for new insights, learning, and cross-fertilization will be lost. Hence the aim of this chapter is to provide an overview and a point of orientation before embarking on more detailed treatments of existing vulnerabilities (chapter 3), the special issue of senior public officials or politically exposed persons (chapter 4), and best international practice (chapter 5).

As noted earlier, rather than seeking to provide an exhaustive coverage, the chapter is confined to the major initiatives with potential for attacking the corruption-money laundering nexus, once again with an emphasis on the Asia-Pacific region. The body of the chapter will review the activities of various international bodies and/or projects, initially focusing on anticorruption initiatives and then on AML, paying particular regard to styles of implementation. The first group is comprised of the Organization for Economic Co-operation and Development Convention for Combating Bribery of Public Official in International Business Transactions (the OECD Anti-Bribery Convention); various governance projects carried out by the World Bank; the United Nations Convention Against Corruption

(UNCAC); the joint United Nations Office on Drugs and Crime/World Bank Stolen Assets Recovery initiative (StAR); and the Asian Development Bank (ADB)/OECD Anti-Corruption Plan for Asia and the Pacific. The second group, coming from an AML perspective, is the Financial Action Task Force (FATF) and the Asia-Pacific Group on Money Laundering (APG). Because there has been a much greater degree of convergence on a single set of AML standards relative to those covering corruption, international AML standards can be summarized more concisely.

The final section is devoted to reiterating two main conclusions. The first is that there are now a large number of organizations and initiatives that have recognized there is currently a disconnect in efforts to counter money laundering and corruption, and have called for this deficiency to be addressed. As welcome as this development is, though, recognizing a problem is clearly not the same as fixing it. The second goal is to draw conclusions on the varying styles of implementation, the means by which international organizations encourage or pressure their member states to live up to their commitments and meet agreed-upon standards, and the varying successes and limitations of the different strategies adopted. This focus on implementation is a recurring theme in the book.

The OECD Anti-Bribery Convention

Aside from the 2003 UNCAC (discussed later), the most important international anticorruption document is the 1997 OECD Convention on Combating Bribery of Foreign Public Officials in International Business Transactions (the OECD Anti-Bribery Convention). As discussed in the previous chapter, the agreement of rich countries that corruption was an issue requiring a coordinated international response set a crucial precedent for subsequent agreements. With the signature of South Africa in June 2007, thirty-seven countries have now committed to the Convention.

In terms of AML content, Article 7 calls upon signatories who have made the offense of bribing a domestic official a predicate offense for money laundering to do the same for the bribery of foreign officials. In the Asia-Pacific, the fact that so few countries beyond the OECD members have criminalized the bribery of foreign officials creates a major problem for investigating and prosecuting these kinds of cases, as discussed in the next chapter. But the Convention is limited in important ways. As the name suggests, the

Convention does not address domestic corruption. Despite the urgings of the International Chamber of Commerce, neither does it deal with private sector corruption, that is, when a person from one private firm bribes another individual in a different firm. Furthermore, it excludes embezzlement and passive corruption. The most valuable aspect of the Convention and the Working Group on Bribery in general, however, is not so much the formal provisions as the method of international monitoring and peer review. This method has been successful in its own right, but has also acted as a model for others to follow. The peer review mechanism is discussed in detail after a consideration of the Working Group on Bribery's recent effort to assess progress so far and identify current areas of weakness.

In May 2006, the Working Group released the *Mid-Term Review of Phase 2 Reports*, a compilation of twenty-one individual country reviews for Phase 2, completed in 2008. While Phase 1 assessed whether members had incorporated the provisions of the Convention into domestic legislation, the current round has sought to ascertain the practical effectiveness of these measures, a vital extra step taken also by the FATF but few other international organizations. The section of this Phase 2 Review most relevant to money laundering (that dealing with Article 7, 85ff), begins by noting that there is an absence of standard data collection techniques among the individual country reports. The resulting lack of comparable data means that it is difficult to draw robust conclusions about common trends. The OECD Review calls for greater efforts to standardize data collection in this area. It also calls for more information on how parties treat the laundering of the proceeds of bribery by the briber, rather than just the bribe itself (page 86, e.g., the profits of a contract won by bribery, OECD 2006). Interviewees indicate that even the countries with the most advanced laws and the greatest practical experience have very little idea as to how to recover the proceeds of bribery.

The OECD Review concisely states a supposition at the heart of the rationale for this book concerning the close links between corruption and money laundering:

> [A] better measure in evaluating the effectiveness of the Convention is whether suspicious transaction reporting systems have led to the discovery of foreign bribery and related money laundering cases. If one assumes that foreign bribery is a prevalent phenomenon, and that the crime frequently involves money laundering (of the bribe or

> the proceeds of bribery), then one could reasonably expect reporting systems to detect foreign bribery cases regularly.[1]

However, the OECD Review immediately goes on to note that in actual fact the results have been "disappointing" as "Suspicious transaction reports (STRs) have not led to bribery investigations in most of the examined Parties."[2] The Review notes the various countries with bribery- or other corruption-related STRs, both foreign and domestic (eighteen in Greece, ten in Luxembourg), and the number of corruption investigations as a result of STRs (seven in Germany, two in Mexico, six in Greece, six in France, twelve in Belgium[3]; additional figures are provided in individual country reviews). The Review does not note any corruption convictions stemming from transaction reports. If results have been disappointing among those countries with the most experience and expertise in countering corruption and money laundering, the results are very unlikely to be more heartening outside the Convention signatories, including most countries of the Asia-Pacific. As such it must be assumed that the failure of STRs to lead to bribery investigations (let alone convictions) to date is a generalized failure, rather than just confined to the OECD members and others that have signed the Convention.

The more important question posed by the OECD Review, then, is why the results have been so disappointing, a failure described as "particularly vexing." The Review discounts the arguments that either there are too few or too many reports (i.e., that financial intelligence units {FIUs} are swamped with a larger volume of reports than they are able to analyse and process).[4] More pertinent, the Review notes, is the fact that very few of these STRs relate to bribery (and by extension other forms of corruption). The Review speculates that this low level of corruption-related intelligence may reflect the fact that when FIUs issue typologies, they rarely include foreign bribery examples. Thus, the FIUs themselves and reporting entities may not be adequately aware of the money laundering-corruption link. Because very few FIUs issue corruption-related examples in their typologies (Belgium and the United States are notable exceptions), reporting entities are much less likely to consider passing on reports of activity that may be suspicious on the grounds of corruption.

Many of the individual country reports for the Phase 2 review process give additional statistics on numbers of corruption-related STRs and money laundering investigations with bribery as the predicate offence. However, judging from interviews, many of the most important details on individual countries' investigations involving international cooperation in fighting corruption-related money laundering offences have been omitted. Rather than reflecting the need for operational security, this omission seems to be a product of political sensitivities, particularly when cases have involved foreign authorities tipping off a government about one of its own officials engaged in corrupt conduct. Keeping such instances from the public eye, or even from the scrutiny of those involved in the peer review process, may spare governments embarrassment, but it hampers the exchange of experience and best practice.

International organizations in general are involved in a great deal of rule-making and standard-setting activity. Unless these rules and standards are to remain a dead letter, they must be implemented or enforced. But in a world of sovereign states with no world government in sight, holding states to their commitments and generally agreed upon international standards is a tall order. The UN Security Council can impose economic sanctions in responding to threats to peace and security, yet this is rare and often ineffective. The European Commission and the World Trade Organization can pass binding legal decisions, but anticorruption and AML bodies have no such prerogatives, and even if they did there is still the problem of enforcement. To the question "why comply?"[5] the OECD has evolved a process of peer review, also referred to as mutual evaluation or peer pressure.[6] Peer review is worth considering in some detail. It is presented as one of the greatest strengths of the OECD Convention, while the lack of such an implementation mechanism is said to be the greatest weakness of the UNCAC, as well as other regional anticorruption agreements such as that of the Organization of American States.[7]

Writing as a member of the OECD secretariat, Pagani defines peer review as follows:

> Peer review can be described as the systematic examination and assessment of the performance of a State by other States, with the ultimate goal of helping the reviewed State improve its policy making, adopt best practices, and comply with established standards and principles. The examination is conducted on a non-adversarial basis, and it relies heavily on mutual trust among the States involved in the review, as well as their shared confidence in the process.[8]

Levi and Gilmore define mutual evaluation in very similar terms as "an international system of periodic peer review."[9] Peer review is more than just information gathering. Instead, countries' compliance is assessed against some benchmark, the Anti-Bribery Convention for the OECD or the 40+9 Recommendations for the FATF. On the other hand, it is not a means by which to coerce countries or settle disputes between them; unlike the World Bank or the International Monetary Fund, the OECD cannot withhold loans. Why, then, would peer review have any impact on motivating states to comply with and enforce international agreements where they otherwise would not? Governmental representatives have regard for the opinions of their peers for at least two reasons. The first is that leaders and public officials want their country to be regarded as modern, advanced, and law-abiding, rather than as backward, criminal, or deviant. As with most others, these individuals like to be liked, that is to say, they gain satisfaction from the esteem of their peers, and conversely seek to avoid public disapprobation or ostracism.[10] The desire to avoid a bad report card is also a product of the relatively tight-knit nature of OECD networks that form a genuine policy community.[11] Second, even if leaders or officials themselves feel no shame about public criticism, being seen to violate commitments or international norms may undermine future negotiating credibility with other states and provide ammunition to opposition at home (remembering that the OECD countries are all democracies).[12]

Peer review has now come to be referred to in some quarters as "the OECD method," and is the basis of the FATF and regional AML bodies' mutual evaluation process. Various regional bodies also have sought to emulate this mechanism, for example, the African Union. Peer review is of course not a panacea. In some instances governments will opt to brazen it out despite the disapproval of their peers, the British government and the BAE al-Yamamah scandal discussed in the next chapter being a good example. Probably more important, though, are those instances where governments may genuinely have the will to fight corruption but not the capacity, and here there is only so much help that peer review can provide.

Aside from the Working Group on Bribery, other divisions within the OECD have also been active in designing better responses to corruption, and implementing standards by peer review. One of the most pernicious features of the old order was not only that multinational companies were free to bribe foreign officials, but, even worse, they could then often count these bribes as legitimate tax deductions. Governments effectively subsidized the corrupt conduct of their firms abroad. The OECD Committee on Fiscal Affairs has since

1996 formally recommended that all members ensure that bribes are not deductible in this manner.[13] Beyond this minimal first step, the Committee has further issued guidance on how tax authorities can assist in detecting corruption.[14] Because the tax system depends on the generation and analysis of vast amounts of financial data, it is a natural source of intelligence on corruption and money laundering. In addition, in most countries tax authorities have strong investigative powers in order to combat tax evasion, which again can be useful in pursuing other types of financial crime. The OECD recommends that tax officials be obliged to report suspicions of corruption to law enforcement authorities,[15] as well as recommending that tax data be available to those responsible for investigating money laundering, and vice versa.[16]

Perhaps even more important are the efforts of the Public Governance and Management group (PUMA) to prevent corruption in public procurement. Public officials placing orders with private firms for goods and services is identified by the OECD as the area most vulnerable to corruption in every region of the world.[17] When the order involves a foreign company this falls under the remit of the Anti-Bribery Convention. But much public procurement involves government orders from domestic firms. Aside from the direct loss caused by the wastage of public money, substandard provision of goods and services by private contractors can put lives at risk. PUMA has published a series of details guidelines on how to mitigate the potential for bureaucrats to place orders so as to maximize kickbacks and bribes, rather than the public welfare.[18]

Finally, the OECD also has a number of regional outreach networks dedicated to fighting corruption. From 1998 these include the OECD Anti-Corruption Network for Eastern Europe and Central Asia. More recently the OECD has begun cooperation with the Organization of American States, building on the Inter-American Convention Against Corruption in 1996. In April 2007 the two organizations signed a memorandum of understanding deepening their cooperation in this and other areas. Most relevant is the joint ADB/OECD Anti-Corruption Plan for Asia and the Pacific, covered separately later.

The UN Convention against Corruption

The United Nations Office on Drugs and Crime (UNODC) is the guardian of the various UN treaties relevant to financial crime: the

1988 Vienna Convention, the 1999 Convention on the Suppression of Terrorist Financing, the 2000 Palermo Convention on Transnational Crime, but especially the 2003 UNCAC. The UNODC has recognized the close links between money laundering and corruption. In its Anti-Corruption Tool Kit, for example, the UNODC states:

> There are important links between corruption and money-laundering. The ability to transfer and conceal funds is critical to the perpetrators of corruption, especially large-scale or "grand corruption." Moreover, public sector employees and those working in key private sector financial areas are especially vulnerable to bribes, intimidation or other incentives to conceal illicit financial activities. A high degree of co-ordination is thus required to combat both problems and to implement measures that impact on both areas.[19]

UNODC subsequently notes:

> Money-laundering statutes can contribute significantly to the detection of corruption and related offences by providing the basis for financial investigations. Identifying and recording obligations as well as reporting suspicious transactions, as is also required by the UN Convention against Transnational Organized Crime and the United Nations Convention against Corruption, will not only facilitate detection of the crime of money-laundering but will also help identify the criminal acts from which the illicit proceeds originated. It is therefore essential to establish corruption as a predicate offence for money-laundering.[20]

Beyond just recognizing the fundamental links between corruption and money laundering, the UNODC is well placed to assist with an integrated response. In addition to its anticorruption responsibilities, the UNODC Global Program on Money Laundering plays an important role in extending AML technical assistance to the developing world. It also hosts the International Money Laundering Information Network (IMoLIN) website of AML resources. The Global Program on Money Laundering lists the money laundering-corruption nexus as one of its priority areas for research. One of the most notable relevant research achievements in this regard is the 1998 report *Financial Havens, Banking Secrecy and Money Laundering* covering a wide variety of financial crimes.[21] The Global Program on Money Laundering is not in the business of carrying out mutual evaluations such as the FATF or regional AML organizations, still less issuing blacklists such as the Non-Cooperative Countries and Territories list discussed later. Rather, it provides technical assistance to developing countries, for example, providing expert advice on the drafting of legislation, often in conjunction with other bodies. The UNODC is a small operation in terms of money and staff, not even in the same league as the World Bank or even the OECD. Yet this smallness may provide an advantage in the closer contact it fosters between those working on AML and anticorruption issues.

As related in the previous chapter, the 1988 Vienna Convention (the United Nations Convention against Illicit Traffic in Narcotic Drugs and Psychotropic Substances) first put the issue of money laundering on the global agenda in calling for signatories to criminalize the proceeds of drug crimes (Article 23). The 2000 Palermo Convention (the United Nations Convention against Transnational Organized Crime) similarly identifies one of its goals as facilitating the fight against money laundering and corruption in the preamble and again calling on parties to criminalize money laundering (Article 6). Article 7 emphasizes the need for customer due diligence and suspicious transaction reporting. The Convention further calls upon parties to set up FIUs and follow the recommendations of international AML bodies.

The UNCAC once again lays out the close links between anticorruption and AML requirements and strategies, beginning from the second clause of the preamble. Some of the most relevant Articles include:

Article 14, which specifies that signatories must set up AML supervisory arrangements, including customer due diligence and establishing beneficial ownership, and a suspicious transaction reporting system; that parties should consider setting up arrangements to monitor the cross-border movement of cash and negotiable instruments; that they should include relevant transaction information on electronic transfers; parties are called upon to follow the standards of existing AML bodies; and ensure international cooperation among law enforcement, judicial, and financial regulatory agencies.

Article 23 specifies that parties must criminalize money laundering.

Article 52 holds that parties must ensure their financial institutions apply enhanced scrutiny to accounts opened or sought by public officials (significantly, making no distinction between domestic and foreign officials) who are or have been carrying out prominent public functions, as well as their families and close associates. Furthermore parties should draw up criteria for the kinds of natural and legal persons to whom this enhanced scrutiny should be applied. Parties should consider setting financial disclosure systems for public officials, including foreign financial accounts, with penalties for noncompliance.

Article 58 encourages parties to set up FIUs to receive, analyze, and disseminate relevant information.

The UNCAC brings to the fore the importance of repatriating stolen assets, and enshrines the principle that these assets should be returned to the "victim" country. Nevertheless, it has received some criticism, and there are particular worries about implementation.[22] Some critics have asserted that the Convention does not go far enough, and that a number of important clauses are voluntary (encouraging parties to take certain measures) rather than obligatory.[23] Thus the Convention encourages, but does not require, parties to criminalize private sector corruption, record cross-border cash transaction, and establish asset registries. The fairly predictable answer to these objections has been that because the Convention did aim to have such broad coverage, compromises were inevitable, and that an imperfect Convention was better than none at all.

Implementation of the UNCAC is a matter of significant concern, as in the absence of a peer review process along the lines of the OECD, there is much less pressure to ensure the practical application of the measures agreed to.[24] As Webb notes: "'Law,' in the sense of a set of formal written documents, will be largely irrelevant if the rules are not embedded in an institutional and organizational structure that favors compliance."[25] The first Conference of Parties in Amman, Jordan, in December 2006 instituted only a weak form of self-assessment.[26] There is some consideration being given to a scaled-down version of a peer review process.[27] Nevertheless, there are also reasons for caution here. The OECD is a much smaller body, its members are far more homogenous, and they have a long history of generally amicable problem-solving discussions, intellectual arbitrage, and exchanges of best practice. Over the past thirty years only six new members have joined (Mexico, the Czech Republic, Hungary, Poland, South Korea, and Slovakia). The OECD Anti-Bribery Convention does include seven nations from outside the OECD (Argentina, Brazil, Bulgaria, Chile, Estonia, Slovenia, and South Africa), but this has not changed the character of proceedings.

In his insider account of peer review, Pagani stresses the requirement that parties trust one another and the impartiality of the process.[28] It is difficult to see how the United Nations, by definition including all states, could come to approximate this community atmosphere of like-minded peers. There is simply not the level of trust among UN members as there is among the OECD countries. Thus although implementation remains a key question for the Convention, simply attempting to cut and paste the OECD peer review process into the UN context seems unrealistic.

The World Bank and the StAR Initiative

In September 2007, the UNODC and World Bank jointly launched a new project that garnered extensive media attention: the Stolen Assets Recovery (StAR) initiative. The report on the initiative begins by emphasizing the scale of the problem of grand corruption and kleptocracy, reciting some of the familiar statistics adduced in the Introduction. The rationale for the project is that efforts to combat grand corruption in developing countries are said to have so far only dealt with one side of the equation: in concentrating on strengthening governance within developing countries, little attention has been paid to the role of actors within developed countries that facilitate this theft.[29] These actors include Western firms offering bribes, foreign financial intermediaries who assist in laundering bribes, and developed country financial centers in which stolen funds are usually invested (although the OECD and Transparency International could fairly claim that Western multinational firms have been in their sights from the beginning). The major obstacles to the recovery of stolen assets are said to be the lack of capacity in developing countries to negotiate the complex legal issues, and the uninterest shown by some developed countries in assisting with the repatriation process. The study contains case studies of corruption and asset recovery from Nigeria, the Philippines, and Peru, as well as tables of the worst offending kleptocrats,[30] reproducing material gathered and released by Transparency International several years earlier.[31] Most broadly, the solutions are said to be first lowering the barriers in developed countries to the repatriation of stolen funds, and second enhancing the capacity of developing countries to successfully mount international asset recovery cases.

In many ways, though, the StAR initiative is less important than the media splash might indicate. Unlike the 1998 UNODC report on financial havens and money laundering, there is little original research. Despite the Action Plan, the report takes care to rule out any role in "investigation, tracing, law enforcement, prosecution, confiscation and repatriation of stolen assets" for the initiative.[32] Instead, the World Bank and UNODC commit to sponsoring a directory and forum for the exchange of best practice in asset recovery, forming a "friends of StAR" group to monitor progress in this area, and provide technical assistance to half-a-dozen developing countries to implement the UNCAC. Beyond this, the initiative aims to keep pressure on governments to ratify the UNCAC and cooperate with international asset recovery cases, in part by mobilizing civil society and like-minded NGO groups. All in all, this is quite a modest program especially, for example, when compared to suggestions from bodies such as the Commonwealth that an international mechanism should be set up to investigate and prosecute serving heads of state.[33] Claims that "StAR would constitute a formidable deterrent to corruption"[34] seem overstated. As for "unequivocally transmitting the signal that corruption does not pay," corruption obviously does pay, or else there wouldn't be so many people engaged in it, and countries would be spared the terrible consequences the report discusses. So far at least, the StAR initiative seems to have its greatest value as a consciousness-raising or hortatory exercise, and in that sense the publicity generated is a positive early sign.

Well before the StAR Initiative, the various component parts of the World Bank Group were instrumental in putting the issue of corruption on the policy agenda in the 1990s, as discussed in the previous chapter, and have produced a prodigious amount of pioneering work on this topic.[35] The World Bank, like the International Monetary Fund (IMF), has had an AML role since late 2001.[36] Rather than being a standard-setter in this area, the World Bank assesses compliance with the FATF 40+9 Recommendations. It does so through such programs as the Reports on Observance of Standards and Codes and the Financial Sector Assessment Program. These are regular surveys of members' financial regulation, equivalent to peer review. In addition the World Bank provides technical assistance to its members to implement the Recommendations. The World Bank also has noted the close link between money laundering and corruption:

> Corruption and money laundering are a related and self-reinforcing phenomenon. Corruption proceeds are disguised and laundered by corrupt officials to be able to spend or invest such proceeds. At the

> same time, corruption in a country's AML institutions (including financial institutions regulators, Financial Intelligence Units (FIUs), police, prosecutors, and courts) can render an AML regime of a country ineffective.[37]

Looking back on its long-standing anticorruption and more recent AML efforts, the World Bank lists the following lessons learned. First that effective customer due diligence under AML requirements, such as providing details on the client's background, the background of the funds involved, and the identity of the beneficiary, plays an important role in promoting general financial transparency and hindering corruption. Second that close cooperation between FIUs, anticorruption agencies, law enforcement, and the private sector is essential to maximizing the impact the AML regime can have on combating corruption. Last that in many countries law enforcement agencies specify corruption as the main underlying offence generating illegal funds to be laundered, and hence AML policy is to a large extent primarily an anticorruption tool.[38] These lessons resonate strongly with the main themes of the book.

Until his departure in 2007, World Bank president Paul Wolfowitz was in favor of taking a particularly tough line against corruption among borrower governments. Breaking with normal diplomatic protocol, Wolfowitz was prepared to name names. Thus in early 2006 he publicly questioned and in some cases stopped the flow of funds to a number of projects on the grounds of corruption. These included a halt on forgiving loans to the Congo after a press report of its president spending $81,000 of public money on himself during a weekend in New York, and an interruption on the granting of new loans to Kenya after the head of its anticorruption unit fled the country.[39] Additional action was taken against Argentina, Bangladesh, Chad, India, and Uzbekistan.[40] This direct approach aroused considerable disquiet among both the World Bank Board and staff (not to mention, of course, those on the receiving end of the criticism). The former demanded a more systematic process before similar action was taken again. Despite the World Bank's reputation for strong-arming vulnerable governments in the Third World, the organization is generally very wary of being seen to bully or publicly insult member states. Although the proximate cause of Wolfowitz's fall was a conflict of interest problem, his aggressive methods for pursuing corruption inside and outside the Bank probably helped to undermine his position. This may be a cautionary tale about the limits diplomatic norms impose on an international organization seeking to confront member governments accused of harboring corruption.

Receiving much less media attention, most of the World Bank's work on corruption and money laundering takes the form of behind-the-scenes policy review and analysis. These surveys, reviews, and reports typify the day-to-day business of most international organizations most of the time. In 2007–2008 three research projects directly relating to the corruption-money laundering nexus were in train. At the time of writing, none of the three reports has been released to the public; international organizations' commitment to transparency only goes so far, though the World Bank is better than most. The first of these projects, hosted by the Financial Market Integrity Unit, looks at the use of AML information for anticorruption purposes. It is comprised of a study of fifteen anticorruption agencies around the world, selected on the basis of geography, size, type, and whether or not there is an internationally accredited FIU present in the jurisdiction. Each was sent a survey focusing on the legal and institutional framework of the anticorruption system, the AML regime, training programs, collaboration with other state agencies, exchange of information, and experience in using AML tools for anticorruption. The end product outlines whether and how countries' anticorruption agencies employ AML data in fighting corruption. It is anticipated that this information will be used to assist other countries in combating corruption via technical assistance, as well as in assisting them to recover the proceeds of corruption.

The second project has been conducted jointly by the World Bank and the Egmont Group on the governance of FIUs as part of the World Bank's wider review and redrafting of its governance and anticorruption strategy. Once again the project is survey based, working from an initial pilot study of twelve Egmont Group FIUs in January 2007. The scope of the survey and project was then revised in light of the feedback received, and the study was extended to all Egmont FIUs. The main priority is to strengthen corruption-prevention measures in FIUs. The third World Bank sponsored project relating to the money laundering-corruption link covers grand corruption and money laundering. The end product comprises twenty-one case studies of grand corruption by politically exposed persons based on court documents and press material, drawing lessons and making policy recommendations on the basis of recurring patterns within these cases. The study examines the instruments and methods used in the laundering of the proceeds of corruption, whether the proceeds were kept on- or offshore, and how the activities were detected, investigated, and prosecuted. The final results may be incorporated in training modules for FIUs.

More than any other of the international organizations considered, the huge financial resources and staff at the disposal of the World Bank give it an extensive reach. It liaises extensively with other international organizations, being an observer or member of many international institutions in its own right (e.g., the FATF), with its office-holders being prodigious networkers. With its regional and country offices and technical assistance programs in dozens of countries, the Bank has a geographical spread all around the globe. Unlike those bodies dominated by the concerns of developed countries, the World Bank has devoted itself to assisting poorer countries (with mixed success), and is thus more used to contexts where governments function poorly or not at all. Despite the tendency to associate the Bretton Woods institutions with rancorous public fights with Third World governments over loan conditionality, the vast majority of their work on money laundering, corruption, and much else is more a quotidian roster of seminars, workshops, questionnaires, reports, assessments, and training programs.

The Asian Development Bank/OECD Anticorruption Initiative for Asia and the Pacific

The ADB/OECD Anti-Corruption Initiative for Asia and the Pacific was established in 1999. It currently includes twenty-eight countries, and its activity has been centered on the Anti-Corruption Action Plan for Asia and the Pacific, adopted in December 2000. This joint enterprise aims to further the cause of anticorruption by facilitating member dialogue, enabling the exchange of best practice, coordinating technical assistance, engaging in policy analysis, and providing a database of anticorruption measures. Along with the organizations listed earlier and others such as the Commonwealth and Asia-Pacific Economic Co-operation, the ADB/OECD aims to help those in the region that have ratified the UNCAC to fulfill its provisions. In contrast to the OECD Anti-Bribery Working Group, countries define their own goals and assess their own progress; the spur of peer review is missing. This absence reflects greater concerns about sovereign prerogatives and, probably, the reluctance to face public criticism in an environment where trust in the objectivity of the peer review process has not had sufficient time to develop. As a result, although there is a great deal of expertise and advice on offer, the pressure for countries to implement common standards and live up to their commitment is weaker.

The Action Plan has stimulated the production of several weighty tomes providing detailed guidance to members on corruption: *Curbing Corruption in Public Procurement* (2004), *Denying Safe Haven to the Corrupt and the Proceeds of Corruption* (2006), and most recently *Mutual Legal Assistance, Extradition and Recovery of Proceeds of Corruption in the Asia-Pacific* (2008). How do these dedicated anti-corruption studies relate to the fight against money laundering? The last-mentioned publication details progress on the direct application of foreign freezing and confiscation orders, a very useful tool for those pursuing international money laundering cases. Indeed, rather than Mutual Legal Assistance Treaties, arrangements for asset confiscation and repatriation are often contained in money laundering laws.[41] Unfortunately, many countries in the region have little provision for asset confiscation in their legislation and regulations, still less for repatriating the proceeds of corruption to the victim country as the UNCAC suggests.

The report notes that even where the framework for international cooperation has attained greater depth and sophistication, in practice it is little used, and thus it is difficult to assess how well it really works.[42] This goes for the network of bilateral treaties, as well as sub-regional arrangements such as the Mutual Legal Assistance among Association of South-East Asian Nation (ASEAN) countries and equivalent agreements among Pacific Islands Forum countries. Examples of successful instances of asset freezing and repatriation like those involving Switzerland and the Philippines (see chapter 6), Kazakhstan, Switzerland, and the United States, and Switzerland and Pakistan are rare exceptions.

A potential solution to the incomplete coverage of formal treaty networks and the legal and practical limitations on their use is the use of less formal agreements, such as memoranda of understanding. Financial regulators in different countries are increasingly likely to be linked in to worldwide bodies such as the International Organization of Securities Commissions and the International Association of Insurance Supervisors.[43] These networks can be used to transmit financial intelligence relating to complex international money laundering and corruption cases involving securities and insurance. But the most valuable such channel is the network of FIUs provided by the Egmont Group. Thus an ADB/OECD publication relates how two Thai men in London sought to buy thirty thousand worth of travellers' checks in cash.[44] Following a suspicious transaction report, the British authorities were able to freeze the funds and then find out from the Thai Anti-Money Laundering Office that the cash had been exchanged illegally in Bangkok. Furthermore, the ostensible justification for the money (buying a Porsche to export back to Thailand) was not credible (Porsches being cheaper in Thailand than in Britain). As a result, in September 2005, a UK court allowed the money to be confiscated.

Of even more direct relevance, the ADB/OECD joint venture aims to help members integrate their anticorruption and AML activities with the Asia-Pacific Group on Money Laundering:

> [T]he Initiative will endeavor to undertake a thematic review jointly with the Asia-Pacific Group on Money Laundering in the framework of the recently launched FATF/APG Project Group on the links between anti-corruption and anti-money laundering and terrorist financing... The thematic review would focus on strengths and vulnerabilities to corruption of member countries' anti-money laundering mechanisms and make suggestions for improvement. This thematic review will be carried out jointly by APG and the ADB/OECD Initiative to complement the research analysis planned by the FATF/APG Project Group. A joint workshop on protecting anti-money laundering institutions and in particular Financial Intelligence Units against corruption would complement the review, and a joint capacity building program with APG would be considered to address the identified challenges.[45]

The main contributions of the ADB/OECD initiative are thus threefold. The first is that the Action Plan works as a form of political commitment for countries in the region to combat corruption, reinforcing similar undertakings made in other contexts. Yet in isolation such commitments are a weak reed, often made and then forgotten. More durable are the detailed studies, sensitive to the corruption-money laundering nexus, that lay out the state of play in the region, identify common deficiencies, and advance practical, specific solutions. Just as important but harder to observe directly, the regular interaction of national officials in this context helps foster the trust that is essential if a more rigorous peer review mechanism is to be put in place in the future.

The Financial Action Task Force and the Asia-Pacific Group on Money Laundering

The final section of this chapter looks at the emerging international framework to tackle the corruption-money laundering nexus from the AML perspective. As well as anticorruption bodies urging more attention to money laundering, the FATF and APG have begun to broaden their focus from money laundering to corruption. Compared with their counterparts dealing with corruption, these AML bodies are much smaller (the World Bank has more staff in its travel booking section than all the world's international AML bodies combined), and they have advanced further on a narrower front. Even with the variety of forms that money laundering may take, and the mission creep into such areas as the financing of terrorism and nuclear proliferation, this area is nevertheless more narrowly bounded than corruption. The FATF has been prepared to take a much more robust attitude to implementation than bodies such as the UNODC, or even the OECD Anti-Bribery Group. Unlike the latter, the FATF has been publicly critical of nonmember states, as well as members, and has even threatened sanctions against countries said to have egregiously substandard AML policies. While this has not endeared the FATF to those on the receiving end of such treatment, and bodies such as the World Bank Board have expressed their reservations, it has worked in forcing policy reform.

The 40+9 Recommendations provide powerful tools for those looking to fight corruption. Specifically, the most useful provisions are those to do with the gathering of financial intelligence, and the use of asset freezing and confiscation measures. A third contribution would be in the provisions for international cooperation, but a discussion of these aspects is held over until chapter 5. Unlike the different anticorruption initiatives sketched out earlier, there is only one set of standards operative for AML policy: the FATF's 40 Recommendations on money laundering and the 9 Special Recommendations on the financing of terrorism. Each of the regional AML bodies pledge to implement the same standards. Similarly, despite their much bigger budgets and longer lineage, the World Bank and the International Monetary Fund defer to FATF standards when assessing the AML systems of their member states. The status of the UNCAC as only the first among equals in relation to the various other regional anticorruption agreements is thus very different from the global uniformity that prevails in AML standards.

The uniformity of standards means that the Asia-Pacific Group on Money Laundering is notable for the different means of implementation rather than any difference in standards. In keeping with the other regional AML bodies pledges, and indeed with the standard practice of international organizations in general, the APG has never engaged in the sort of public blacklisting represented by the Non-Cooperative Countries and Territories regime. Within the limits of its small six-person secretariat, it extends technical assistance and acts as a clearing house for best practice both during and between its annual plenary. The APG does engage in a process of mutual evaluation (peer review), which does not shy away from giving bad grades. Given the recent adoption of AML standards in many member countries, Mutual Evaluation Reports commonly give long strings of Non-Compliant or Partially Compliant ratings. Up until 2007 such reports have not been made public, representing the reticence many members feel about public criticism. However, spurred on by the fact that every other regional AML body had followed the FATF lead in making these reports public (in theory at least: some regional groups don't post the reports on the website), the APG has now made public mutual evaluation reports from 2005 onward. Aside from negative evaluation reports, in extreme cases the APG has the options of either suspending or expelling members, in the same way the FATF threatened Austria with suspension of its membership in 2000 unless it abolished anonymous bank accounts. The APG came very close to adopting these measures in 2007 against one of its members that had repeatedly missed deadlines to introduce legislation criminalizing the finance of terrorism. A last-minute back-down by the state defused the problem. In general, governments are reluctant to lose face in front of their peers by being singled out as substandard or noncompliant.

More than the FATF, the APG was an early adherent to the view that AML standards could and should be used to combat corruption and corruption-related laundering. In late 2003 the APG Typologies Workshop in Kuala Lumpur focused on corruption-related money laundering issues for the first time. The Workshop agreed on a program of work, including a survey and typology, with the goal of preparing a scoping paper to identify significant issues related to the money laundering-corruption nexus in the Asia-Pacific region. As a result of this work, Hong Kong and Pakistan, under the auspices of the Typologies Working Group, volunteered to cooperate with all APG members to prepare a paper considering types of corruption-related money laundering, current measures taken to combat corruption-related money laundering, and challenges and opportunities for countering this problem. APG members were asked to provide detailed information on existing legislative measures to combat interlinked instances of money laundering and corruption, further case studies of related typologies, and examples of practical steps to implement effective AML measures. The draft paper was prepared in September 2004 on the basis of material provided by member jurisdictions.

Subsequently, the Typologies Working Group sought further detailed responses from jurisdictions on the definition of corruption, the type and nature of legislation in place, and case studies relating to corruption and money laundering. Parallel to this work, at the Joint Plenary Session of the FATF and APG in Singapore in June 2005, the two organizations agreed to combine their efforts in exploring the relationships between AML and anticorruption efforts, with particular reference to how corruption might undermine AML implementation. The FATF and APG formed a project group to carry out a study of the links between corruption and money laundering. Following interest from a number of countries and organizations, the project group is comprised of Argentina, Australia, France, Hong Kong, India, Indonesia, Korea, Malaysia, the Netherlands, Pakistan, South Africa, and Thailand, as well as a plethora of international organizations, including the UNODC, OECD, and various other regional AML bodies. Notwithstanding this large membership, a report on corruption and money laundering excepted, the project group seems to be active only sporadically.

The discussion in the preceding sections of this chapter considered the international standards drawn up and propounded in the campaign against corruption, which now also offer considerable potential in fighting money laundering. Now it is time to consider how AML standards may be useful in attacking the corruption-money laundering link. As covered in chapter 1, the practice of AML involves collecting and analyzing large quantities of financial data, and results in a substantial increase in overall financial transparency. Corruption is a crime that depends on secrecy, and one where the victims are typically unaware of their loss. As a result, countering corruption may be viewed as in large part a problem of information. Because most (but not all) corruption, and all grand corruption, involves the transfer of money or assets, gathering and analyzing financial information is vital. To the extent that parties involved in corruption can render their financial dealings opaque to the outside world, the chances of catching them out, or deterring others with similar inclinations, drop dramatically. With this in mind, the significance of the huge amounts of financial information generated and collated in the AML system with regards to fighting corruption can be appreciated.

Perhaps the central tenet of AML systems is the requirement that private financial firms report suspicious transactions. At first limited to banks, this responsibility has been expanded to encompass credit unions, insurance companies, wire transfer offices, bureaux de change, casinos, dealers in gems and precious metals, and others. Examples of what constitute a suspicious transaction might include depositing or paying with a large volume of cash, moving money through a series of accounts with no apparent business purpose, major purchases inconsistent with reported income, or transacting with individuals, firms, or jurisdictions that are themselves under suspicion. These reports, which may number in the tens or even hundreds of thousands every year, are passed on to the FIU for analysis.[46]

More general requirements seek to ensure that each particular activity within the financial system is linked with a specific, identifiable person. Opening a bank account requires multiple forms of confirming identification (such as a passport, national identity card, driver's licence, and utility bill), with copies kept on file in the bank. Wire transfer agencies must include and record the full details of the sender and the recipient. Those crossing borders with large amounts of cash (typically $10,000 or more) must declare this fact. Any corporate vehicle (most usually a company, but also including trusts, partnerships, foundations, and so on) must be able to be linked with those individuals enjoying beneficial ownership or control. Just as important as these new sources of information, the requirements also remove some of the barriers to accessing financial data that have previously impeded investigations. Financial institutions in general have a duty to keep their customers' information confidential, and some may have a more general fiduciary duty to act in their customers' best interests, but AML reporting supersedes these rules. Even in the countries that have become known for their particular banking secrecy (e.g., Switzerland, Liechtenstein, Panama, and other tax havens), the duty to report suspicious transactions and provide information on account-holders for money laundering investigations is paramount.[47] In countries such as the United Kingdom and Australia even lawyer-client confidentiality is suspended with reference to STRs, although some other countries such as Canada, France, and the United States have decided against this measure.

As can readily be appreciated, collecting mountains of data by itself does little if anything to stop crime. It is the responsibility of the FIUs to receive, collate, analyze, and disseminate this information. In fulfilling this role the FIU may check transactions against lists of individuals under suspicion of committing financial crimes, or analyze networks of transactions between specific people or companies. They may ask for further details from the reporting institution, and pass the resulting information on to various law enforcement agencies. The police and, depending on national circumstances, tax authorities and intelligence agencies may request information from the FIU regarding persons of interest.

Often investigations into money laundering, corruption, or other kinds of financial crime have been stymied due to the slowness of the investigatory process relative to the speed with which ill-gotten gains can be spirited out of the country and laundered. Confiscating the proceeds of corruption may act as one of the most effective deterrents, as criminals are sometimes willing to spend time in jail rather give up the funds they have illicitly acquired. The freezing and confiscation measures that are a major focus of the response to money laundering can help to remedy both of these problems. To comply with international standards, those within the global AML regime must be able to expeditiously freeze funds connected with ongoing investigations (covered in FATF Recommendation 38). Even more powerful are the methods provided to the authorities to confiscate laundered money, including that deriving from corruption offences. In keeping with the vast sums of money looted by corrupt officials, the assets recovered may even be sufficient to make a significant contribution to the national budget. For example, President Mohamed Suharto of Indonesia is estimated to have looted between $15 and $35 billion during his thirty-one-year rule.[48] Jean-Claude Duvalier, dictator of Haiti, is estimated to have stolen funds equivalent to between 1.7 and 4.5 per cent of national GDP every year he was in power. In Nigeria $505 million of the money stolen by Sani Abacha has been repatriated from abroad (in addition to $800 million recovered within Nigeria), while the Philippines recovered $624 million stolen by former president Marcos and his family.[49]

In the past, even where laws have allowed for the confiscation of the proceeds of crime (initially in the United States for drug offences), they have proved difficult to apply in practice. Historically, confiscation generally required the case to be proven beyond a reasonable doubt, and the money or assets in question had to derive directly from criminal activity. Both of these propositions are difficult to establish in corruption cases. Recent changes, however, have lowered the threshold under which seizure may occur. In addition to confiscation based on a criminal conviction, governments can now use non-conviction based civil forfeiture and civil law measures. Generally, civil forfeiture cases brought by the government against a corrupt official's assets on money laundering grounds are required to meet a lower threshold of proof for recovery of funds, namely on the "balance of probabilities" rather than "beyond a reasonable doubt" (explained in chapter 5). Under a non-conviction based approach, the case proceeds against an individual's assets directly, rather than seeking to expropriate the assets as a by-product of successfully prosecuting the individual.[50] Thus in pursuing the assets of Vladimir Montesinos, the former Peruvian intelligence chief who fled after being accused of demanding bribes in return for defense contracts, the United States seized and repatriated $20 million. Those responsible for prosecuting the case in the United States are adamant that if conviction-based asset confiscation measures had been the only option, the money could not have been recovered.[51] The Philippines government has also enjoyed recent success against corrupt domestic officials using the same technique.

The FATF's standards on countering money laundering thus provide a great deal of potential in fighting corruption-related money laundering. Enhancing this potential is the fact that so many countries have committed to observing these principles, at least 180 and rising. Unlike the UNCAC, the FATF has developed a robust, perhaps even aggressive, style of ensuring that states live up to their commitments in this area. This is further embodied in the process of peer review in the FATF and its regional offshoots, as well as in the incorporation of the 40+9 Recommendations in the various World Bank and IMF assessments. In some ways, though, the FATF is a victim of its own success. It has proven so successful at strengthening its standards, making them more rigorous, expanding the coverage of money laundering (from drug profits to all crimes), and diffusing the Recommendations across the globe, that it may be suffering from overstretch. This is all the more so as the United States has successfully sought to broaden the remit of the FATF to include first the financing of terrorism (2001), and then the financing of nuclear proliferation (2007). As a result the body has little energy and few resources for other priorities. Particularly as there are so many organizations with a dedicated anticorruption mission, although the Recommendations are very useful for fighting all sorts of financial crimes, with intermittent exceptions the FATF has been happy to leave corruption alone.

Here there is an interesting divergence between rich and poor countries. Developing countries such as South Africa and Brazil are supportive of devoting much more attention to the relations between money laundering and corruption. The same is true of several of the regional AML bodies, including the APG. Thus the regional groups for Eastern and South Africa as well as West Africa have both declared that investigating and responding to corruption as a source of money to be laundered is a central priority for their future work.[52] The World Bank study quoted earlier indicates why this emphasis makes good sense: for developing countries, corruption is probably the single greatest source of illicit monies. Yet the developed countries are notably less enthusiastic about, as they see it, asking the already over-burdened AML system to cope with one more responsibility outside the central focus. According to this perspective, dealing with corruption is someone else's job. This situation of developing world enthusiasm for a new attack on corruption counterposed with developed world relative indifference is a fairly sharp role reversal of the conventional picture. This view would have it that rich countries have to push and prod reluctant poor nations to adopt the maxims of good governance and corruption-fighting, often using the threats of withholding aid and cheap credit. But when it comes to using the AML system to attack corruption, it is developing countries that are currently doing most of the pushing.

Conclusions

Governance at the international level tends to be messier than that within states. Rather than a single authoritative source of laws and policy, disparate, partially overlapping, and sometimes directly conflicting standards obtain. While enforcement and implementation pose a challenge for nearly all governments, putting the various global and regional covenants and treaties into effect is qualitatively more difficult. This chapter has laid out the broad outlines of the current international regimes designed to counter corruption and money laundering. Increasingly, the organizations and officials involved in drawing up and seeking the implementation of these regimes are aware both of the intimate links between corruption and money laundering, and the need for an integrated response. But despite the potential benefits of such an integrated response, the reality has not yet lived up to the aspirations.

The ambitious commitments enshrined in documents such as the UNCAC pose major implementation headaches. The UNCAC and regional anticorruption agreements such as those of the Organization of American States and the African Union lack a rigorous peer review or equivalent mechanism to make sure that countries live up to the commitments they have made. Although the OECD Anti-Bribery Working Group has such a review process, the fact that some prominent members have yet to obtain a single conviction for international bribery raises questions about effectiveness. The media profile of the StAR initiative and the World Bank's periodic public confrontations with borrower states over corruption belie the fact that most of its work tends to be incremental attempts to build anticorruption capacity in developing states, and studies and assessments of current policies and regulations, often undertaken jointly with other more specialized international institutions. Turning to AML agencies, no one could accuse the FATF of a lack of energy in both diffusing and enforcing its standards worldwide. Its uncompromising approach is epitomized by the Non-Cooperative Countries and Territories blacklist from 2000. The FATF's achievements have been shored up by the eight regional AML bodies. The 40+9 Recommendations provide very valuable tools with which to attack corruption and corruption-related money laundering. But the FATF has had only an intermittent interest in fighting corruption, perhaps understandably in view of its small secretariat and heavy responsibilities. The push to link responses to money laundering with those from corruption has tended to come from the regional bodies: those in Africa, and especially the Asia-Pacific Group on Money Laundering.

Moving from this high-level coverage of the various international initiatives to the specific solutions presented in chapters 4 (on senior public officials) and 5 (best practice for international cooperation) requires a better understanding of where the existing system is failing. What are the points of vulnerability that currently allow those involved in money laundering to corrupt the overall AML system, and corrupt officials to obscure the illicit origins of bribes, kickbacks, and stolen assets? Parts of the answer have been foreshadowed, especially a lack of integration and implementation failures, but this is not sufficiently concrete for an adequate grasp on the problem. It is with this in mind that the next chapter is devoted to diagnosing the major points of vulnerability in the existing system of anticorruption and AML standards.

CHAPTER 3

POINTS OF VULNERABILITY

Introduction and Overview

Corruption and money laundering are alike in that few of those committing these crimes are convicted, and only a very small proportion of the money involved is seized. Many countries in the Asia-Pacific are yet to record a single conviction for money laundering, but it is unlikely this is because there is no money laundering going on. Similarly, the fact that countries such as the United Kingdom and Australia have yet to record a single conviction for the bribery of foreign officials is probably not because no such bribery has occurred. To what extent could the increased use of intelligence, laws, and institutions of the anti-money laundering (AML) regime enhance efforts to counter corruption? To what extent is the fight against money laundering being held back by corruption? If there are problems in these areas, what can be done to ameliorate them? This chapter is largely devoted to investigating the second and third issues: examining vulnerabilities to corruption in the AML system, and proposing how these risks might be managed.

In assessing the vulnerability of the AML regime to corruption, it is important to adopt a broad view. Fighting money laundering effectively and maintaining the integrity of the system depends on a whole range of institutions, not just specialized financial intelligence units (FIUs). To the extent that judges or prosecutors can be bribed, convicting wealthy or well-connected money launderers will be difficult or impossible. Even if the judicial system as such functions well, unless it is insulated from political interference, prosecutions, or trials can be prevented or sabotaged. But the potential vulnerabilities of the AML system to corrupt practices extend further. The private sector plays a crucial role in providing financial intelligence. Through sins of omission and commission, private firms can shield money launderers. Criminals may induce firms with a duty to report suspicious transactions to turn a blind eye when criminal money enters the legitimate financial sector. Even worse, there are instances where banks and company formation agents have deliberately connived to launder illicit funds.

In part the modest results achieved so far in combating corruption and money laundering are due to legal gaps. To the extent that countries have not ratified and legislated the provisions of the various international conventions on money laundering and corruption examined in chapters 2 and 5 this represents a significant shortcoming. Certainly there are some glaring problems as a result of incomplete legislation. Prominent among these is the failure to make corruption a predicate offence for money laundering purposes.[1] In the Asia-Pacific region only Australia, China, India, Indonesia, Korea, Malaysia, Singapore, and Thailand have done so. Only Australia, Indonesia, Korea, and Japan have legislated the criminal liability of firms (legal persons) for financial crimes.[2] With the exception of Hong Kong and Singapore, no country in the region has comprehensive legislation against private sector corruption.[3] Just four countries in the region (Australia, Japan, Korea, and Singapore) have criminalized the bribery of foreign public officials. Because most international legal cooperation such as extradition requires that behavior constitutes a criminal offence in both jurisdictions (the dual criminality criterion, see chapter 5), this scant coverage makes the prosecution of complex international corruption and money laundering cases problematic.[4] Outside these four countries, bribes given to foreign officials are commonly tax deductible.[5]

Asset confiscation is a central pillar of efforts to fight corruption and money laundering. Confiscation establishes the principle that people should not profit from their illegal actions, functions as a deterrent, and may also provide significant funds to the public purse. But no country has resolved the thorny legal issues surrounding confiscation of the proceeds of bribery, as opposed to the bribe itself. If a multinational firm gives a minister $1 million to approve a new mine site, it is relatively easy to then confiscate the bribe. The legal issues surrounding any efforts to expropriate the mine itself are much more difficult, especially under criminal law.[6]

But aside from legislative deficiencies, interview sources stress the centrality of implementation. It seems probable that even "state of the art" legislation will do little to reduce interlinked instances of corruption and money laundering in the absence of effective implementation. For example, Indonesia's FIU (the Indonesian Financial Transactions and Report Center) and anticorruption body (the

Corruption Eradication Commission) enjoy broad legal powers, including, unusually, provision for close cooperation between the two. Yet so far little progress has been made in prosecuting individuals involved in the massive corruption of the Suharto era or recovering the money stolen. Reviews of measures to fight corruption and money laundering by international organizations commonly devote most of their attention to legislation. This chapter seeks to correct this imbalance by putting questions of implementation in the foreground.

The first section reviews international best practice in corruption prevention with reference to FIUs. What are the general rules for strengthening the integrity of public institutions, and to what extent might these general principles make FIUs less vulnerable to corruption? To the extent that best practices have not been adopted by FIUs, they may be prone to improper influence. A related issue is the trade-off between FIU independence and capacity, especially in developing countries.

In keeping with the broad view of the AML system, the following section looks at susceptibility to corruption in the judiciary, including political interference in the decision to prosecute. In rich and poor countries alike, where government attorney-generals or justice ministers have the final say on prosecutions, there is a danger that this prerogative will be used to advance a self-serving political agenda or foreign policy interest, rather than uphold the rule of law. This issue is explored with reference to the British cabinet's decision in December 2006 to cancel the investigation of British Aerospace System's alleged bribery of Saudi government officials in return for an $86 billion arms purchase.

In the private sector, corrupt banks officials may passively or actively subvert AML rules. A prominent instance of such occurred when senior Bank of New York officials colluded with Russian criminals to conceal illegal funds from U.S. and Russian law enforcement bodies. The presence of unregulated corporate service providers (CSPs) providing chains of anonymous shell corporations also facilitates the laundering of bribe money. The final major point of vulnerability is the disconnect or compartmentalization that tends to undermine potential synergies in the fight against money laundering and corruption.

Before turning to a detailed investigation of the impact of corruption on the AML system, a few caveats are in order. In developing countries especially the AML system has a short track record.

Among those interviewed from the various international organizations by the authors, the degree of political support, resource constraints, and relations with law enforcement and prosecutors were all held to have as great an influence in facilitating or impeding efforts to fight money laundering as corruption. As such, even where the AML system has been in place for some time, modest results in countering money laundering may be a result of these kinds of factors, rather than corruption. Developing countries are already struggling to fulfill global AML requirements in an environment where there are many other competing demands on public funds. Given this fact, promoting expensive, complex solutions to make AML bodies more corruption-resistant may be unrealistic, and perhaps even counterproductive. Too often rich Western countries and international organizations foist complex and expensive regulatory regimes on developing countries without any effort to assess the patterns of costs and benefits, or the opportunity cost of the alternative uses to which given resources could be employed.[7]

Financial Intelligence Units: Points of Vulnerability and Solutions

As discussed in chapter 1, fighting the "scourge" or "cancer" of corruption has been a global policy priority since the mid-1990s. Some countries, such as Hong Kong, recognized this problem and took robust action domestically decades before.[8] However it is an open question as to whether there is any less corruption now than previously. Writing in 2003, Bhargava and Bolongaita note that "Early indicators of progress in controlling corruption in Asia are not encouraging."[9] There is, however, a growing body of knowledge about general guidelines for making government agencies more resistant to corruption.[10] It is believed that certain features of institutional design and organizational practice can make public bodies more or less susceptible to corruption. Many of these corruption prevention principles have been formalized in the OECD Anti-Bribery Convention, the United Nations Convention Against Corruption (UNCAC), and the various regional anticorruption arrangements (as discussed in the preceding chapter).

This section outlines best practice in general corruption prevention for public bodies. These lessons may be able to enhance the integrity and effectiveness of FIUs. Best practices are drawn primarily from the experiences of the Hong Kong Independent

Commission Against Corruption (ICAC) and the United Nations Office for Drugs and Crime Anti-Corruption Toolkit. The ICAC is regarded as one of the world's most effective anticorruption bodies, and its structure and practices (if not success) have been widely emulated elsewhere.[11] To the extent that FIUs have not adopted some version of some of these principles, they are more susceptible to improper influence. As ever, different countries need to adapt any generalized guidelines to local circumstances. Previously an unreflective copying of foreign models has led to disappointing results, for example, the spread of independent anticorruption bodies in the absence of domestic political and societal support has had little effect on the scale of corruption.[12] Although the evidence is so far incomplete, it seems that in practice the majority of FIUs in the Asia-Pacific region more widely fail to adhere to important corruption-prevention principles.

Asset Registries and Illicit Enrichment

Experts in the field suggest that perhaps the single most important corruption-prevention tool for public institutions is a register of officials' assets and income.[13] When officials are hired they must make an exhaustive declaration of all their assets and liabilities, any sources of income apart from salary, and beneficial ownership or control of corporate entities (e.g., being a company director or trustee). These declarations must be updated and audited regularly. Because their baseline, legitimate wealth is known when they commence employment, public officials who subsequently accept large bribes are more likely to be found out, or at the very least will have to go to the extra trouble of concealing their illicit gains. As is discussed in detail in chapter 6, the discrepancy between Ferdinand Marcos's declared wealth on entering politics and his assets at the time of his overthrow was a central plank of the case to recover assets he stole. Individuals with conflicts of interest, or who are financially vulnerable (perhaps with large debts), may also be identified. Declarations of assets may also include the spouses or immediate families of those taking up sensitive senior positions (see chapter 4). Asset registries (or registers) can comprise an important measure for safeguarding the integrity of FIUs. But their application is potentially much wider. Depending on national circumstances, such a registry may include politicians and senior public officials, judges, police, and members of the anticorruption body.

Such registries are not a new idea. This approach is recommended in several international anticorruption agreements. The 1996 Inter-American Convention against Corruption Article III 4 calls for a registry of the income, assets, and liabilities of public officials. The UNCAC also calls for a similar registry in Article 8 (5) under the rubric of dealing with conflicts of interest among public officials. They are common in many governments, legislatures, and anticorruption bodies around the world.[14] In the Asia-Pacific region Bangladesh, Cambodia, Fiji, India, Kazakhstan, the Kyrgyz Republic, Malaysia, Mongolia, Nepal, Pakistan, the Philippines, and Vanuatu require all public officials to declare their assets on a regular basis. The Kyrgyz Republic, Nepal, and the Philippines extend this requirement to officials' families as well. In Australia, China, Japan, Korea, and Papua New Guinea only senior public officials and those in sensitive positions must declare their assets, with Thailand and Vietnam also requiring the same information about these officials' families.[15]

The effectiveness of these registries is severely compromised, however, unless underpinned with certain supporting measures. It is often not so much the absence of asset registries that is the issue, as problems of implementation. In particular, three conditions typically need to be fulfilled. First, there must be meaningful (preferably criminal) penalties for those making false, misleading, or incomplete declarations. Second, there must be an obligation for registries to be regularly updated, preferably on an annual basis at least. Third, these registries should be cross-checked for accuracy regularly using AML and tax information. Unless these conditions are fulfilled, registries are unlikely to be effective in deterring and detecting corrupt practice.

Judging on the basis of available evidence, most registers do not satisfy these conditions.[16] Even in developed countries, there are serious problems of implementation. For example, the Australian Transactions Report and Analysis Center (the local FIU) conducts only a partial investigation of new employees, and this information is not regularly checked for continuing employees. More broadly, it seems that the AML intelligence and information from tax authorities necessary for robust and effective asset registers are rarely combined to verify the accuracy of officials' declarations.

More far-reaching than the idea of asset registers is the offence of illicit enrichment. Rather than merely requiring public officials to declare assets and liabilities, the possession of unexplained wealth by these officials becomes a criminal offence. For example, an official is stopped with $50,000 on her person. Unless she can explain a legitimate source for the money, punitive action can be taken. Under these circumstances there is a reversal of the usual burden of proof: individuals must prove that they acquired funds legally, rather than it having to be proved that they acquired them illegally. Once again, various international instruments recommend this approach. The UNCAC asks signatories to consider criminalizing illicit enrichment: "a significant increase in the assets of a public official that he or she cannot reasonably explain in relation to his or her lawful income" (Article 20). Several countries in Asia have long had this kind of law on the books: Hong Kong, Malaysia, Nepal, the Philippines, Singapore, Thailand, and India from as far back as the 1940s. In part this reflects the tendency of British colonial administrations to introduce illicit enrichment laws, though such a law was never considered appropriate for the United Kingdom itself.

For some countries, however, a reverse onus clause in a criminal offence would violate the constitutionally protected presumption of innocence. The Canadian Charter of Rights and Freedoms, for instance, would prohibit any such law on this ground. More broadly, there are concerns in countries such as the United States about giving governments such sweeping powers.[17] Of course, if governments could be trusted to exercise these powers and their other prerogatives wisely, impartially, and with restraint, there would be no need for anticorruption strategies in the first place.

General Corruption Prevention Principles

Both asset registries and illicit enrichment may be powerful tools with which to protect the integrity of FIUs. To the extent that such measures are not introduced, FIUs will tend to be more vulnerable to corruption. But there are other organizational features that may increase or decrease an FIU's vulnerability to corruption. These measures, discussed briefly in the following paragraphs, include codes of conduct, and policies on conflicts of interest and the handling of sensitive information. These corruption-prevention methods may well overlap with, and should complement, the measures summarized earlier.

Codes of conduct provide written guidelines to employees of an organization as to how to perform their duties according to the organization's standards and principles. It further outlines the disciplinary measures that will be taken against an employee if a breach of the code of conduct occurs (the provision for such a code is expressed in UNCAC in a discretionary measure, Article 7d). Also included may be guidelines on receiving gifts and benefits. These codes reduce the chances that well-meaning officials will unintentionally breach standards by clearly laying out expectations.

Closely related to codes of conduct is the regulation of conflicts of interest. Properly managing conflicts of interest is critical to maintaining an image of integrity and high ethical standards in public agencies such as FIUs. The public's perception that a government official, and hence the official's agency, has acted in a biased or unfair way because of personal interest can be just as detrimental to the confidence in that agency's work as an unlawful act. Conflicts of interest may be pecuniary (in which case asset registers may again be useful) or non-pecuniary. Rules governing such situations may extend beyond the period of officials' employment in the public sector. A notable conflict of interest (now remedied) concerned Thai law enforcement officers pursing money laundering. The Thai authorities sought to provide officers with an enhanced incentive to find and confiscate laundered money. Various law enforcement agencies in the United States are able to retain a share of criminal money recovered thanks to their efforts. In the Thai case, however, the incentive of retaining a portion of recovered funds was offered to individual officers, rather than to the agency as a whole. Although no cases of abuse were publicly reported, there was a strong incentive for officials to frame innocent individuals in order to gain a share of any funds confiscated.[18]

Ensuring the proper handling of confidential information is particularly relevant for FIUs given their role in collecting, analyzing, and disseminating financial intelligence. The unauthorized release of confidential information may have serious consequences. Tipping off by a corrupt official might sabotage ongoing investigations. Past practices suggest that information policy should incorporate provisions for the classification of sensitive information, and the "need to know" principle should be applied internally to regulate the access to restricted information. FIUs may benefit from adopting the dual control "four-eyes" principle of risk management. This principle refers to such safeguards as dual control of assets, requiring two signatures on key documents, and a general presumption of cross-checking, review, and segregation of functions. Such arrangements minimize the chances of malfeasance (as well as innocent error). However, dual control may be particularly challenging for small, developing countries where staff shortages are already pronounced. For example, several Pacific island states have a one-person FIU, including Niue with a total population of just thirteen hundred.

A hypothetical (to the authors' knowledge) example of what could go wrong was provided by one interview source. An FIU official in country A receives a request from an FIU in country B for financial intelligence with respect to a particular individual. The official in country A is the only person in the FIU who knows about the request for this information. This official may then be tempted to contact the individual in question to give advance warning of the investigation, to improperly refuse the request, or to falsify the answer, in each case in return for a bribe. A dual control system would not entirely eliminate this vulnerability (the two officials could collude), but it would make such abuses more difficult to conceal.

Financial Intelligence Unit Independence and Capacity

A clear necessity for the insulation of FIUs from improper influence is operational independence. This criterion is emphasized by the Egmont Group, the international club of FIUs. Financial intelligence units that do not possess operational independence in law and fact represent a major point of vulnerability to corruption. At a minimum, independence requires the autonomous ability to hire and fire personnel, preserve basic pay and conditions, and decide which cases to investigate, prosecute, and/or pass on to prosecutorial authorities (depending on the structure and prerogatives of the FIU). Beyond these basic prerequisites, there is some disagreement as to the trade-off between independence and capacity, particularly in the developing world where resource constraints are tight.[19]

Some international organizations indicate that especially in small, developing countries, having a stand-alone FIU may be too expensive. Creating a stand-alone FIU to ensure independence may be false economy if that FIU is untenable because of a lack of resources. Such an agency may lack even the most basic facilities (e.g., electricity supply), and thus be ineffective. One of the reasons that there have been so few examples of corruption in FIUs reported in developing countries (apart from their relative novelty) may be that these bodies have not yet become effective enough to be worth corrupting. If understaffed and under-resourced FIUs do not pose much of a deterrent to corrupt activities, those engaged in corrupt practice have little need to exert improper influence over them.

One alternative is to house the FIU within the central bank. This option provides the advantage of association with one of the best-functioning institutions in low-capacity countries. Furthermore, the central bank can be expected to have a close working relationship with the private financial sector.

A further extension of nesting FIUs within other independent bodies would be to co-locate the FIU within the national anticorruption agency. An example is Nigeria's powerful Economic and Financial Crimes Commission, which has responsibility for both money laundering and corruption (though there is also a separate Nigerian anticorruption office).[20] Mauritius adopted a similar approach in its 2000 legislation against economic crimes, though this has since been updated to create more distinct AML and anticorruption roles.[21] This would be one solution to the common problem of a lack of communication (or even acquaintance) between anticorruption and AML bodies that this book identifies as one of the most serious problems affecting efforts in these interlinked areas. Conceivably, this solution might also be more economical than having two separate bodies. Another potential positive is that the FIU would be subject to the same integrity safeguards as apply to the anticorruption agency. The extent to which these potential benefits have actually eventuated for countries adopting this solution, however, or would eventuate for countries that might emulate Nigeria and Mauritius in this fashion is not known. Those interviewed generally saw greater communication and joint training between anticorruption and AML agencies as being preferable to a full merger of the two. This ambivalence perhaps reflects reservations concerning a perceived politicization of the anticorruption process in Nigeria.

The Judicial System

Reflecting several decades' experience of endemic corruption, a Kenyan proverb suggests "Why hire a lawyer when you can buy a judge?" Even the best financial intelligence will not be sufficient to make an impact on money laundering if the judicial system is corrupt. In response to this priority, this section covers two main topics: the vulnerability of judges to corruption, and the susceptibility of the prosecutorial system to improper political influence. The United Nations, the Commonwealth, and especially Transparency

International have over the last few years produced voluminous and valuable material on preventing corruption in the judiciary. Turning to the issue of the prosecutorial system, one of the starkest illustrations of the problems that can arise is the current controversy over the British government's decision to cancel an investigation of the al-Yamamah arms deal.

Among the common vulnerabilities to judicial corruption identified by the Commonwealth are: a lack of public guidelines on judicial ethics; a lack of judicial training and mentoring programs in ethics and anticorruption; threats to the principles of appointment and promotion on merit through a competitive and transparent process; court hearings that are not open to the public; judges' salaries that are too low to provide a secure livelihood; and the reluctance of judges to undergo training in anticorruption principles, especially when the training is conducted by non-judges. The UNCAC calls for measures to strengthen judicial systems in the following terms: "Each State Party shall, in accordance with the fundamental principles of its legal system and without prejudice to judicial independence, take measures to strengthen integrity and to prevent opportunities for corruption among members of the judiciary" (Article 11). In 2006 the UN Economic and Social Committee endorsed the Bangalore Principles for Judicial Conduct. Further detailed guidance is provided by the Commonwealth Limassol Recommendation on Combating Corruption within the Judiciary.[22]

In 2007 Transparency International released its Global Corruption Report with the special theme of corruption in the judiciary. This contained many of the same recommendations on corruption prevention already covered under the section on FIUs (asset registers, codes of conduct, conflicts of interest, etc.). Also emphasized are transparent and merit-based principles of appointing, promoting, and sanctioning judges. In general, the corruption threats to the judiciary in relation to money laundering cases are little different from those judges face in other kinds of cases. To the extent that there are vulnerabilities specific to the money laundering-corruption nexus, they reflect the complexity of these cases, and the tendency to require cooperation from two or more countries. If the judiciary in any one country involved is corrupt, this will tend to hinder legal remedies in the other jurisdictions also. For example, if a jurisdiction is perceived as having a corrupt judiciary, it is unlikely that other countries will permit individuals to be extradited to that jurisdiction. This will also tend to endanger asset recovery cases.[23]

According to the 2007 Global Corruption Report, judicial corruption may produce a spiral of unaccountability: poorly paid judges become susceptible to corruption; the corrupt judiciary undermines efforts to attack corruption and money laundering; this failure in turn prevents either successful deterrence of financial crime or asset recovery from abroad; the country becomes still more impoverished; judges' pay remains low.[24]

Also included are salutary examples of judicial corruption and irregularities in relation to money laundering cases. In Mexico two armed individuals with connections to known drug traffickers were detained with $7 million in cash and a further $500,000 in valuables after attempting to evade the police. In contravention of the criminal code the judge ordered both individuals freed, even though further investigations in progress against them meant they should have been held. The same judge freed the son of the local drug cartel boss after he was accused of money laundering and murder. Transparency International alleged that these decisions, both reversed on appeal, were a direct result of criminal influence over the judge.[25] The same report also refers to a case in Nicaragua where $600,000 was seized after five individuals were convicted of money laundering. While the individuals were serving their sentences, their representatives managed to withdraw this money with the authorization of the Supreme Court.[26] Once again, Transparency International alleges that this was a result of judicial corruption. The Supreme Court in Nicaragua has a monopoly on initiating investigations of judicial irregularities. It chose not to initiate an investigation in this case.

Complementing the general corruption prevention measures covered elsewhere in this chapter and the Commonwealth Limassol recommendations, Transparency International makes several other specific and compelling recommendations. The process for hearing complaints and taking disciplinary action against judges should be transparent. The reasoning behind judicial decisions should be published. Judges should declare conflicts of interest, and may be included in asset registries, again with the requirement that to be effective asset registers must be regularly updated and cross-checked against data collected by tax and AML authorities. It is important, though, that these measures are applied in a proportionate manner that does not undermine public confidence in the judiciary.

Turning to prosecutorial independence, for the most serious and large-scale instances of corruption-based money laundering, there is a real danger that high-ranking political officials will be able to sabotage the proper functioning of the AML system. This might take the form of cabinet-level officials withholding permission to prosecute, even once sufficient evidence for a prosecution has been gathered. The failure to prosecute corrupt officials was the main factor that precipitated the resignation and flight of Kenya's anticorruption head in 2005. But this kind of failure may occur in developed as well as in developing countries. The topic of senior public officials is one of the most important concerns of this book, and is dealt with separately at length in chapter 4, but prosecutorial independence as part of the AML system is discussed later in this chapter.

British Aerospace and the Al-Yamamah Case

It is important that the loophole of declining to prosecute cases on grounds of "national security" be carefully investigated, as is currently being done by the OECD Working Group on Bribery. The problem has recently come to the fore in the case of the United Kingdom's decision to abandon a corruption investigation against British Aerospace Systems (BAE) involving arms sales to Saudi Arabia. Traditionally, along with the minerals industry, the arms business has been widely portrayed as blighted by systematic corruption.

Responding to this al-Yamamah case, the OECD has noted: "a number of questions remain unanswered and the Working Group maintains its serious concerns as to whether the decision was consistent with the OECD Anti-Bribery Convention."[27] Mark Pieth, the head of the OECD Working Group, became involved in a heated exchange with the U.K. government over the al-Yamamah case and the British government's attempts to undermine Pieth in response to his tough line.[28] The credibility of the British government, and individual U.K. citizens in international organizations, on corruption issues has been significantly eroded by this scandal.[29]

The facts of the BAE case are still bitterly disputed. Undoubtedly more information will emerge once ongoing investigations have been concluded, including one by the U.S. Justice Department. But thanks to the diligent investigation of two reporters for the *Guardian* (David Leigh and Rob Evans), it is possible to establish the outlines of how BAE allegedly arranged its corrupt payments to officials from Saudi Arabia and other BAE customers in return for arms orders.[30] According to Leigh and Evans, BAE paid its bribes through a front company Novelmight, until 1999 registered in the United Kingdom, thereafter reincorporated as a British Virgin

Islands International Business Company. Novelmight has its office in Geneva and uses the Swiss branch of Lloyds Bank. Decisions to make particular deals were made by senior BAE executives traveling to Novelmight's offices. The contracts with the agents that actually transferred the bribe payments were arranged by Swiss lawyers, with payments routed through separate offshore companies. Prominent among these were Red Diamond and Poseidon Trading Investments (again incorporated in the British Virgin Islands, incorrectly referred to by Leigh and Evans as a "financial black hole"). These companies each had bank accounts in Switzerland, the United Kingdom, and the United States, and had been formed by Liechtenstein Corporate Service Provider ATU.

In September 2003 the U.K. Serious Fraud Office began a formal investigation into al-Yamamah under the Anti-Terrorism, Crime and Security Act of 2001. This decision followed media publicity accorded to corruption allegations made by a former BAE employee. In July 2006 the National Audit Office again refused to release the results of a 1992 investigation of earlier corruption allegations made against BAE, the only such investigation ever suppressed in this manner. By November–December, the Serious Fraud Office was making progress in its attempts to access bank records from Switzerland, but there were also rumors that the Saudis were threatening to cancel a ten-billion-pound follow-on order for seventy-two additional fighter planes unless the investigation was quashed. On December 14, 2006, Attorney General Lord Goldsmith announced the termination of the investigation. Prime Minister Blair explained that there had not been sufficient evidence to bring the case to a conclusion, and that continuing the investigation would jeopardize intelligence ties with Saudi Arabia (both these claims were later contradicted by the Serious Fraud Office and MI6, respectively[31]). Blair also emphasized the jobs at stake, but carefully ruled this out as a factor in the decision; economic interest is specifically forbidden as a defense in the OECD Anti-Bribery Convention.

Groups opposed to the arms trade appealed the decision to the high court. Dismissed by one of its opponents as "a hopeless challenge brought by a bunch of tree-hugging hippies," the appeal scored an unlikely success in April 2008 when the High Court ruled that the decision to stop the investigation was unlawful. Going beyond this decision, the judges excoriated the government, lamenting that "so bleak a picture of the impotence of the law invites at least dismay, if not outrage." Criticizing the craven submission of the U.K.

government, the attorney general and the prime minister personally to Saudi threats in terms widely reported in the press. The verdict went on:

> No one suggested to those uttering the threat that it was futile, that the United Kingdom's system of democracy forbad pressure being exerted on an independent prosecutor whether by the domestic executive or by anyone else; no one even hinted that the courts would strive to protect the rule of law and protect the independence of the prosecutor by striking down any decision he might be tempted to make in submission to the threat.[32]

As embarrassing as this outcome has been, the government as yet has not been forced to reopen the investigation.

Even if the description earlier of the corrupt payments is accurate (which of course BAE vigorously denies), is there a money laundering aspect? From the perspective of corrupt officials, the problem arises in laundering their bribes. The current U.S. Department of Justice investigation into the al-Yamamah specifically targets the question of whether U.S. banks were used to launder bribes paid to Saudi officials (interestingly, Britain has refused to provide information requested by the U.S. government for this investigation).[33] One solution, allegedly practiced by BAE, was to fund lavish holidays for officials (wining and dining potential clients has a long and disreputable history in the arms business[34]). However, intermediary agents paying the bribes may also assist corrupt officials in hiding their illicit gains. Thus in 1996 a Qatari official admitted to receiving a £6 million bribe from BAE in an offshore account. In 2007 Sailesh Vithlani admitted to being the agent for a $12 million BAE kickback in return for an order for a $40 million radar from Tanzania. The money was deposited in a Swiss account in the name of a shell company.[35] In this case the British government has opted not to stifle the investigation, so far at least.

Beyond this particular imbroglio, national security is such an elastic concept that it could conceivably be used by highly placed corrupt officials to sabotage almost any kind of investigation. Sani Abacha, along with many other corrupt governments, justified his massive looting of the Nigerian government treasury on national security grounds. The more general problem exposed by the al-Yamamah case relates to the prosecutorial function in Commonwealth countries such as the United Kingdom (and many of the fifty-two other Commonwealth nations). At issue is the dual position of the attorney general, both a member of the cabinet and an independent legal officer, whose permission is required to prosecute senior public officials for corruption. Such a dual role creates a serious conflict of interest: the decision to bring charges against one government minister depends on the assent of a fellow minister. One solution is contained in the 2003 Report of the House of Lords /House of Commons Joint Committee on the Draft Corruption Bill that ministerial involvement in the prosecutorial decision in corruption cases should be avoided.[36] The two roles could be separated, reassigning the prerogative to bring charges to a genuinely independent legal official outside the government, such as the director of public prosecutions. In a move that speaks volumes about its priorities, however, the British government has instead moved to make it easier for the attorney general to block investigations if the government feels they might compromise national security.

Problems associated with political discretion over corruption prosecutions is by no means exclusive to common law countries. During its implementation review reports, the Council of Europe's GRECO has highlighted potentially serious deficiencies in this area in a large number of its members. Politically appointed prosecutor generals in civil law countries often enjoy wide discretion in deciding to initiate, continue, or terminate prosecutions. Similar to the situation with judges, GRECO has also emphasized the need for a transparent, objective, and merit-based system for the appointment, promotion, and disciplining of prosecutors in order to avoid political interference.

Private Sector Corruption and Money Laundering: Banks and Corporate Service Providers

Combating money laundering is above all a problem of information. Most of the information necessary to successfully attack money laundering is in the hands of private sector firms. Although it is FIUs that collate, analyze, and disseminate intelligence, the raw material is provided as suspicious transaction reports by banks and other firms. Because the private sector is such a crucial component of the AML system, if firms intentionally or unintentionally fail to play their role, the effectiveness of the overall system is severely compromised.

Historically, corruption was regarded as the abuse of public office for private gain. The bribery of one private party by another was made a criminal offence in the United States in the late nineteenth century and in the United Kingdom in the early part of the twentieth century. However, in both countries, commercial corruption was a low priority for law enforcement. Countries such as Hong Kong and Singapore have been exceptional in giving equal importance to combating both private and public sector corruption. The organization that has done most to address this general gap is the Paris-based International Chamber of Commerce. The UNCAC recommends in Articles 21 and 22 that states adopt a comprehensive law that prohibits all manifestations of private corruption.

This section examines the importance of the private sector in the money laundering-corruption nexus. Unsurprisingly, banks are key players. One of the simplest ways to launder relatively small sums of money in developed countries is to bribe a bank teller not to record a cash transaction as suspicious.[37] On a much larger scale is the Bank of New York case, examined below, that illustrates how private sector corruption can involve large-scale money laundering. Just as important, though with a much lower media profile, are CSPs: firms that set up, service, and sell shell corporations, trusts, and similar corporate vehicles. Although a perfectly legitimate business, CSPs may facilitate the process of laundering through constructing complicated chains of corporate vehicles. Similar to the BAE scandal sketched out earlier, some of the largest cases of money laundering, corruption, tax evasion, and corporate fraud have been characterized by the intimate involvement of these corporate intermediaries.

The Bank of New York, Nauru, and Russian Money Laundering

One particularly well-publicized private sector corruption and money laundering case involved the unlikely combination of the Bank of New York, Russian organized crime, and the tiny South Pacific island republic of Nauru. This Bank of New York case epitomizes the danger of deliberate private sector involvement in the corruption-money laundering nexus. Aside from the direct legal fallout, after 1999 the publicity from the scandal inspired a major U.S. Senate investigation,[38] and reinforced the FATF's determination to blacklist recalcitrant financial centers.

The basic details of the scheme used reveal the typical use of chains of interlocking firms and other corporate vehicles (in this instance, banks) to obscure the link between the illegal origins of the funds and the ultimate beneficiary. The money in question derived from the murky privatizations in Russia from the early 1990s, as well as tax evasion, kidnapping, and may have also included money loaned to Russia by the International Monetary Fund. As a first step, two Russian banks, Sobinbank and MDM, created two new Russian banks, Depozitarno-Kliringovy Bank [Deposit-Clearing Bank] and Flamingo Bank. These latter two banks were used as conduits to pass the funds to a Nauruan shell bank (that is, a bank with no tangible presence, no office, and no employees) called Sinex. Sinex set up a bank-to-bank correspondent account with the Commercial Bank of San Francisco, and made a series of payments to a variety of Delaware shell companies (again, a company with no physical presence, no office, and no employees) set up especially to receive these funds. The Delaware companies had accounts with the Bank of New York. Finally, these Delaware shell companies dispatched the money to several offshore centers where the money was registered as legitimate funds from U.S. corporations.[39] Although the scheme had originally been designed by Russian bankers, it was operated by Lucy Edwards (born Ludmilla Pritsker in then Leningrad), a vice president of Bank of New York, and her husband Peter Berlin. The Bank of New York itself had an impeccable pedigree in the U.S. financial system, having been established in 1784 by none other than Alexander Hamilton. Using this network Edwards and Berlin processed one hundred and sixty thousand transactions over a three-year period worth $7 billion. In return, they were paid $1.8 million, money that they hid in the Isle of Man.

Initial news reports stressed that Nauru had played a pivotal role. Indeed, speaking of the building that acted as the legal residence of Nauru's shell banks, a *New York Times* article reported on "the billion-dollar shack . . . that some say brought Russia to its knees and destroyed it as a modern nation."[40] Supporting this notion of Nauru's cataclysmic impact on the Russian economy, the Russian Central Bank claimed that in 1998 alone $70 billion from Russia had been laundered through Nauru's banks. These claims seem overstated. For all the exoticism of the South Pacific connection, and the undoubted recklessness of Nauru's government, the Nauruan bank was but one link in a very long chain substantively based in Russia and the United States.[41] The Russian Central Bank has never provided any evidence to support its $70 billion claim (which has repeatedly been quoted at face value in government and media reports), and was subsequently shown to have engaged in some highly irregular financial activity of its own, also involving tax havens. Russia itself, like Nauru, was blacklisted shortly after the scandal by the FATF for having deficient AML laws.

The deliberate collusion between a senior Bank of New York official and foreign criminals clearly illustrates how private corruption and money laundering can be linked. As a result, in 2005 the Bank of New York was fined $26 million and forced to pay an additional $12 million to reimburse other banks for their losses. The bank was put under a special monitoring regime to check on its AML policies. In 2007 the Russian Customs Service decided to pursue legal action against the bank for $22.5 billion.[42] Even more direct evidence of this link is provided by the conduct of the two original Russian banks, Sobinbank and MDM, where it seems it was the whole corporate structure rather than just one or two rogue officials that was deliberately involved in criminal activities. In response to Sobinbank's protestations of innocence in the affair, a U.S. judge noted: "The court cannot fathom how billions of Sobinbank's dollars could have been transferred out of its constantly replenished B.O.N.Y. account, to accounts in the United States, without Sobinbank's knowledge or wilful blindness."[43] While the conduit banks DKB and Flamingo were closed down by Russian authorities, no penalties were applied to Sobinbank or MDM, which continue to operate today.

Corporate Service Providers and Anonymous Shell Companies

Complex money laundering schemes (including the al-Yamamah and Bank of New York cases) often involve companies and trusts as part of the layering process to camouflage the trail of evidence. The use of corporate vehicles in hiding various kinds of financial crimes has been a long-standing concern for a variety of international organizations. This is evidenced by the coverage in the 1998 UNODC report *Financial Havens, Banking Secrecy and Money Laundering*; the 2001 OECD study *Behind the Corporate Veil: Using Corporate Entities for Illicit Purposes*; and most recently the 2006 FATF study *The Misuse of Corporate Vehicles, Including Trust and Corporate Service Providers.*

The first page of the 2006 FATF study *The Misuse of Corporate Vehicles, Including Trust and Corporate Service Providers* states the following:

> Organized crime groups or individual criminals tend to seek out the services of professionals to benefit from their expertise in setting up schemes that the criminals then use for illicit purposes. Criminals may seek advice from trust and company service providers...as to the best corporate vehicles or jurisdictions to use to support their

> schemes, with [service providers] having varying degrees of awareness of or involvement in the illicit purposes underlying their clients' activities.

For the majority of cases involving the use of corporate vehicles to assist in money laundering, including laundering the proceeds of corruption, CSPs were wittingly or unwittingly involved in obscuring the illegal nature of the funds. Commonly this is done through the provision of shell companies, particularly international business companies (IBCs). However, other corporate vehicles, such as trusts, foundations, and partnerships, may also be used in this manner to launder the proceeds of corruption.

As well as setting up shell companies, CSPs may then assist in opening overseas corporate bank accounts through which to channel funds. Or such companies may be used in generating false invoices, fictitious consultancy fees, or bogus loans. Corporate service providers are often not covered by the requirement to report suspicious transactions. To the extent CSPs who are covered by this requirement fail to lodge a report in the expectation of personal gain, or are bribed to actively assist in laundering money, this kind of private sector corruption represents a key risk to the integrity of the AML system.

In addition to multilateral organizations raising the matter of regulating CSPs as a law enforcement and money laundering priority, various U.S. government studies on the subject have come to a similar conclusion. Thus a Government Accountability Office study from 2000 indicated that CSPs were active in providing hundreds of Delaware shell corporations to groups of organized criminals from Russia. These Delaware corporations were then used to open U.S. bank accounts and through them launder the proceeds of corruption. Further studies by the Treasury in 2005, the Government Accountability Office in 2006, and the Financial Crimes Enforcement Network in 2007 again drew attention to the threat posed by U.S. shell corporations. Exacerbating this danger is the fact that it is impossible to establish the beneficial (real) ownership of such entities under the laws of forty-seven of fifty U.S. states.[44] The combination of unlicensed CSPs and corporate vehicles for which it is difficult or impossible to establish the beneficial owner represents a serious danger to the ability of a jurisdiction to meet FATF standards (particularly Recommendation 33) and Egmont Best Practice (see Legal point 7). It also represents a danger to the integrity of the financial sector as a whole. The identity of shell companies' real owners may be hidden when bearer securities are allowed, or when companies can be formed online without the need for supporting documentation (e.g., notarized copies of a passport). The same holds true when there is no obligation to disclose the beneficiary or settlor of a trust.

It is possible to discern the state of play with regards to licensing CSPs with the data presented in the 2006 FATF report. Of the jurisdictions surveyed, twenty-two allow intermediaries to form corporate vehicles but do not include them within the AML regime.[45] A majority of the seventeen jurisdictions in the sample that allow trusts do not regulate them (e.g., in terms of identifying beneficiaries). Sixteen jurisdictions allow anonymous bearer shares, many in combination with corporate and nominee directors, enabling anonymous companies to be established.[46] In nearly all cases, information on ownership in company registries covers only legal, not beneficial, ownership. In fourteen jurisdictions it is not mandatory to keep the information with company registries regularly updated (including the United States and Germany). Only nine jurisdictions regulate CSPs with a license system. These intermediaries are regulated in the Bahamas, Jersey, Guernsey, the Isle of Man, and Gibraltar, but unregulated in the United States and the United Kingdom.[47]

How can this serious shortcoming be addressed? The FATF study of the misuse of corporate vehicles recommends that CSPs should be subject to a licensing requirement, including a test of fit and proper persons, and explicitly brought under the suspicious transaction reporting regime, including where the grounds of suspicion relate to corruption. This report was accepted at the February 2007 FATF Strasbourg Plenary, but no specific action to encourage members to license CSPs in this manner was taken. As long as no action is taken, this crucial vulnerability will persist.

Some have raised doubts that such a licensing regime would be impractical, overly expensive, or threaten the commercial viability of CSPs. Yet the experience of imposing similar requirements on small jurisdictions such as the Bahamas, Jersey, the Isle of Man, and the British Virgin Islands indicates that such worries are overstated. If such small jurisdictions can successfully implement a robust system of CSP licensing, there is no reason why all FATF members cannot do likewise. Indeed, even very small developing jurisdictions such as Vanuatu (which has had registered trust formation agents since the 1970s) has recently introduced a licensing system for CSPs modeled on that in place on the Isle of Man. An example of best practice in CSP regulation can be taken from the Isle of Man's Corporate Service Providers Act of 2000 and Fiduciaries Act of 2005 (including trust providers), a model that the U.S. Government Accounting Office has proposed should be emulated among American states.[48] The Isle of Man legislation covers those who are professionally involved in the formation of companies or trusts; the sale, transfer, or disposal of companies; providing a registered office for a nonresident company; acting as a director, agent, or registered secretary of a company or trustee of a trust; acting or arranging for others to act as a nominee member of shareholder; or offer administrative services for nonresident companies or trusts.[49]

Returning to private sector corruption in banks, a familiar theme from private sector sources is that commonly implementation difficulties tend to be a greater threat to the proper functioning of the AML regime than obsolescent or incomplete legislation.[50] Nor are implementation problems confined to developing countries. For example, the tardy response to the repeated failure of Riggs Bank to observe the stipulations of the Bank Secrecy and USA Patriot Acts, and the active collusion of bank officials in assisting former Chilean dictator Augusto Pinochet to open accounts under false names and hide assets from foreign law enforcement officials using linked trusts and shell companies show that implementation failures can be important even in highly regulated sectors of developed country financial systems.[51]

Even granted that CSPs are licensed, fall within the suspicious transaction reporting regime, and are honest, it is still necessary to inculcate knowledge about corruption-related money laundering. Firms may not be sensitized to report transactions that are suspicious from a corruption-related point of view. To the extent that relevant case studies and typologies are unavailable, that AML training does not include fostering an awareness of corruption issues, and that CSPs making reports in this area do not receive follow-up information from FIUs, it is unlikely that much progress will be made in remedying this weakness in the AML system. Given the artificial and unhelpful isolation that often exists between anticorruption and anti-money laundering agencies this lack of awareness is not surprising.

Conclusion

To the extent that the AML system is corrupted it will not be effective. This chapter has analyzed vulnerabilities to corruption in the

AML system broadly conceived and suggested possible remedies. Three areas are particularly important: the FIU; the judicial system (including prosecution); and the private sector. The chapter has summarized best international practice in corruption prevention to provide pointers in strengthening the integrity of FIUs. To the extent that these practices are not already being applied in FIUs and other public bodies in the AML system this represents a point of vulnerability to corruption. These practices include codes of conduct, and policies relating to conflicts of interest, and security of confidential information. Asset registers comprise an especially valuable tool for ensuring the integrity and proper functioning of FIUs. For maximum benefit asset registers should be regularly updated, cross-checked with data from AML and tax authorities to ensure accuracy, and there should be criminal penalties for false, misleading, or incomplete declarations. For small and developing countries the requirement for operational independence does not preclude the FIU being housed within the central bank. Otherwise, a stand-alone FIU may be ineffective due to basic resource constraints.

Judicial corruption presents a serious threat to the proper functioning of the AML regime and the justice system generally. Where judges are poorly paid, appointment and promotion procedures are opaque or arbitrary, hearings are held in secret, and there is a lack of ethics and anticorruption training, and judges will be vulnerable to improper influence. In complex corruption-related money laundering cases spanning two or more jurisdictions even one corrupt judge may jeopardize the whole effort. The situation in which the decision to prosecute senior public officials for corruption lies with a government minister or political appointee creates a serious conflict of interest. Prosecutorial authority in this context should be vested in an independent legal authority outside the government.

The quality and quantity of financial intelligence received from the private sector form the foundation of any successful AML system. To the extent that officials in banks or other firms can be bribed to assist in laundering, tens of thousands of criminal transactions may be hidden. The often unlicensed and unregulated status of CSPs represents a serious risk to the integrity of efforts to counter money laundering. This vulnerability is acute in jurisdictions where there is no legal provision for private sector corruption, and where CSPs may form corporate vehicles for nonresidents where the beneficial owner remains hidden. In response it was suggested that jurisdictions that have not already done so move to license CSPs and bring them within the AML system.

CHAPTER 4

SENIOR PUBLIC OFFICIALS AND POLITICALLY EXPOSED PERSONS

Introduction and Overview

An important new strategy in combating serious forms of international corruption is anti-money laundering (AML) regulations governing high-level political figures. The Swiss authorities were the first to recognize the connection between grand corruption and money laundering, largely as a result of their experience in dealing with the illicit assets of Philippine president Ferdinand Marcos. The U.S. Patriot Act in 2001, the Financial Action Task Force (FATF) in June 2003, the United Nations (UN) in December 2003, and the European Union (EU) in 2005 have enacted measures addressing the challenge of senior public officials to AML systems. The new international and national standards recognize that senior public officials, who are frequently called politically exposed persons (PEPs), pose a higher risk of money laundering, especially in connection with corruption. In turn, the Basel Committee on Banking Supervision has identified grand corruption as posing a significant reputational risk to banks, financial centers, and to the international banking system.

This chapter explores why senior public officials should be managed as part of AML obligations. It deals with the question of whether domestic senior public officials have inhibited the adoption and the effective implementation of adequate AML measures. It outlines the vulnerabilities of AML institutions to PEPs. A major challenge is that there is no single agreed-upon definition of PEPs, or even a consensus that this is the best term. Questions of terminology aside, perhaps the best-developed definition of PEPs is that contained in the EU Third Directive on Money Laundering. This definition is more precise than FATF standards, in particular its treatment of legal persons connected to PEPs by beneficial ownership or control.

Gaps in the existing coverage of PEP rules are the omission of subnational leaders (e.g., regional governors in federal systems), senior figures in political parties, military and security police leaders, those directing public enterprises, and politically connected religious leaders and managers of charities. Effective laws require that these categories are included within regulations governing senior public figures. The reality of extended families or clans in some cultural contexts, and extramarital affairs, are further complications to be considered.

A more serious omission, however, is the restriction of PEP regulations in a large majority of countries to cover only foreign officials, and not domestic ones (exceptions including Brazil, Mexico, and Belgium). But Article 52(1) of the United Nations Convention Against Corruption (UNCAC) does not distinguish between foreign and domestic public officials. As such, there is an expectation (if not an international legal obligation) that all those countries ratifying the UNCAC should broaden their PEP coverage to include domestic or national officials. This will most likely be controversial, as earlier some governments refused to pass AML laws while these laws contained national PEP provisions. In fulfilling this new expectation, governments can learn from the best available practice from countries such as Mexico and Brazil in applying enhanced scrutiny to national PEPs in preparation for legislation in this area.

Evidence from the private sector further suggests that the coverage of PEPs in FATF Recommendation 6 is no longer state-of-the-art, and is therefore no longer the best guide for national law. Prominent private sector firms regard the different PEP definitions in play as a secondary issue compared with the lack of implementation of "know your customer" provisions. Complementing the provisions of the UNCAC with regard to domestic PEPs many firms already apply a similar risk-based approach to foreign and domestic PEPs. Multilateral standard-setters and national regulators have fallen behind superior private sector practice.

At present just how PEPs are to be identified is under-specified and largely delegated to the private firms, who will often not have sufficient expertise and resources to perform this task adequately. This gap is even more pronounced given the likelihood of the PEP category being expanded. At the very least, governments must be prepared to give more and more specific guidance to private firms on identifying PEPs, if not become directly involved in drawing up PEP lists.

Why Manage Senior Public Officials as Part of Anti-Money Laundering Obligations?

The FATF first examined the risks posed by senior public officials to the financial sector in 2001 when it analyzed the money laundering vulnerabilities of private banking. Senior public officials who used the private banking services of international financial institutions posed a risk because of the possibility that the source of their deposits was illicit, especially corruption. The FATF's perceptions were influenced by the landmark hearings and report of the U.S. Senate into private banking where it was revealed that U.S. multinational banks had facilitated the laundering of the corrupt proceeds of the political leaders of Nigeria, Mexico, Pakistan, and Gabon.[1] In 2003 the FATF identified PEPs as requiring additional scrutiny because of the higher risks of money laundering and terrorist financing. Following a review of the FATF Recommendations, it was decided that Revised Recommendations would be issued in 2003. From the perspective of the FATF, the money laundering risks associated with PEPs were spelt out in its 2003–2004 Typologies Report:

> the sources for the funds that a PEP may try to launder are not only bribes, illegal kickbacks and other directly corruption-related proceeds but also may be embezzlement or outright theft of State assets or funds from political parties and unions, as well as tax fraud. Indeed in certain cases, a PEP may be directly implicated in other types of illegal activities such as organized crime or narcotics trafficking. PEPs that come from countries or regions where corruption is endemic, organized and systemic seem to present the greatest potential risk; however, it should be noted that corrupt or dishonest PEPs can be found in almost any country.[2]

The FATF Typologies Report contained four case studies demonstrating the linkage between corruption and money laundering. These studies show that the "techniques employed by PEPs to launder illegal proceeds [are] very similar to those of other criminal money launderers. PEPs may use distinctive banking arrangements to assist them in creating a complex or sophisticated network of transactions to protect illicit assets they may have generated."[3] The implication of these findings was that financial institutions should be obliged to perform enhanced due diligence on those customers identified as senior public officials or PEPs. The FATF view, which is enshrined in its revised Recommendations, is that increased surveillance on the financial activities of senior public officials acts as a deterrence to serious corruption and improves the chances of detection of corruption through the reporting of suspect transactions.

The Bank for International Settlements (BIS), the world's central bank for national central banks, has focused on the risks posed by senior public officials to the international banking system. The BIS's Basel Committee on Banking Supervision expressed its concerns as to the reputational consequences of grand corruption and money laundering:

> Accepting and managing funds from corrupt PEPs will severely damage the bank's own reputation and can undermine public confidence in the ethical standards of an entire financial centre, since such cases usually receive extensive media attention and strong political reaction, even if the illegal origin of the assets is often difficult to prove. In addition, the bank may be subject to costly information requests and seizure orders from law enforcement or judicial authorities (including international mutual assistance procedures in criminal matters) and could be liable to actions for damages by the state concerned or the victims of a regime. Under certain circumstances, the bank and/or its officers and employees themselves can be exposed to charges of money laundering, if they know or should have known that the funds stemmed from corruption or other serious crimes.[4]

Since one of the key aims of bank regulation is prudential supervision, the Basel Committee's focus is on the impact of PEP money laundering cases on the safety and soundness of banks and the integrity of the banking system. Where a multinational bank is involved in a corruption-related money laundering scandal, the impact is frequently not limited to a specific country. There is the potential for contagion risk, which may undermine confidence in the international banking system and have a spiraling effect on business confidence and the underlying "real economy."

Power and Immunities of Senior Public Officials

Special Status and Immunities

Senior public officials enjoy a special status in their country of origin because of their executive, legislative, judicial, military, and/or bureaucratic power. They are in a unique position of influence in their nation state and perhaps also diplomatically when they are acting abroad. The enactment and implementation of AML laws and systems are potentially vulnerable to PEPs because such measures may threaten the financial interests of PEPs.

One unique legal problem that senior public officials present is that of legal immunities. In corruption cases, senior public officials and politicians accused of corruption will frequently object to civil and criminal jurisdictional claims on the basis that they are protected by specific privileges or immunities. International legal instruments provide some guidance on the scope of immunities. For example, Article 40(2) of the UNCAC provides:

> Each State Party shall take such measures as may be necessary to establish or maintain, in accordance with its legal system and constitutional principles, an appropriate balance between any immunities or jurisdictional privileges accorded to its public officials for the performance of their functions and the possibility, when necessary, of effectively investigating, prosecuting and adjudicating offences established in accordance with this Convention.

Article 40(2) of the UNCAC gives a state a wide measure of discretion as to how it regulates the immunities of its senior public officials. This article does not require states to change their domestic laws. This is unfortunate became many countries provide what may be considered excessive immunities to their heads of state, senior government officials, members of parliament, and state governors. Some countries, for example, Gambia,[5] have passed constitutional laws giving former heads of state immunity from legal prosecution even after they have left office, while others such as Turkey make it nearly impossible to remove immunities from senior officials.[6]

National constitutions frequently provide immunities to certain constitutional position holders while they are in office.[7] For example, under Article 68 of the French Constitution, the president is immune for acts committed in the exercise of the functions of the office, except for the crime of high treason. This functional immunity is designed to protect incumbent French presidents from the inconvenience or disturbance of their functions while they are in office, and to protect the independence of the executive office. The French courts have further held that the French president cannot be investigated or required to testify before a court while in office; in effect, any investigation is suspended until the president's term of office expires.[8] This happened in the case of French president Jacques

Chirac when between 1999 and 2001 French examining magistrates unsuccessfully sought to question him concerning his knowledge of financial transactions involving his political party, *Rassemblement pour la République*. After Chirac's ten-year presidency ended in May 2007, French magistrates revived their investigations into Chirac's case. One of these investigations focused on Chirac's role in approving what is alleged to be bogus work contracts handed out to political supporters while Chirac was mayor of Paris from 1977 to 1995. Several of Chirac's political allies, including former prime minister Alain Juppé, have been convicted over scams relating to Chirac's years as mayor of Paris.

Perhaps the most controversial case of immunities involves the current prime minister of Italy, Silvio Berlusconi.[9] Under Article 68 of the Italian Constitution, members of parliament enjoy immunity from criminal prosecution for offences committed in the exercise of their functions; but this immunity does not apply to offences committed prior to the assumption of office. Silvio Berlusconi was one of Italy's richest entrepreneurs prior to becoming a member of parliament and prime minister. In November 1999 Berlusconi and his attorney Cesare Previti (who subsequently became Berlusconi's defense minister) were indicted for allegedly bribing a judge during a takeover battle for control of the state-owned supermarket chain SME. In June 2003, the Italian parliament passed a law that provided the five most senior office holders in Italy (the head of government, the president of the republic, the president of the constitutional court, and the speakers of the houses of parliament) immunity from criminal prosecution until after they had completed their terms of office. Berlusconi as the head of government was the only one of the five office holders who was then subject to criminal prosecution in Italy. This law was branded by the Italian opposition as "*lex Berlusconi*." In April 2004 the Italian Constitutional Court ruled that this law was unconstitutional in that it violated the guarantee of equal treatment for all citizens and due process. Consequently, the criminal prosecution of Berlusconi was resuscitated. Subsequently, Berlusconi was acquitted of a number of charges and won appeals against various convictions. For instance, he was formally acquitted in April 2007 of charges relating to the corruption of judges in relation to the SME affair; Previti had previously been acquitted in relation to the same matter. However, Berlusconi is still facing criminal charges in Italy relating to embezzlement, false accounting, and tax fraud.

Laws bestowing high ranking officers with immunities from prosecution have presented challenges to developing countries as well. Nigeria has had major difficulties in bringing politicians to account where they enjoy constitutional immunities. Under section 308 of the Nigerian constitution, the serving president, vice president, governors of the thirty-six states and their deputies enjoy immunity from prosecution while they are in office. These immunities apply within the territorial jurisdiction of Nigeria, but have no extraterritorial application. Many of the Nigerian governors have been accused of corruption but have avoided prosecution because of their constitutional immunity. Here are some case examples[10]:

In 2004 Nigerian governor Joshua Davies from the central state of Plateau was arrested and questioned by the London Metropolitan police for the alleged offence of money laundering. He was released on bail, returned to Nigeria, where he has refused to answer any further questions from the London police, relying on his immunity;

In 2005 governor Diepreye Alamieyeseigha of the oil-producing southern state of Bayelsa was arrested in Britain and charged with laundering £1.8 million. While on bail, he escaped to Nigeria where he cannot be extradited to Britain because of his immunity; and

In 2007 a Nigerian federal high court struck out the name of Dr. Emmanuel Ewetan Uduaghan (the governor of the oil rich state of Delta) from a suit instituted by some indigenes of the state requesting the Economic and Financial Crimes Commission (EFCC), to investigate an allegation that Uduaghan conspired with Chief James Ibori to divert over N120 billion of public funds

The Nigerian cases illustrate the challenge faced by prosecutors in corruption-related money laundering cases.[11] Since the immunity is found in the Nigerian constitution, it cannot be waived by the legislature. In practice corrupt governors can only be removed from office by the complex and arduous process of impeachment. However, more recently, eight former governors have been detained after being indicted for corruption charges.

Sometimes national courts are prepared to lift immunities. For example, General Augusto Pinochet who ruled Chile as president of the junta from 1973 to 1990 was on his retirement bestowed with immunity by virtue of his appointment as "Senator for life". In 2005 the Santiago Court of Appeals removed Pinochet's congressional immunity in circumstances where Pinochet was under investigation for embezzlement of public funds. In a separate decision, the Court of Appeals also lifted Pinochet's immunity on tax evasion charges relating to his foreign bank accounts. The Chilean courts had previously, in 2000, removed Pinochet's immunity from prosecution for grave human rights crimes.

Impact of Senior Public Officials on Anti-Money Laundering Laws

One way of evaluating the power of senior public officials is to examine whether they have had any influence on the adoption and/or effective implementation of AML laws. Presumably if senior public officials are corrupt, they are likely to resist the enactment of AML laws that could be used to identify, freeze and confiscate their corrupt monies. Some of our interviewees suggested that certain governments in Africa and the Pacific initially resisted the enactment of AML laws because of the impact of such laws on their political and economic power. There was some opposition by countries to the implementation of the new AML standards because of concerns that this might be the "thin edge of the wedge." If the politicians in country A had close political and economic links with politicians in a neighboring country B, then increased scrutiny of PEPs from country A by financial institutions in country B could have a "boomerang effect" exposing the hidden monies of PEPs from country B. It was for this reason that some national politicians were concerned that new AML measures relating to foreign PEPs might ultimately lead to the application of PEP requirements to national PEPs. The fact that the FATF standards do not cover national PEPs provided a loophole that could allow corrupt local politicians to prosper. This provides an additional argument why international standards on PEPs should apply to both foreign and national PEPs. This issue is discussed in detail later.

Senior public officials are in a unique position to undermine the effective implementation of FATF international standards governing national AML laws. In some countries PEPs have considerable financial power and may own or control significant sectors of the economy, including major financial institutions and the media. For example, it has been alleged that the former prime ministers of

Italy and Thailand, both of whom are billionaires, had the capacity to and may have obstructed investigations into their financial activities. Whatever the truth of these allegations, there is no doubt that wealthy senior public officials may pose a significant potential obstacle to the effective implementation of AML standards. Although the authors are not aware of any specific case of PEPs interfering in the reporting of suspect transactions involving their own illicit financial activities, the fact that such reports are rare should not lead policymakers to become complacent about the potential for PEPs to obstruct the detection and investigation of corruption.

Inertia and lack of political will may contribute to a lackluster investigation of a foreign senior official who is perceived as a friend of or is linked to senior officials or politicians of the current government. Investigations of the foreign PEP may not be handled in a timely fashion or may be subject to such formalistic and inflexible requirements that the investigation may be halted or rendered ineffective in supply of any timely information.[12]

There are additional challenges, as noted by the FATF:

> Because of the special status of PEPs . . . there is often a certain amount of discretion afforded by financial institutions to the financial activities carried out by these persons or on their behalf. If a PEP becomes involved in some sort of criminal activity, this traditional discretion given to them for their financial activities often becomes an obstacle to detecting or investigating crimes in which they may be involved.[13]

The introduction of risk management systems in customer due diligence standards will impose increased legal responsibility on the private sector to detect corruption-related money laundering. But this will not completely solve the problem of detecting financial crime in which senior public officials may be involved.

Investigation Only after Senior Public Official Departs from Office

There is some evidence that the power and the special status of senior public officials may prevent the detection of illegal financial activities in which they or their business associates are involved. In nearly all recent cases of grand corruption, the detection and investigation of the criminal activity of senior political figures occurred only after there was a change of government. While the PEPs were in power, there was no real opportunity for domestic law enforcement agencies to investigate the financial crimes of government leaders. Examples of this include:

President Ferdinand Marcos was investigated by the new government of President Corazon Aquino after he was forced to flee the Philippines in 1986 (see chapter 6);

General Sani Abacha was investigated by a new Nigerian Government in 1998 only after he died of a heart attack (see chapter 5);

President José Arnoldo Alemán Lacayo of Nicaragua was subject to an investigation prompted by his successor Enriques Bolaños, leading to formal charges of corruption in December 2002 (see chapter 5).

When there is a change in government, there is usually an incentive to blame economic problems on the previous regime. This will often include allegations of corruption and economic mismanagement. The successor regime has an obvious interest in exposing and investigating illicit activities of their political enemies. The reliability of accusations made by new governments concerning former senior public officials must be carefully assessed because this may represent a "political settling of scores" rather than a genuine effort to obtain criminal justice.

There have been rare cases where a criminal investigation and prosecution against a sitting head of state or head of government has occurred while they were still in power. The examples of Prime Minister Berlusconi of Italy and President Chirac of France were considered earlier.

Who is a Senior Public Official?

An examination of the international legal instruments and influential international guidelines shows that there is no consistent terminology or comprehensive definition of a senior public official. The FATF and EU Third Money Laundering Directive refers to PEPs, the United States Patriot Act refers to senior public figures, while other texts refer to senior politicians, senior public officials, and/or senior public servants. Although there is some diversity in the requirements, there are some common elements in the definitions of PEPs.

Natural Persons

Both the FATF and the EU Third Money Laundering Directive's initial focus is on PEPs as individuals or natural persons who are in positions of power. For instance, Article 3(8) of the EU Directive defines PEPS as "natural persons who are or have been entrusted with prominent political functions and immediate family members or persons known to be close associates of such persons." The PEP definition in the EU Directive definition was based on the PEP definition in the FATF Recommendations.

Public Officials

The UNCAC, which addresses corruption by public officials and the private sector, does not define senior public figures, but in Article 52(1) refers to "individuals who are, or have been entrusted with prominent public functions." Article 52(1) imposes legally binding obligations on states in dealing with officials who have been given "prominent public functions." There is no definition of this phrase in the UNCAC. The idea of public functions is linked to the definition of public official, which is found in Article 2:

> "Public official" shall mean: (i) any person holding a legislative, executive, administrative or judicial office of a State Party, whether appointed or elected, whether permanent or temporary, whether paid or unpaid, irrespective of that person's seniority; (ii) any other person who performs a public function, including for a public agency or public enterprise, or provides a public service, as defined in the domestic law of the State Party and as applied in the pertinent area of law of that State Party; (iii) any other person defined as a "public official" in the domestic law of a State Party. However, for the purpose of some specific measures contained in chapter II of this Convention, "public official" may mean any person who performs a public function or provides a public service as defined in the domestic law of the State Party and as applied in the pertinent area of law of that State Party.

The wide definition of "public official" in the UNCAC is consistent with a key aim of the Convention to "promote integrity, accountability and proper management of public officers and public property." With the exception of certain limited provisions in the UNCAC, there is no distinction between the obligation of states with respect to foreign and domestic public officials. The UNCAC also encompasses "officials of a public international organization," which is important in that it recognizes the potential for international civil servants to be engaged in corrupt behavior. The necessity for PEP rules to cover international organizations is illustrated by the conviction of two UN officials, including the Russian ex-chairman of the UN's budget oversight committee, for assisting in the laundering of bribes in the oil-for-food scandal.[14]

Prominent Public Functions

The UNCAC, the FATF, and the EU Directive refer to senior public officials as individuals who occupy "prominent public functions." This reference emphasizes the reputational risks of accepting clients who may have been involved in large-scale corrupt activities. Although there are legal and compliance costs, such as fines for failure to carry out adequate PEP due diligence, the underlying reason for implementing a PEP program is to avoid reputational damage. This view is reflected in the Wolfsberg's definition of PEPs: "The term should be understood to include persons whose current or former position can attract publicity beyond the borders of the country concerned and whose financial circumstances may be the subject of additional public interest."[15] The Wolfsberg Group is a voluntary group of leading multinational financial institutions that have promulgated international standards on AML, private banking, and corruption.

The idea of prominent public functions is linked to the position or function exercised by the public official. That is, only senior public officials or persons occupying high-level positions are caught by the definition of PEPs. The international instruments dealing with PEPs and national regulations generally provide a list of examples of high-level positions, so as to assist financial institutions in their interpretation of this requirement. The list varies from the modest examples given by the FATF to the more comprehensive list of the EU Directive. National regulations also differ, with member states of the EU implementing the EU Directive list, which differs from the list in the US Patriot Act. The following list has been compiled based on the relevant international instruments and national legislation. It provides a more comprehensive list of PEPs:

1. heads of state, or heads of government;
2. government ministers;

3. members of the legislature;
4. senior bureaucrats;
5. senior officials of a major political party;
6. ambassadors and charges d'affaires;
7. high-ranking officers in the armed forces;
8. senior members of law enforcement and intelligence agencies;
9. members of the boards of central banks; and
10. senior executives of state-owned enterprises.

No Requirement of Actual Influence or Control of Public Assets

It is sometimes suggested that the definition of a PEP should include the additional requirement that the office of the PEP involves actual influence or control of public assets where there is an increased risk of corruption. For example, the European Commission originally proposed that PEPs would be "natural persons who are or have been entrusted with prominent public functions and whose substantial or complex financial or business transactions may represent an enhanced money laundering risk." However, this definition was considered less precise than the FATF definition and so was altered to remove this requirement.[16] In contrast, industry lobby groups, such as the European Banking Industry Committee, favored the original EU definition because it targeted not PEPs per se but only those PEPs whose transactions involved an "enhanced money laundering risk." The European Banking Industry Committee argued in 2005 that the proposed PEP definition and categorization were inconsistent with the risk-based approach of the EU Directive in that it was over-prescriptive in approach.[17] Similarly the Wolfsberg Group stated in 2008 that "only individuals holding senior, prominent or important positions with substantial authority over policy, operations or the use or allocation of government-owned resources can be PEPs."[18]

Religious Leaders and Charities

The list of PEP categories stated earlier does not address the question of whether senior religious leaders and/or heads of charity organizations connected to senior political figures should be included in the definition of PEPs. In countries where religious leaders hold senior political positions in the executive, parliament, administration, or judiciary, then they should be treated like any other senior public official. A religious leader may also be treated as a PEP when exercising de facto political power or controlling or managing substantial public funds, thereby presenting opportunities for corruption.

The relationship between charities and senior public officials also requires attention. The misuse of charities or religious foundations for money laundering purposes is not a new problem. In 1979 the Shah of Iran was accused in a New York lawsuit of utilizing his Pahlavi foundation as a vehicle for illicit personal and family enrichment. That civil claim, which was launched by the Islamist government of Ayatollah Khomenei, was dismissed on the ground that the United States was not the appropriate forum for the legal suit. More recently, the Attorney General's Office in Indonesia brought a civil suit claiming Rp 15 trillion (US$ 1.6 billion) losses and damages from the Supersemar foundation, which was one of President Suharto's charitable foundations. The Supersemar foundation was established by government regulation for the purpose of providing scholarships to students, but substantial funds were channeled to private businesses. In 2008 the South Jakarta District Court ordered the Supersemar foundation to repay $110 million to the Indonesian government on the basis that the foundation had illegally used government funds for business purposes. However, the Court held that Suharto, who was chairman of the foundation, was not legally responsible for the misuse of the charity funds because all relevant decisions were approved by the board of the foundation, not Suharto.[19] The implication of the Suharto case is that organizers or managers of charities should be subject to additional scrutiny where they are associated with political power, and that one mechanism to do this would be to include them within the definition and categorization of PEPs. The case for including charities within the scope of the PEP rules is stronger given the heightened awareness of the misuse of charities for the purposes of terrorist financing.

Middle-Ranking Public Officials

The FATF definition of PEPs specifically states that it is not "intended to cover middle- ranking or more junior individuals." This limitation on the definition of PEPs suggests that the major concern of the AML systems is to combat the most serious forms of international corruption, such as grand corruption by senior political leaders. There is a clear linkage between corruption by senior PEPs and reputational risk, while petty corruption or corruption by more junior officials is not viewed as important from the reputational risk perspective.

The exclusion of middle-ranking public officials from the FATF definition is a matter of practical sense. If such individuals were included in a PEP definition, then millions of individuals would be subject to PEP due diligence. Although these individuals are outside the enhanced PEP diligence requirements, financial institutions are required to apply increased diligence to public officials in certain circumstances. For example, a financial institution would be obliged to file a suspect transaction report with a government agency, if a middle-ranking public official deposited substantial and unexplained funds into a bank account. It is a well-known typology that middle-level public servants who have significant responsibilities dealing with public monies or major contracts may be prone to corruption, especially when their salaries are low and the bribes are high.[20] However, in order for a financial institution to file a suspect transaction report, it would need to know the job or occupation of its client, and have a system that allowed monitoring of accounts.

Subnational Political Figures

The international definitions of PEPs do not expressly include senior public officials operating at the subnational level of government. The issue is whether a public official who is in a senior position at a state (province or canton) level of government, or even at a local level of government, may be considered a PEP. Both the FATF and the EU definitions refer to individuals with "prominent public functions," which would suggest that it is possible to be a PEP at a subnational political figure. The EU Directive provides:

> Public functions exercised at levels lower than national should normally not be considered prominent. However, where their political exposure is comparable to that of similar positions at national level, institutions and persons covered by this Directive should consider, on a risk-sensitive basis, whether persons exercising those public functions should be considered as politically exposed persons.

The FATF Recommendations and EU definitions of PEPs are not intended to exhaustively deal with the risk of laundering the proceeds of corruption. It was never intended that the FATF or EU definitions would automatically exclude subnational political figures. The failure by a financial institution to consider whether a subnational leader is a PEP would be inconsistent with the risk-based approach to identifying PEPs, which both the FATF and the EU have endorsed. The EU test of "political exposure" as determining whether to include a subnational figure as a PEP would capture high-risk local or state politicians. This recognizes that corruption by heads of regional governments, regional government ministers, and large city mayors are no less pernicious than corruption by prominent national figures. Subnational political figures in some countries have access to more funds than national leaders in other states. They will often have significant opportunities for corrupt behavior. There have been several PEP cases involving mayors in populous cities in South America who have allegedly laundered their illicit funds in offshore jurisdictions. A recent case is that of Paulo Maluf, the former mayor of the city of Sao Paulo, Brazil, and currently a federal deputy in the National Congress of Brazil. In 2007 a New York City grand jury indicted Maluf for allegedly laundering $11.6 million of illicit kickbacks and funds embezzled from a public project in Brazil through banks in New York and in the Channel Island of Jersey.[21]

Extended Definition of Senior Public Officials

Family Members and Relatives

The FATF PEP definition states that "business relationships with family members or close associates of PEPs involve reputational risks similar to those with PEPs themselves." Although family members are not expressly part of the FATF definition of PEPs, they are required to be subject to increased scrutiny to the extent that they entail increased risks. The UN Corruption Convention is more specific in requiring enhanced due diligence of families of PEPs. The EU Directive applies to "immediate family members" of PEPs, including the spouse or any partner considered by national law as equivalent to a spouse; the children and their spouses or partners; and the parents. The U.S. Patriot Act definition of senior public figure includes the immediate family member of a senior foreign political figure, such as parents, siblings, spouses, children, and in-laws.

These definitions are limited to immediate family members and do not take into account extended family and kinship obligations that may facilitate nepotism and corruption in developing countries in Asia, the Pacific, Africa, and the Middle East. Although the narrow definition of family members may be justified on the basis that it reduces the potential target group for PEP risk assessment, it is oversimplistic in its understanding of the complexity of family relationships throughout the world.

The restriction of the EU definition to a "partner considered by national law as equivalent to a spouse" is formalistic and legalistic. Why should the legal status of a de facto partner determine the definition of a spouse for the purpose of PEP reviews? From a risk perspective, a nation state's family laws and attitude to divorce and non-married partners is only one consideration that should influence a bank's PEP risk assessment. An illustration of the limitation of the EU definition is the case of the Philippines, which has no divorce laws, and does not recognize de facto relationships. In 2007, Josef "Erap" Estrada, the former president of the Philippines, was convicted of plunder, in that being a public official Estrada amassed immense wealth through a combination of criminal acts in violation of public trust. It was the Philippines Center of Investigative Journalism that first revealed in 2000 that Estrada had laundered his illicit funds from gambling through properties that were acquired for the use and benefit of his mistresses and their children.[22] If a restrictive definition of family members had been applied to Estrada, then financial institutions in the Philippines would be entitled to ignore the president's de facto relationships.

The important issue is whether a person's family connections to a PEP are likely to be exploited by a PEP for money laundering purposes. The prevention of corruption requires a definition of PEPs that is consistent with the actual and functional relationship of a family and relatives in any given country. In this way international standards would seem to be falling behind the best practices of industry. One leading international financial institution incorporates a broader range of family members who may be subject to PEP guidelines.[23] For example, this multinational financial institution has compiled a detailed list of categories of relatives who may be included in a PEP assessment. That list includes grandparents, grandchildren, aunts, uncles, nephews, nieces, in-laws, and step-parents. The financial institution considers that the list of relatives is neither exhaustive nor compulsory. Senior managers of the financial institution in each country in which it operates are required to adapt the list to local circumstances. The decision whether a person is a relative of a PEP for the purpose of AML rules will thus depend on the application of a global standard taking into account local knowledge of family relationships.

Close Associates and Business Associates

In practice, business associates have played two roles in facilitating corruption. First, they may act as fronts for senior political figures in concealing and laundering the proceeds of corruption. As the FATF has noted:

> PEPs, given the often high visibility of their office both inside and outside their country, very frequently use middlemen or other intermediaries to conduct financial business on their behalf. It is not unusual therefore for close associates, friends and family of a PEP to conduct individual transactions or else hold or move assets in their own name on behalf of the PEP. This use of middlemen is not necessarily an indicator by itself of illegal activity, as frequently such intermediaries are also used when the business or proceeds of the PEP are entirely legitimate. In any case, however, the use of middlemen to shelter or insulate the PEP from unwanted attention can also serve as an obstacle to customer due diligence that should be performed for every customer. A further obstacle may be involved when the person acting on behalf of the PEP or the PEP him or herself has some sort of special status such as, for example, diplomatic immunity.[24]

Second, business associates of senior public officials may use their political connections to obtain favorable commercial opportunities, such as licenses or monopolies. The business associates may enjoy the corrupt benefits of "crony capitalism" and as such are legitimate targets for corruption-related AML investigations. An illustration of this phenomenon is the Philippines under the Marcos regime and Indonesia under the Suharto administration.

Nearly all definitions of PEPs include individuals who are close associates or business associates of a PEP. For instance the EU Directive provides that a person who is a close associate includes "any natural person who is known to have joint beneficial ownership of legal entities and legal arrangements, or any other close business relationship" with a PEP. Section 312 of the U.S. Patriot Act refers to a close associate who is "widely and publicly known to maintain an unusually close relationship with the senior foreign political figure." There is no explanation as to the meaning of an "unusually close relationship," but it is broad enough to capture significant personal advisers and consultants to PEPs, as well as persons who profit from such a relationship. The Patriot Act definition of a close associate also includes a "person who is in a position to conduct substantial domestic and international financial transactions on behalf of the senior foreign political figure." International private bankers of senior public figures would be encompassed by this requirement.

Private Corporate Interests

The challenge of corporate service providers (CSPs) and anonymous shell companies in countering corruption-related money laundering has been discussed in chapter 3. Senior public officials will frequently use shell companies, foreign legal entities, opaque legal arrangements, and offshore banks, located outside the country of the origin of the PEP. The purpose of such arrangements is to disguise the identity of the beneficial owner and/or controller of the illicit funds. The question is whether and when such corporate entities or arrangements should be incorporated into a PEP definition. The international regulations in this area are not very helpful. There are varying requirements in different countries. For instance, PEPs may include "companies related to them" (Hong Kong) or companies "established by or for the benefit of PEPs" (EU countries). It would seem that both cases would include an entity beneficially owned or controlled by a PEP.

Our knowledge of the behavior of senior public officials would suggest that PEP-related corporate entities should be caught by the PEP requirements. In nearly all cases of grand corruption, senior public officials, including heads of state and heads of government, have used corporate entities to conceal their illicit income and assets; see, for example, chapter 6 on President Ferdinand Marcos.

Should National Senior Public Officials be Subject to Anti-Money Laundering Rules?

The FATF definition of PEPs is limited to foreign PEPs. It refers specifically to individuals with "prominent public functions in a foreign country." Although there is no obligation under the FATF standards to provide for enhanced due diligence to domestic PEPs, the FATF does encourage the application of its PEP standards to domestic PEPs. The FATF in its interpretative note to Recommendation 6 states: " Countries are encouraged to extend the requirements of Recommendation 6 to individuals who hold prominent public functions in their own country."

Unfortunately, despite the exhortatory suggestion of the FATF, few FATF member jurisdictions have taken up this suggestion. The EU Directive requires financial institutions to apply enhanced due diligence procedures to foreign PEPs and PEPs residing in another European member state, but not to national PEPs. In contrast, the UNCAC does not distinguish between domestic and foreign PEPs in its definition of "public officials." Article 52(1) of the UNCAC provides:

> Without prejudice to Article 14 of the Convention, each State Party shall take such measures as may be necessary in accordance with its domestic law, to require financial institutions within its jurisdiction to verify the identity of customers, to take reasonable steps to determine the identity of beneficial owners of funds deposited into high-value accounts and to conduct enhanced scrutiny of accounts sought or maintained by or on behalf of individuals who are, or have been entrusted with prominent public functions and their family members and close associates. Such enhanced scrutiny shall be reasonably designed to detect suspicious transactions for the purpose of reporting to competent authorities and should not be so construed as to discourage or prohibit financial institutions from doing business with any legitimate customer.

Article 52(1) imposes an international legal obligation on state parties to enact measures to "conduct enhanced scrutiny of accounts . . . of individuals who are, or have been entrusted with prominent public functions and their family members and close associates," irrespective of whether those individuals are domestic or foreign. According to the text of Article 52(2), it is arguable that this international obligation is not satisfied if the implementing laws are confined to foreign PEPs. However, our research indicates that apart from Canada, no state that has ratified the UN Corruption Convention has made any declarations or reservations to Article 52 of the Convention. Under international law, those countries that have ratified the UN Corruption Convention without making a reservation in respect of Article 52 are obliged to implement this provision in full. We have found that few of the state parties to the UN Corruption Convention have implemented Article 52 so as to impose enhanced due diligence obligations on national PEPs. There is a major compliance gap in implementing Article 52 of the Convention, which should be addressed. One way of achieving this is to change the definition of PEPs in domestic AML laws to include national PEPs.

Presently, the vast majority of countries that have AML laws governing senior public officials have limited their coverage to foreign senior public officials because they are viewed as more risky as compared to domestic or national officials. The idea that foreign PEPs are high risk compared to national PEPs is linked to two ideas. First, in the case of developed countries, national PEPs are perceived to be less likely corrupt than foreign PEPs, so that there is no need to apply enhanced due diligence standards to national PEPs. Second, PEPs are more likely to conceal their illicit funds by using banking services in foreign jurisdictions because they are not as well known and have a greater opportunity of masking their identity and illicit gains. For example, the U.S. Patriot Act compels financial institutions to apply "enhanced scrutiny" to the accounts of current and former senior foreign political figures, but imposes no such similar requirement on senior U.S. political figures. U.S. law also targets the misuse of private bank accounts where there is laundering of the proceeds of foreign corruption, a problem highlighted in several U.S. Congressional hearings. Section 312 of the Patriot Act and its associated regulations require financial institutions to conduct specified due diligence for private banking accounts maintained by or on behalf of a non-U.S. person (which includes preventing the acceptance of the proceeds of foreign corruption). Financial institutions in the United States are also required to take reasonable measures to identify the nominal and beneficial owners of and the source of funds deposited in such private accounts.

Our research indicates that the following countries have laws, regulations, or guidelines that require financial institutions to apply enhanced due diligence to national PEPs as well as foreign PEPs: Afghanistan, Belgium, Brazil, Mexico, Solomon Islands, Sri Lanka, and East Timor.[25] For instance, in 2004 Mexico enacted an AML law that defined a PEP as "any individual who performs or has performed important public functions in a foreign country or within the nation's territory, including among others, chiefs of state or government, political leaders, high-ranking government, judicial or military officials, senior executives of state-owned companies or officers or important members of political parties."[26] Under Mexican law obligated entities must "develop mechanisms for determining the degree of risk of operations carried out with PEPs, and for this purpose will determine whether the transactional behavior corresponds reasonably to their functions, level and responsibility."[27] Mexican financial institutions are also obliged to establish a system of alerts in order to detect changes in the transactional behavior of PEPs and report unusual or suspicious transactions as evidenced by that behavior.

This raises the question of whether there should be any differentiation in AML rules between national and foreign PEPs. There is an international legal expectation (and some would argue an international legal obligation) of countries that have ratified the UNCAC to extend the PEP obligation to national public officials. There are strong policy arguments supporting an extension. National PEPs can be as corrupt as foreign PEPs, and may launder illicit proceeds in the local economy, for example, through real estate and financial transactions. By imposing enhanced AML obligations on financial institutions that deal with national PEPs, countries with major corruption problems would be assisted in their fight against corruption and money laundering.

The international standards of the FATF concerning PEPs are falling behind the actual practice of major financial institutions. Several multinational financial institutions headquartered in the United States and Europe apply the same standard of enhanced scrutiny to senior domestic public officials as they do to foreign public officials.[28] The leading private PEP database service providers have stated that their clients should not distinguish between domestic and foreign PEPs.[29] The history of money laundering scandals, illicit political funding, and bribery and corruption cases pertaining to domestic politicians is extensive and continuing. This is found in both developed and developing countries. The legal and reputational risks involving national politicians who abuse taxpayers' funds or personally enrich themselves through corrupt behavior may in some cases be more significant than those pertaining to foreign PEPs. Empirical evidence and logic suggest that there is no real justification for distinguishing between national and foreign PEPs.

In our opinion the international AML standards on PEPs as expressed in the FATF Recommendation are not sufficiently rigorous in countering corruption-related money laundering. Limiting AML measures to foreign PEPs establishes an unfortunate precedent, especially for developing countries. If developed countries do not require enhanced scrutiny of their national politicians, why should developing countries not follow their example and apply the same minimum due diligence standards to their national politicians? This undermines international efforts to prevent corruption in poorer countries. If corruption is to be effectively prevented, then measures of accountability through the process of customer due diligence should apply equally to both national and foreign PEPs. This has been recognized by the Commonwealth Working Group on Asset Repatriation, which has recommended that enhanced scrutiny should apply to both foreign and domestic PEPs.[30]

Anti-Money Laundering Rules and Processes

The most important international regulations concerning senior public officials are found in FATF Recommendation 6, Article 52 of the UNCAC, and Article 13(4) of the EU Third Money Laundering Directive. There are essentially four requirements:

1. Apply appropriate risk-based procedures to determine whether the customer is a senior public official.
2. Take reasonable measures to establish the source of wealth and source of funds that are involved in the business relationship or transaction.
3. Require senior management approval for establishing a business relationships with such customers.
4. Conduct enhanced ongoing monitoring of the business relationship.

Know Your Client and the Risk-Based Approach

Financial institutions are required to have "appropriate risk management systems" in place to identify both existing and future clients who may be classified as PEPs. The principal international source of guidance on risk management for financial institutions in AML is found in policy documents issued by multilateral institutions, such as the one adopted by the FATF in 2007. The *FATF Guidance on the Risk-Based Approach to Combating Money Laundering and Terrorist Financing* deals with high-level principles and procedures that are applicable to supervision by public authorities and self-regulation by financial institutions. The FATF Guidance on risk management by the private sector has been implemented by several national governments, such as those of the United States and the United Kingdom, through policy instruments issued by national regulators and self-regulatory organizations.

The FATF Guidance recognizes that identification of PEPs is a complex problem for financial institutions. There is the difficulty in defining PEPs, which we have considered earlier. There is the challenge of identifying whether a customer is a PEP, including whether a person is a family member or close associate, or whether a corporate entity is PEP-owned or -controlled. This information is frequently not publicly available because of the desire of PEPs to maintain the privacy of their family and business relationships. The problem is further exacerbated in the case of de facto wives, husbands, and children, and offshore financial interests. Further, there is a compliance issue of identifying higher risk PEPs since an underlying assumption of AML systems is that not every PEP is high risk and thereby requiring additional scrutiny.

There are several possibilities in identifying a PEP. Customers may be required to disclose their PEP status, and this may be verified from freely available public information, such as through Internet searches. This self-reporting or self-certifying process is advantageous from the cost viewpoint, but it is not clear whether this is a sufficient risk management measure. In the case of products or services that are regarded as low-to-medium risk and where the person is identified as a national of a country with a low risk perception, it might be appropriate to carry out limited procedures to identify a PEP. Alternatively, or as an additional measure, all new customers are checked through private PEP databases and other information sources that are available to the financial institution. This is a more costly measure that may be required where the nature and scope of a financial institution's business or geographical locations are high risk. Recent FATF assessments indicate that acceptable PEP customer due diligence measures range from relying on customer declarations on account opening forms to checking internal and external databases.

Applying a risk-sensitive approach to identifying PEPs would suggest that "not all customers must be screened for PEP purposes."[31] This is a practical perspective in the application of PEP risk measures. However, where a person may be identified in hindsight as a PEP from public sources, the financial institution may suffer reputational damage if in fact a corrupt PEP uses its services. There is the difficulty that financial institutions will not generally have the information within their own internal databases to recognize PEPs. Financial institutions collect vast quantities of information concerning customers so as to provide them with services; they do not (or should not) collect data on politicians or persons operating in the political sphere for their own sake. Information about national PEPs is more readily obtainable for a financial institution, than information about foreign PEPs. The challenge is even more acute for nonfinancial institutions, professionals, and others who are now required to take measures to prevent money laundering, including implementing PEP rules.

The identification of who a person is will not necessarily result in identification of a person as a PEP. Potential clients are not likely to volunteer information about their political status, connections, or relationships unless these are already well-known. Indeed, it is likely that some PEPs will go to extraordinary lengths to avoid disclosure of their political relationships if they believe that this will result in increased scrutiny and disadvantage them in their dealings with financial or nonfinancial businesses. The authors endorse the suggestion of the IMF that in implementing compliance with FATF Recommendation 6, "it is important that the supervisory authorities draft texts implementing the Law which spell out in more detail the particular measures for identifying PEPs for all non-financial professions."[32] The absence of specific guidelines hinders effective compliance with international AML standards.

From an AML perspective, financial institutions when applying their risk assessments must not only consider whether a person fits within the PEP definition, but also whether a PEP is employed in an institution or in a country where there is an endemic culture of corruption. Judgments about institutional or country risks of corruption are inherently subjective, and often rely on perceptions concerning corruption risks, rather than on any quantitative evaluation of the actual risks. There are several sources of information on national levels of corruption, such as Transparency International's Corruption Perceptions Index.

What is important is that financial institutions apply risk assessments that take into account all relevant information at their disposal. For example, any risk assessment of the identification of PEPs is also linked to the requirement of disclosure of beneficial ownership of companies and other legal entities. It is important that the risk assessment be made at the time of opening the account so that there is adequate documentary evidence of the beneficial owner or controller of the bank account. In most grand corruption cases, the PEP bank account is owned by or controlled by an offshore entity, such as a company, a trustee of a trust, or a partner of a partnership, which makes it vital to document beneficial ownership and control of account owners and users.

Source of Wealth and Income

Prior to establishing a business relationship with a PEP, financial institutions are expected to obtain information that identifies the source of funds that are deposited in or transmitted through a PEP account. There is an initial obligation to establish the source of wealth of the PEP. It is best practice for financial institutions at the time of opening a PEP account to gather information directly from the client. This will include information such as the transaction authority of family members and close associates over the PEP bank account, and the purpose, as well as expected volume and nature of PEP account activity. A financial institution should reach an agreement with the PEP as to the expected level of deposits in the account and should have sufficient knowledge of the sources of income and capital of the PEP to justify the actual level of banking activity.

Senior Management Approval

Since 1987 Swiss banks have been required to obtain senior management approval when opening bank accounts on behalf of foreign PEPs. In 1998 the Swiss Federal Banking Commission formalized this rule, which then became part of the country's Money Laundering Ordinance. In June 2003 the FATF adopted the Swiss requirement in its Recommendation 6 and the EU enacted this obligation in 2005 in Article 13(4) of the Directive. Given the significant reputational and legal risks of PEPs, it is necessary for senior management of financial institutions to take responsibility for the decision to take on a PEP as a client and to agree to the form and extent of the business relationship between the PEP and the bank. The decision to support a PEP account requires an understanding of the risks involved, and this will require consideration by senior management of whether it has the resources to adequately manage such risks.

The requirement that senior management approves the acceptance of a senior public official as a customer ensures that the management of PEP risk is not merely a back-office function or the sole responsibility of wealth management advisers. PEP risk is a matter of concern for senior management who must ensure that risk management systems are in place to identify, quantify, control, monitor, and report AML activities. International best practice requires senior management to supervise a risk assessment of all PEP accounts. For instance, the U.S. Bank Secrecy

Act's AML Examination Manual sets out a matrix of factors that financial institutions should take into account when evaluating their clients' overall PEP risk, including the type of services and products sought, the geographic coverage of its customer base, the source of funds and level of financial activity. For those financial institutions that have PEP accounts, it is important that there is a central internal database of PEPs, which may be reviewed by senior management or regulators. In one survey carried out by the British Financial Services Authority, it was found that many financial institutions could not produce on request a centrally managed PEP list.

Ongoing Monitoring

The obligations to carry out due diligence on PEPs do not cease at account opening. The requirements of FATF include "enhanced ongoing monitoring of the business relationship" of PEPs. The U.S. Bank Secrecy Act's AML Manual[33] emphasizes the importance of implementing systems that monitor bank account activity against anticipated transactions, so as to highlight discrepancies that may result in a suspect transaction report. In 2001 the U.S. government issued specific guidance on enhanced scrutiny for transactions that may involve the proceeds of foreign official corruption.[34] The guidance sets out a list of red flags for suspicious activities involving PEP accounts:

> request by a PEP to establish a relationship with, or the routing of a transaction through, a financial institution that is unaccustomed to doing business with foreign persons and that has not sought out business of that type;
>
> request by a PEP to associate any form of secrecy with a transaction, such as booking the transaction in the name of another person or a business entity whose beneficial owner is not disclosed or readily apparent;
>
> routing of transactions involving a PEP into or through a secrecy jurisdiction or through jurisdictions or financial institutions that have inadequate customer identification practices and/or allow third parties to carry out transactions on behalf of others without identifying themselves to the institution;
>
> routing of transactions involving a PEP through several jurisdictions and/or financial institutions prior to or following entry into

an institution in the United States without any apparent purpose other than to disguise the nature, source, ownership or control of the funds;

use by a PEP of accounts at a nation's central bank or other government-owned bank, or of government accounts, as the source of funds in a transaction;

rapid increase or decrease in the funds or asset value in an account of a PEP that is not attributable to fluctuations in the market value of investment instruments held in the account;

frequent or excessive use of funds transfers or wire transfers either in or out of an account of a PEP;

wire transfers to or for the benefit of a PEP where the beneficial owner or originator information is not provided with the wire transfer, when inclusion of such information would be expected;

large currency or bearer instrument transactions either in or out of an account of a PEP; and/or

deposit or withdrawal from a PEP's account of multiple monetary instruments just below the reporting threshold on or around the same day, particularly if the instruments are sequentially numbered.

The idea is that banks providing private banking services to senior public officials will collect considerable information about their clients and should have computer monitoring systems in place to compare anticipated transactions with actual transactions. Where account activity is inconsistent with information supplied by customers about their sources of funds, the stated purpose, or expected uses of accounts, the bank will need to take additional measures to verify the legitimacy of the transactions and sources of funds. Compliance managers are expected to review PEP transactions on a regular basis throughout the term of the relationship. Senior managers also have a role in ongoing monitoring of PEPs, and annual reviews may be necessary.

It is not only ongoing monitoring of PEP transactions that is required, but also continuous updating of the PEP status of clients. A significant challenge is that a senior public official may not be identified at the account opening stage, or the existing status of a customer may change over time so that a PEP status is acquired. Each year there are dozens of elections throughout the world, resulting in senior political figures gaining or losing political office. There is also turnover of senior public officials without any election. Consequently, it is important that financial institutions regularly review their customer database against PEP lists or other privately held or publicly available information, so that they uncover new PEPs. Particular care must be taken to ensure that there is monitoring of important changes in the client circumstances and the business relationships of the clients. This was emphasized by the Jersey Financial Services Commission in its review of the island's financial institution's involvement with associates of the former president of Nigeria General Sani Abacha. An example of changed circumstances is "where an individual client becomes a Cabinet Minister with responsibility for government contracts, and where trading structures commence sensitive activities. Structures created to hold wealth that are subsequently used to conduct trade without warning are also a potential risk."[35]

Role of Governments in Identifying Senior Public Officials

Article 52(2) of the UNCAC sets out the measures that state parties are required to implement in order to comply with Article 52(1). These measures have been influenced by "relevant initiatives of regional, inter-regional and multilateral organizations against money laundering," for example, the FATF Recommendations and the EU Directive. The measures include the issue of advisories concerning the types of persons to whose accounts financial institutions are expected to apply enhanced scrutiny, and the notification to financial institutions of the identity of particular persons to whose accounts such institutions will be expected to apply enhanced scrutiny.

The UNCAC requirements raise the issue of whether the government should have a more important role in identifying their own national PEPs so as to prevent money laundering. The private sector in nearly every jurisdiction has complained that their national governments are not doing enough to assist in complying with their new PEP obligations.[36] The argument is that the government, the public service, and law enforcement authorities have superior knowledge concerning the identity of PEPs and are in a better position to assess the risks of corruption by PEPs holding specific offices or occupying particular functions. Indeed, governments in some countries, such as Australia, have carried out detailed fraud and corruption risk assessments concerning government departments as a fraud and corruption prevention tool. Unfortunately, governments do not share their knowledge of public sector corruption risks with the private sector, and yet they expect the private sector to apply a risk-based model in managing corruption-type risks involving senior public officials.

The information and the intelligence that governments possess on these subjects are not communicated to the private sector so that the latter is deprived of important information that would assist in the assessment of the risk of PEPs. Despite having superior information advantages, governments have refused to compile lists of national PEPs or risk categories concerning specific public offices. The failure of governments to carry out such steps illustrates the lack of political will to tackle public sector corruption and the comfortable belief that there is no real corruption problem in their jurisdiction.

Up till now governments have resisted creating national PEP lists on the grounds that it is not cost efficient, although the real reason may be that it is too politically sensitive. In effect, governments have taken the position that the private sector should shoulder the entire responsibility for PEP intelligence by relying on publicly available information or expensive privately created PEP databases. If governments are serious about corruption and money laundering, then more needs to be done by the public sector in developing PEP information. Governments are in the best position to identify their own PEPs and to provide this information to the private sector.

That national governments are in a position to create lists of national PEPs is illustrated by the experience of one FATF member jurisdiction, Mexico. In order to facilitate financial institutions and other bodies to comply with their AML obligations, the Ministry of Finance of Mexico has prepared an "initial list of national PEPs made up of the position held by public officials" covered in Article 110 of its AML law. The Mexican Ministry of Finance regarded this list as "illustrative, rather than exhaustive," so that the ultimate responsibility for risk management of PEPs is placed on the reporting entity. We consider that governments should develop national PEP lists that will assist both local and foreign institutions in combating both corruption and money laundering. The experience of the government of Mexico in developing PEP intelligence should be studied by governments and international AML institutions.

Conclusions

Corrupt political elites are one of the most significant obstacles to economic development and good governance. Financial institutions in a globalized economy may facilitate serious corruption by political leaders by being used wittingly or unwittingly for money laundering services. A new idea is that international AML systems may be used to prevent the laundering of corrupt proceeds. This chapter has examined the evidence of emerging international norms subjecting senior public officials or PEPs to AML rules.

In devising appropriate PEP rules, there are difficult questions as to the definition, scope, and content. We have argued the case for a comprehensive rules-based treatment for the definition of PEPs encompassing de facto family relationships, close associates and business associates, and PEP-related corporate vehicles. The greatest weakness in this area is the failure to apply PEP standards to national PEPs. Our research has shown that the international standards are falling behind the actual practice of major multinational financial institutions.

We have also analyzed the PEP rules and processes, including the role of the risk-based approach in identifying PEPs, the significance of obtaining senior management approval for all PEP clients, and the impact of ongoing monitoring of PEP transactions so as to detect suspicious activities relating to corruption and other crimes. Finally, it is arguable that the governments should play an increased role in assisting financial institutions in detecting corrupt activities by supplying information relating to both domestic and foreign PEPs.

This chapter on senior public officials provides an introduction to the next two chapters. In chapter 5 the scope of international cooperation in the investigation of corruption-related money laundering by PEPs is considered, as well as the tracing and recovery of illicit assets. Best practices in the exchange of intelligence, evidence, suspects, and monies are analyzed. We provide examples of international cooperation, such as the cases of Peruvian intelligence chief Vladimir Montesinos, Ukrainian prime minister Pavlo Lazarenko, and Nigerian president Sani Abacha. In chapter 6 we present a detailed case study of one of the richest PEPs of the twentieth century, Ferdinand Marcos, who ruled the Philippines for twenty years accumulating billions of dollars of illicit income and laundering it through domestic and foreign financial institutions. Litigation concerning the Marcos assets and the criminal prosecution of Imelda Marcos continues even today. The Marcos case illustrates the importance of comprehensive AML rules. If the FATF standards had been applied during the rule of Ferdinand Marcos, banks in the Philippines would not have been under an obligation to apply enhanced due diligence procedures to the local Marcos bank accounts because the FATF standards only apply to foreign PEPs, not to national PEPs.

CHAPTER 5

BEST PRACTICE FOR INTERNATIONAL COOPERATION

Introduction and Overview

Grand corruption and money laundering are inescapably international phenomena. As such it is not uncommon for the proceeds of corruption, the evidence of the crimes, and the criminal actors to be located in different countries. Any adequate response to these problems is fundamentally premised on international cooperation. Some of the most important issues are the exchange of intelligence, evidence, suspects (extradition), and monies (asset repatriation) across borders. Investigations in transnational corruption and money laundering cases may be complex, resource intensive, and require unprecedented assistance. The chapter surveys relevant international treaties and conventions to give a succinct account of best international practice in these areas.

The challenge of international cooperation in money laundering and corruption cases is similar to the problem of investigating transnational financial crimes in general. The common problems are the detection of secret criminal activity, investigation in multiple jurisdictions, and the collection of admissible evidence for court proceedings. There is de facto banking secrecy that remains intact in some countries through quirks of national jurisprudence or the failure to establish beneficial ownership of corporate vehicles that have entered the banking system. There is also the additional difficulty that political leaders who are engaged in grand corruption have access to significant governmental, legal, accounting, and financial resources to conceal their crimes and to prevent recovery of the bulk of their looted assets. The privileges enjoyed by political elites through doctrines of immunity may inhibit effective law enforcement and undermine international cooperation.

The recovery of funds stolen by corrupt officials and stashed abroad is one of the most important goals of mutual legal assistance. It is an area of pronounced interest among developing countries in Asia and elsewhere, as in the last few years hundreds of millions of dollars have been repatriated to the Philippines and Nigeria. In particular, courts in Switzerland and the United States have been common venues for complex grand corruption and asset recovery cases. The main challenges to asset recovery are the lack of admissible evidence, coupled with the delays and expense associated with this kind of international legal action. This chapter analyzes these challenges by providing practical case studies of Peruvian intelligence chief Vladimir Montesinos and Ukrainian Prime Minister Pavlo Lazarenko, while chapter 6 focuses entirely on Philippine President Ferdinand Marcos. These chapters demonstrate how best policymakers can use anti-money laundering (AML) intelligence and asset confiscation provisions to recover these funds.

The implementation and effectiveness of international initiatives such as the United Nations Convention Against Corruption (UNCAC), the ADB/OECD Action Plan and associated work, and the OECD Anti-Bribery Convention are examined. We welcome the shift represented by the UNCAC that enshrines the principle of stolen assets being returned to the "victim" country, rather than being kept by the country whose cooperation is requested in effecting this return. This principle does not, however, preclude requested countries being compensated for extraordinary expenses in tracing, freezing, confiscating, and returning assets. Complementary or alternative measures for victim states might be taking civil action in the foreign jurisdiction, or assisting the foreign jurisdiction to bring money laundering charges against local persons and financial institutions.

Challenges to International Cooperation

The ADB/OECD Anti-Corruption Initiative for Asia and the Pacific has produced two valuable reports to assist countries in improving international cooperation in this field. The first report, published in 2006 under the title *Denying Safe Havens to the Corrupt and the Proceeds of Corruption*,[1] is a major study of the mechanisms, obstacles, and practices of international cooperation in relation to corruption and money laundering, focusing not only on the Asia-Pacific experience, but also on major traffic mutual assistance countries, such as Switzerland. The second ADB/OECD report published in 2007, under the title *Mutual Legal Assistance, Extradition and Recovery of Proceeds of Corruption in Asia and the Pacific*,[2] provides a thematic review of the framework and practices for mutual legal assistance, extradition, and the recovery of the proceeds of corruption among twenty-seven Asian and Pacific jurisdictions: Australia, Bangladesh, Cambodia, China, Cook Islands, Fiji, Hong Kong, India, Indonesia, Japan, Kazakhstan, South Korea, Kyrgyz Republic, Macao, Malaysia, Mongolia, Nepal, Pakistan, Palau, Papua New Guinea, Philippines, Samoa, Singapore, Sri Lanka, Thailand, Vanuatu, and Vietnam.

Both the 2006 and 2007 ADB/OECD reports detail a series of challenges to international cooperation, including the following:

> misunderstandings of the differences in legal systems resulting in inadequately drawn requests for assistance or even "self censorship," where a requesting state decides not to make a Mutual Legal Assistance (MLA) request;
>
> requirement of dual criminality, which requires that the conduct alleged by the requesting country amounts to a crime in the requested state: this causes problems because of the wide variety of offences of corruption throughout different jurisdictions;
>
> differences in evidentiary procedures between the requested and the requesting state, which may result in evidence supplied by the requested state not being admissible in court proceedings in the requesting state;
>
> wide range of grounds for refusing assistance listed in treaties and legislation, such as the concept of "national security" or "essential interests of the state";
>
> excessive delays in obtaining evidence from the requested state (often caused by multiple appeal procedures in the requested state) which may stymie a prosecution for corruption-related money laundering, and in some cases result in prosecutors abandoning a criminal case; and
>
> the costs of investigating, tracing, freezing, confiscating and returning the proceeds of corruption.

There is the challenge of carrying out an investigation into corrupt conduct and illicit assets where the target is an influential politically exposed person (PEP) or a powerful business figure with political connections. In the case of grand corruption it may well be impossible to obtain the approval of the requested country for any legal mutual assistance where its PEPs are implicated. The problem is compounded because of the wide range of reasons for refusing assistance, such as "sovereignty, security and essential national interests," immunities of office, or even a claim that the foreign investigation is politically motivated. There is a risk that corrupt government officials or judges may utilize these grounds to reject a mutual assistance request.

Another important international policy-making body is the Commonwealth Working Group on Asset Repatriation, established by the Commonwealth Secretariat with the mandate "to examine the issue of the recovery of assets of illicit origin and repatriation of those assets to the countries of origin, focusing on maximizing co-operation and assistance between governments."[3] The Working Group consists of representatives from the UNODC, IMF, World Bank, as well as Transparency International and the International Bar Association.

The Commonwealth Working Group on Asset Repatriation has made a number of suggestions that may limit or reduce the vulnerability of AML and anticorruption systems to political interference. We endorse the following suggestions that have been adapted from the Commonwealth Working Group Report:

impose an obligation of enhanced scrutiny for both domestic and foreign PEPS (see chapter 4);

create independent and effective mechanisms to investigate, prosecute, and recover assets of current heads of state or government who are allegedly involved in corruption; and

establish an international and/or regional ad hoc peer review mechanism for monitoring allegations of corruption by serving heads of state or government.[4]

International Treaties and Instruments

The starting point for analyzing international cooperation is to assess the level of commitment of states as demonstrated through international agreements. There are a number of international instruments that are relevant to international cooperation in combating corruption and money laundering (see also chapter 2). Prominent regional examples are: Council of Europe Convention on Laundering, Search, Seizure and Confiscation of the Proceeds from Crime 1990; Organization of American States Inter-American Convention against Corruption 1996; Council of Europe Criminal Law Convention on Corruption 1999; Council of Europe Civil Law Convention on Corruption 1999; and the African Union Convention on Preventing and Combating Corruption and Related Offences 2003. The industrialized developed world has sought to limit the demand-side of corruption through the landmark OECD Convention on Combating Bribery of Foreign Public Officials in International Business Transactions. The key universal multilateral instruments are those that have been sponsored by the United Nations: United Nations Convention against Illicit Traffic in Narcotic Drugs and Psychotropic Substances 1988 (Vienna Convention); International Convention for the Suppression of the Financing of Terrorism 1999; United Nations Convention Against Transnational Organized Crime and its supplementing protocols 2000 (Palermo Convention); and the United Nations Convention against Corruption 2003 (UNCAC).

Each of these multilateral instruments provides mechanisms for international cooperation between the parties. They provide a gateway for cooperation between states that may have no bilateral extradition or mutual assistance arrangements. The failure of states to sign, ratify, and effectively implement these instruments reduces the potential level of cooperation and may result in the creation of corruption and/or money laundering havens. It is highly desirable that as many states as possible accede to and ratify these multilateral instruments so that the international network of cooperation is maximized. FATF Recommendation 35 requires countries to take "immediate steps to become party to and implement" the Vienna Convention, Palermo Convention, and the United Nations International Convention for the Suppression of the Financing of Terrorism. Regional AML bodies have pointed out that the harmonization of mutual legal assistance laws and treaties increases international cooperation in tracing and confiscating the proceeds of crime and pursuing criminals.[5]

In terms of fighting international corruption, including the laundering of the proceeds of corruption, the three most important instruments for countries in the Asia Pacific region are the UNCAC the ADB/OECD Action Plan, and the OECD Anti-Bribery Convention. Table 5.1 provides information as to the status of these multilateral instruments among member jurisdictions in the Asia Pacific Group

Table 5.1 Legal status of international instruments on corruption—APG members

Jurisdiction	*UNCAC*	*ADB/OECD action plan*	*OECD Anti Bribery Convention*
Afghanistan	Ratified		
Australia	Ratified	Endorsed	Ratified
Bangladesh	Ratified	Endorsed	
Brunei	Ratified		
Cambodia	Ratified	Endorsed	
Canada	Ratified		Ratified
Cook Islands		Endorsed	
Fiji	Ratified	Endorsed	
Hong Kong	China ratify	Endorsed	
India	Signed	Endorsed	
Indonesia	Ratified	Endorsed	
Japan	Signed	Endorsed	Ratified
South Korea	Ratified	Endorsed	Ratified
Laos			
Macao	China ratify	Endorsed	
Malaysia	Ratified	Endorsed	
Marshall Islands			
Mongolia	Ratified	Endorsed	
Myanmar	Signed		
Nepal	Signed	Endorsed	
New Zealand	Signed		Ratified
Niue			
Pakistan	Ratified	Endorsed	
Palau		Endorsed	
Philippines	Ratified	Endorsed	
Samoa		Endorsed	
Singapore	Signed	Endorsed	
Solomon Islands			
Sri Lanka	Ratified	Endorsed	
Taiwan			
Thailand	Signed	Endorsed	
Tonga			
United States	Ratified		Ratified
Vanuatu		Endorsed	
Vietnam	Signed	Endorsed	

ADB: Asian Development Bank; APG: Asia Pacific Group on Money Laundering; OECD: Organization for Economic Cooperation and Development; UNCAC: United Nations Convention Against Corruption.

on Money Laundering (APG), which is the regional AML body for Asia/Pacific countries:

United Nations Convention Against Corruption

In fighting corruption, the most significant international measure is the commitment of states to the UNCAC, which was adopted by the General Assembly on October 31, 2003, was open for signature on December 9–11, 2003, and entered into force on December 14, 2005. As of January 20, 2009 there were 140 signatories, and 129 ratification/accessions to the UNCAC.[6] Within a relatively short period of time, most member states of the United Nations have acceded to the UNCAC. Signatories to the UNCAC have included 26 of the 35 APG member jurisdictions, such as Bangladesh, Indonesia and Philippines, where anticorruption is a key development goal. A number of the less developed countries within Asia and the smaller island states in the Pacific have not yet signed the UNCAC, reflecting their lack of resources and inadequate legal infrastructure. In the case of the 34 FATF members, all countries with the exception of Iceland have signed the treaty. China, which is a member of the FATF and the Eurasian Anti-Money Laundering Group, has signed and ratified the UNCAC.

The record on ratification/accession to the UNCAC is not as impressive, although ratifications/accessions have grown from 98 countries in 2006 to 129 in 2009. The most disappointing omission is that several developed countries within FATF that have not ratified the UNCAC, such as Germany, Ireland, Japan, New Zealand, Singapore, and Switzerland. Given the leadership role of the FATF, it is important that all its members proceed to ratification as soon as practicable.

The UNCAC has been presented as a landmark in international cooperation in the fight against corruption and the laundering of corrupt funds. It has been described as the "first genuinely global, legally binding instrument on corruption and related matters, that is the first to be developed with an extensive international participation and with a broad consensus of signatory States and international private sector and civil society organisations"[7] That gainsaid, the UNCAC represented a compromise between developing states that sought the rapid and unencumbered return of assets looted by their former political leaders, and developed states that insisted that the recovery of such assets be subject to the procedural and substantive safeguards imposed by their legal systems.

The UNCAC requires all state parties to give the widest measure of international cooperation in combating, investigating, and recovering the proceeds of corruption. A key aim of the UNCAC as stated in Article 1(b) is "to promote, facilitate and support international co-operation and technical assistance in the prevention of and fight against corruption, including in asset recovery." Chapter IV (Articles 43–50) contains provision on extradition, mutual legal assistance, law enforcement cooperation, joint investigations, and special investigative techniques, such as controlled delivery. These provisions assist in the detection, investigation, extradition, and prosecution of persons who are suspected of committing Convention corruption offences. Although chapter IV of UNCAC is modeled on several international criminal law treaties, it has several innovative provisions that seek to reduce the obstacles to more timely and effective international cooperation. These include the UNCAC provisions on asset recovery, which are considered here.

The UNCAC recognizes that international cooperation between states depends on enhancing national criminal laws and national law enforcement agencies. It provides for a wide range of national measures, including:

- improving anticorruption prevention (chapter II), including measures to prevent money laundering (Article 14);
- the criminalization of a variety of corruption offences (chapter III, Articles 15–28), including the criminalization of laundering of proceeds of crime (Article 23) and the liability of legal persons (Article 26);
- the implementation of a wide range of law enforcement strategies (chapter III), including the freezing, seizure, and confiscation of the proceeds of crime (Article 31), the protection of witnesses, experts, victims, and reporting persons (Articles 32 and 33), and the creation of specialized authorities to combat corruption (Article 36); and
- the enhancement of cooperation with national law enforcement authorities (Article 37), between national authorities (Article 38), and between national authorities and the private sector (Article 39).

The UNCAC acknowledges that international cooperation depends on the effectiveness of national institutions, such as anticorruption agencies (Article 6) and AML bodies (Article 14). Thus states are required under Article 14(1) (a) to institute a "comprehensive domestic regulatory and supervisory regime for banks and non-bank financial institutions... in order to deter and detect all forms of money laundering." In establishing a regulatory regime, states are called upon to use as a "guideline the relevant initiatives of regional, interregional and multilateral organizations against money laundering." This would include the international standards recommended by the FATF and FATF-style regional bodies.

OECD Anti-Bribery Convention

The background and key features of the OECD Convention have been summarized in chapters 1 and 2. Few APG members are parties to the OECD Convention, which is understandable given the origin of the Convention. Presently, the only APG members that are parties to the OECD Convention are the six members of the OECD: Australia, Canada, Japan, South Korea, New Zealand, and the United States. Several non-OECD members have signed the OECD Convention, such as Bulgaria and South Africa, while other non-OECD countries have laws that would enable prosecution of foreign bribery in certain circumstances. For example, in Hong Kong, it is an offence for any person to offer a bribe to a foreign public official in Hong Kong, and it is also an offence for a foreign public official in Hong Kong to solicit or accept a bribe. The Hong Kong law requires a physical nexus or territorial connection in that the offending conduct must take place within the local territorial jurisdiction. Another case is that of Taiwan, which criminalizes the bribery of local public officials and foreign public officials, regardless of where the criminal conduct occurs. The Taiwanese anti-bribery offences have a wide extraterritorial scope in that they apply to public officials, even if there is no law punishing such offences in the place where the crime took place.

One of the limitations of the OECD Convention is that it has a narrow focus on the supply side of bribery (i.e., the active briber or payor), and ignores the demand side of bribery (i.e., the bribee or the recipient). Despite this limitation, we are of the opinion that newly industrialized countries and any country that has multinational corporations should seriously consider ratifying the OECD Convention. Alternatively, countries may criminalize foreign bribery, without becoming a party to the OECD Convention, an option that is contemplated by the UNCAC.

The OECD Convention provides an international framework for countries to criminalize the payment of foreign bribes and to assist states to carry out effective international investigations into those offences. All thirty-seven countries that have ratified the OECD Convention have criminalized foreign bribery. This is a requirement arising from Article 1 of the Convention, which provides:

> Each Party shall take such measures as may be necessary to establish that it is a criminal offence under its law for any person intentionally to offer, promise or give any undue pecuniary or other advantage, whether directly or through intermediaries, to a foreign public official, for that official or for a third party, in order that the official act or refrain from acting in relation to the performance of official duties, in order to retain business or other improper advantage in the conduct of international business.

Whereas Phase 1 of the OECD review process examined the legislation of Convention states, Phase 2 focuses on the implementation of the OECD Convention among convention countries. In 2006 the OECD published a midterm study of phase 2 reports.[8] The study found that of the twenty-one states examined under the review process, nearly all states have laws that criminalize acts of bribery through intermediaries. This measure is important since much of bribery is executed through third parties and does not involve a direct monetary exchange between the briber and the bribee.

The OECD study also found that almost all examined parties have provided prompt legal assistance to other parties as required by Article 9 of the Convention. Mutual legal assistance is not only available for the purpose of criminal investigations and proceedings, but also for non-criminal proceedings brought against a legal person. The obligation of states under Article 2 of the Convention to establish the liability of legal persons (e.g., corporations) for the offence of foreign bribery is critical in that it ensures that all legal actors are accountable for corruption.

In many of the successful foreign bribery prosecutions, important evidence of bribery was obtained from another party to the Convention.[9] This highlights the practical value of the Convention. There is, however, a problem of gaining timely cooperation and the difficulty of obtaining any effective legal assistance from nonparties to the Convention. The unavailability of mutual legal assistance from a foreign jurisdiction in which a foreign bribe transaction takes place was cited as the "single most important reason for terminating an investigation" into foreign bribery.[10] The absence of mutual legal assistance may arise because there is no treaty relationship between the requested and requesting state. In order to overcome this difficulty, the United States has entered into ad hoc arrangements (referred to as "Lockheed-style Agreements") with other countries, which allow mutual assistance in specific cases of foreign corruption. There are also practical problems arising from the dual criminality principle, such as the varieties of definition of public officials and public enterprises, and the coverage of bribery laws in relation to foreign officials of a subdivision of government.[11]

ADB/OECD Anti-Corruption Action for Asia and the Pacific

The main features of the ADB/OECD Anti-Corruption Action for Asia and the Pacific have been discussed in chapter 1. Most countries in the Asia-Pacific region have endorsed the ADB/OECD Anti-Corruption Action. Of the twenty-seven countries of the region that have formally endorsed the Action Plan and are committed to its goals, twenty-four are APG member jurisdictions. It is surprising that several developed countries, such as the United States, Canada, and New Zealand, which are APG member jurisdictions, have not endorsed the Plan.

International Best Practice

The international dimensions of AML and anticorruption laws and operations raise a series of commonalities. Anticorruption and AML strategies have a shared objective to promote international cooperation in targeting criminals and their proceeds of crime. The identification of the vulnerabilities for corruption in AML institutions in relation to the provision of effective mutual legal assistance is necessary so as to limit the effects of such vulnerabilities. There is a need to measure progress in tackling corruption and money laundering in states. One way of achieving this is to compare countries against a standard of international best practice. International agencies are attempting to benchmark effective systems for mutual legal assistance, extradition, confiscation, and seizure of assets and to limit safe havens for criminals and assets arising from criminal activities.

FATF Recommendations 35–40 set out international best practice for international cooperation in dealing with money laundering. The

FATF standards cover mutual legal assistance, extradition, and other forms of cooperation. Recommendation 36 provides that "countries should rapidly, constructively and effectively provide the widest possible range of mutual legal assistance" in relation to money laundering. FATF members must ensure that the powers of competent authorities to obtain documents and information for investigative, prosecutorial, and related actions under Recommendation 28 are also available for use in response to requests for mutual legal assistance. It is also a requirement that mutual legal assistance should not be subject to unreasonable, disproportionate, or unduly restrictive conditions.

The ADB/OECD 2006 and 2007 reports referred to earlier provide numerous examples of international best practice. The 2007 report analyzed the framework and practices for mutual legal assistance, extradition, and recovery of proceeds in twenty-seven Asian and Pacific jurisdictions. The report allows a direct comparison between countries. Besides the comparative value of the book, it is a very valuable practical resource for national law enforcement agencies in dealing with transnational crime.

Another useful source is the 2001 report of the UN-sponsored informal expert working group on mutual legal assistance.[12] The 2001 report made a series of best practice recommendations, which we believe will enhance international cooperation:

strengthening the effectiveness of central authorities for mutual legal assistance: likewise financial intelligence units (FIUs) need to be made more effective;

ensuring awareness of national legal requirements and best practice for domestic and foreign officials involved in the mutual legal assistance process;

expediting mutual assistance through use of alternatives to formal mutual legal assistance requests, for example, the use of joint investigative teams; and

maximizing personal direct contact between officers in different countries, together with eliminating or reducing technical impediments to execution of requests in the requested state.

Jurisdiction Over Crimes

One measure to improve the deterrent effects of criminal laws dealing with bribery is the expansion of the jurisdictional net so as to empower more states to prosecute the same criminal act. For example, "if bribery of a foreign official is criminalized in both the countries where the bribe giver and the bribe recipient are located and under the law of the nationality of the participants in the bribe, there will be an improvement in detection and punishment."[13] What this would mean is that if the country that has territorial jurisdiction over the corrupt transaction was unable or unwilling to prosecute the offence, other countries could fill the jurisdictional gap and commence an investigation leading to a potential prosecution.

A number of states have national laws with wide jurisdictional reach in implementing the OECD Anti-Bribery Convention. Article 42 of the UNCAC is less ambitious in that it permits but does not require states to adopt comprehensive bases of jurisdiction over Convention offences. However, states are obliged to establish jurisdiction based on the territorial principle, that is, jurisdiction based on the physical location of the crime. States under the UNCAC may also assert jurisdiction based on the nationality of the alleged offender (nationality principle) and the nationality of the victim (passive personality principle).[14] There is also under the UNCAC an obligation imposed on a state to take measures to establish its jurisdiction over Convention offences when the alleged offender is present in its territory, and it does not extradite the person on the ground that it does not allow the extradition of its citizens.

Immunities and International Cooperation

The problem of immunities of public officials was highlighted in chapter 4 on PEPs. In addition to domestic laws, international law also provides immunities for heads of state, which affect all forms of international cooperation in criminal matters. Under customary international law heads of state enjoy absolute immunity from the criminal law process. This means that a head of state is immune from criminal investigation or prosecution by another state. For example, in 1989 the Swiss Supreme Court ruled that Ferdinand Marcos, the former president of the Philippines, enjoyed head of state immunity from criminal jurisdiction for both official acts and "private acts" (which would include looting of assets). However, the Swiss Supreme Court held that because the Philippine government had waived the immunity, Marcos could not assert this immunity. Similarly, the Swiss Supreme Court ruled that Jean-Claude Duvalier, the former "President for Life" of Haiti was not entitled to immunity from jurisdiction because of the waiver by the government of Haiti. In contrast, the French Cour de Cassation (the highest court in the French judiciary) held that the claim for restitution of funds from Duvalier was not maintainable because this would involve the enforcement of claims of foreign states based on their public laws.[15]

An important policy question is whether crimes of grand corruption committed by heads of state should continue to enjoy absolute immunity from the criminal process. Since 1997 the Institute of International Law has called for limits on the immunity of heads of state in cases of "misappropriation of assets of the states which they represent." The Commonwealth Working Group on Asset Repatriation suggested that governments "should strive for a position where there are no immunities" not only for heads of state and government, but for all public officials. The justification for eliminating immunities is that they violate the "fundamental principle that all persons are equal before the law." We are of the opinion that legal immunities in the international context should be narrowly confined to those cases demanded by international law, such as diplomatic immunity.

It may be expected that the increasing international concern with public corruption, money laundering, and terrorist financing may lead to the development of state practice which curtails the abuse of immunities by heads of state and senior politicians and public servants in criminal cases of grand corruption. Until this is the case, heads of state who deposit illicit monies in foreign bank accounts will be protected by the traditional immunity in criminal matters.

The Extradition of Suspects

Extradition is the oldest form of international cooperation and is considered to be the most intrusive form of cooperation because it entails the direct removal of a suspect to another country. The extradition of a person wanted for prosecution raises a series of challenges:

- difficulty of entering into bilateral arrangements with states whose legal systems are based on different ideological and political perspectives, resulting in an absence of trust, which is the very cement of any effective extradition relationship;
- prima facie or probable cause evidentiary requirement, which is a long-standing extradition requirement of common law jurisdictions;
- principle of non-extradition of nationals, which is applicable in most civil (non-common law) jurisdictions; and

the wide grounds for refusing extradition, such as severe penalties (e.g., death penalty), and the humanitarian principle that certain states adhere to.

Extradition is often a time-consuming, expensive, and an inefficient mechanism for international cooperation. FATF Recommendation 39 encourages countries to "simplify" extradition by allowing extradition based on warrants of arrest or judgments. FATF Recommendation 39 suggests that "international best practice" requires countries, if permitted by their legal system, to eliminate the prima facie/probable cause evidentiary rule of extradition. In effect the FATF has endorsed the model of extradition found in the European Convention on Extradition, which allows more intense cooperation between states that have similar developed legal systems and are subject to the European Court of Human Rights. For over 150 years the prima facie or probable cause evidentiary requirement has been an essential component of extradition for Anglo-American common law countries. However, since the mid-1980s, the prima facie rule in extradition proceedings has been slowly disappearing in extradition treaties and state practice. An exception to this trend is the United States, where constitutional requirements prevent the elimination of an evidentiary (probable cause) requirement in extradition cases.

Refusing to extradite nationals or citizens is one of the major differences between countries from the common law and the civil law traditions. Civil law countries such as France and Spain have a longstanding legal prohibition on the extradition of its citizens. In some countries there is a constitutional prohibition against extradition of nationals. In the Asia region, non-common law jurisdictions such as China, Cambodia, Macao, Mongolia, Japan, and South Korea have laws that prevent the extradition of their nationals.[16] Several civil law countries in South America have modified their historical refusal to extradite their citizens, but this has largely been as a result of pressure from the U.S. government. Generally, the civil law countries have maintained their opposition to the extradition of their citizens. Where extradition is refused on the ground of nationality, the requested state is usually obliged under bilateral or multilateral extradition treaties to prosecute the alleged offender instead of granting extradition. In such a case the country that refuses extradition will need to obtain evidence of the crime from the place where it allegedly occurred. This may be problematic in cases involving common law and civil law jurisdictions.

Sometimes the definition of a citizen for the purposes of extradition is given a liberal interpretation. For example, Japan refused to respond to Peru's seven-hundred-page request to extradite Alberto Fujimori, the former president of Peru, even though Fujimori allegedly committed the crimes of murder, kidnapping, illicit enrichment, and embezzlement of $371 million, at a time when he did not appear to have Japanese nationality.[17] Fujimori was born in Peru, but as his Japanese parents registered him with the Japanese consulate in Lima, he was able to claim Japanese nationality when in 2000 he fled from Peru for Japan. This conclusion has been questioned by legal experts because Japanese law does not recognize dual nationality, and Fujimori was a Peruvian national for his entire adult life until his exile from Peru.[18] Since Japan has no bilateral extradition treaty with Peru, the Japanese government asserted that it has no international obligation to extradite its nationals (including Fujimori) to Peru.

Dual criminality presents another potential problem in extradition of persons suspected of corruption. Dual criminality is a long-standing requirement in extradition law and practice of nearly all countries. It is a mandatory exception to extradition, so that if the requirement of dual criminality is not satisfied extradition is not permissible. Under the dual criminality principle, an act is not extraditable unless it constitutes a crime under the laws of both the state requesting extradition and the state from which extradition is sought. The justification for the principle is that it protects the freedom of individuals when their conduct is not criminal in the state in which they are physically located, that is, the state receiving the extradition request.

There is a wide variety of practice among states in applying the dual criminality principle in extradition cases. Some states take a very technical approach to dual criminality so that there must be some correspondence or conceptual similarity between the offence in the requesting and requested states. For example, if a requested state does not recognize the offense of possession of proceeds of crime, as distinct from money laundering, extradition may be refused because the foreign offense is unknown to its law.

Most countries do not require that the corresponding offense in the requested state be described by the same name as the alleged offence in the requesting country. Nor is it necessary that the crime be conceptually similar in both countries. In practice, there has been some relaxation of the dual criminality requirement by virtue of the adoption of the "conduct test" in international treaties, national legislatures, and courts. For example, Article 43(2) of the UNCAC, which applies to extradition and mutual legal assistance, provides:

> In matters of international co-operation in criminal matters, whenever dual criminality is considered a requirement, it shall be deemed fulfilled irrespective of whether the laws of the requested state shall place the offence within the same category of offence or denominate the offence by the same terminology as the requesting state, if the conduct underlying the offence for which assistance is sought is a criminal offence under the laws of both State Parties.

Article 43(2) of the UNCAC adopts a flexible conduct-based approach to dual criminality. It provides the same international standard for dual criminality as is found in modern bilateral and multilateral treaties, as well as in FATF Recommendation 37. This does not remove all the difficulties; the dual criminality principle may require a "translation or substitution of certain factors, such as locality, institutions, officials and procedures."[19] This entails complex legal questions in criminal fraud cases where the alleged conduct is committed in relation to an institution that is of a purely parochial character, and that is unrecognizable by the requested state.

The United Nations Office on Drugs and Crime has described the dual criminality principle as "cumbersome," "time wasting," and as an "obstacle to an efficient and effective extradition system."[20] There is no doubt that the dual criminality principle has provided defendants with a legal basis for challenging their extradition and in some cases have considerably delayed the extradition process. Although it is rare for an extradition case to fail on the ground of dual criminality, the time delays in processing extradition have resulted in some cases of countries withdrawing their extradition requests and abandoning prosecution. The Australian Government's Attorney-General's Department, which is currently reviewing Australia's extradition law and practice, has questioned whether dual criminality should continue to be a mandatory ground for refusing extradition.[21] The suggestion is that national courts should no longer be empowered to deny extradition on the basis of lack of dual criminality. Instead, the relevant government minister would have a discretion to refuse extradition "on the basis of dual criminality on a case-by-case basis where there are concerns about the nature of the offence for which the country seeks extradition."[22]

Dual Criminality in Legal Mutual Assistance Cases

There is a much weaker case for retaining dual criminality as a requirement in legal mutual assistance because mutual assistance is less intrusive on the rights of an individual, compared with extradition. In terms of international cooperation in tackling money laundering, FATF Recommendation 37 provides that countries should, to the greatest extent possible, provide mutual legal assistance, notwithstanding the absence of dual criminality. Multilateral mutual assistance treaties take the same approach. For example, the Harare Scheme of mutual legal assistance between the fifty-three members of the Commonwealth has no mandatory dual criminality requirement. Instead, under the Harare Scheme, countries have a discretion to refuse mutual legal assistance on the ground of dual criminality. Similarly, Article 46 (9)(b) of the UNCAC provides that states may decline to render legal mutual assistance for Convention corruption offenses on the dual criminality principle. This provision represents an advance on previous international treaties concerning crime in that it also provides that a "requested State Party shall, where consistent with the basic concepts of its legal system, render assistance that does not involve coercive action." The effect of this provision is that noncoercive measures, such as interviewing witnesses or taking evidence from voluntary witnesses, providing publicly available or government sourced documents, or identifying assets without using compulsory measures, will be available even if the principle of dual criminality is not satisfied. In contrast, mutual legal assistance measures such as the execution of search and seizure warrants, the obtaining of bank documents under court orders, and the freezing, seizure, and confiscation of assets are coercive measures that some states (e.g., Switzerland) will not grant unless the principle of dual criminality is satisfied.

The application of the principle of dual criminality may cause problems, as illustrated by certain Convention offences. Article 20 of the UNCAC provides:

> Subject to its constitution and the fundamental principles of its legal system, each State Party shall consider adopting such legislative measures as may be necessary to establish as a criminal offence, when committed intentionally, illicit enrichment, that is, a significant increase in the assets of a public official that he or she cannot reasonably explain in relation to his or her unlawful income.

The obligation in Article 20 requires countries "to consider" criminalizing illicit enrichment. Several countries have already done so, for example, member states of the Organization of American States (OAS) that have ratified the Inter-American Convention Against Corruption are required under Article IX to criminalize illicit enrichment. The United States and Canada, parties to the OAS Corruption Convention, have declared that they cannot create an illicit enrichment offense because this would violate the presumption of innocence guaranteed under their constitutions. A number of Asian jurisdictions including Hong Kong, Indonesia, Malaysia, Pakistan, Singapore, and India have criminalized illicit enrichment. In several cases in Asia, the illicit enrichment offense was enacted as part of the law while the United Kingdom was the colonial power. In the case of the Philippines, which has been strongly influenced by U.S. legal traditions, there is no criminal offense of illicit enrichment, which has been a handicap in the prosecution of Imelda Marcos (see chapter 6).

The challenge of dual criminality in cases of illicit enrichment requires further explanation. The offense of illicit enrichment imposes on public officials the burden of proving that any increase in their assets was derived from lawful earnings. Anti-money laundering tracing powers may be utilized to show that the resources of the public officials are not commensurate with their declared assets and income. Where the illicit assets of the officials are in a foreign country, international cooperation will be required to obtain evidence of such assets. If legal mutual assistance is refused because of the principle of dual criminality, then the evidence to establish this crime may not be available.

There are several ways of limiting the impact of the dual criminality principle on international cooperation. Practical experience shows that where the underlying offense in the requesting state is illicit enrichment, the request for legal assistance to the requested country should not be confined to the evidence relevant to the offense of unjust enrichment.[23] It is important for the requesting state to draft its mutual assistance request to reflect the totality of conduct, not merely what is criminal under the law of the requesting state. In several grand corruption cases, the Swiss authorities provided assistance where the foreign country's request for mutual assistance was not confined to factual allegations about the income and assets of the senior politicians, but also contained detailed allegations of bribes, kickbacks from government contracts, and embezzlement of public funds. For example, the Supreme Court of Switzerland upheld the decision to grant mutual assistance to Nigeria and Philippines in regard to General Sani Abacha and President Ferdinand Marcos, finding that dual criminality was established.

Mutual Legal Assistance and Bank Secrecy

It is well recognized that bank secrecy has provided a difficult and, in some cases, insuperable obstacle to the obtaining of financial information in international corruption cases. Several international reports commissioned by the United Nations, FATF, and EU, as well as American congressional enquiries have identified bank secrecy as the single greatest obstacle to international cooperation in criminal matters. Since the 1970s financial havens and bank secrecy jurisdictions have spread to all parts of the globe, including the Caribbean, Europe, Asia, the Pacific, the Middle East, and Africa.[24]

A variety of international initiatives have successfully targeted banking secrecy as an obstacle to international legal cooperation. These include the OECD "Increasing Access to Bank Information for Tax Collection Purposes" and "Harmful Tax Practices" initiatives and the FATF Non-Cooperative Countries and Territories exercise. The EU Savings Tax Directive has sought to reduce the attractiveness of European-based bank secrecy jurisdictions for tax evasion, which may include undeclared illicit income from corruption. Since the EU Savings Tax Directive applies to the Caribbean dependencies of the United Kingdom, such as the Cayman Islands, it has increased international cooperation from tax haven countries outside Europe. The EU and the OECD are now pressuring countries in the Asian region, such as Singapore, to reduce their bank secrecy in tax evasion cases. This has implications for cooperation in corruption investigations because cases of corruption will often coincide with tax evasion in that the bribe or the proceeds of corruption will not be declared.

There are several important provisions in the UNCAC which are designed to counter bank secrecy. Article 31(7) requires states to empower their courts to "order that bank, financial or commercial records be made available or seized" in cases of international cooperation. Article 40 requires states to ensure that in domestic criminal investigations of the UNCAC offenses, there are appropriate mechanisms to "overcome obstacles that may arise out of the application of bank secrecy laws." Article 46 (8) of the UNCAC provides that countries "shall not decline to render mutual legal assistance ... on the grounds of bank secrecy." This provision may require states to change their domestic laws so that there are mechanisms to overcome bank secrecy. Countries are expected under the UNCAC to empower their courts and/or government institutions to order financial institutions to reveal the secrets of their customers in corruption cases. The effect is that financial institutions in a corruption investigation may not rely on bank secrecy as a legitimate reason for failing to comply with a court order to search, seize, or confiscate the proceeds of crime.[25]

Although the UNCAC eliminates bank secrecy as a ground for refusing assistance, this may not be sufficient to overcome the incidental consequences of bank secrecy. One unclear issue is the effect of the bank secrecy provisions of the UNCAC on countries such as Switzerland. Under Swiss law, bank secrecy per se has never been a ground for refusing mutual legal assistance. Disclosure of information that involves a Swiss bank secret is permitted in Switzerland where a competent Swiss court orders disclosure pursuant to a mutual legal assistance request. However, Swiss jurisprudence has applied its principles of mutual assistance, such as the principles of dual criminality, specialty, and proportionality, as "firewalls in protecting fiscal secrets," with collateral damage to cooperation in international corruption cases.[26] It is permissible under Swiss law for an examining magistrate to edit the bank's documents so as to eliminate details concerning third parties, prior to the dispatch of bank documents to a requesting country. The redaction process may eliminate the most significant investigatory leads and undermine the tracing of missing illicit monies. Under the rubric of protecting financial privacy, the Swiss authorities have the capacity to curtail international financial investigations involving Swiss-based institutions. In this way de facto bank secrecy continues to be an obstacle to effective international cooperation despite the formal provisions in the UNCAC.

The Challenge of Delays and Costs

One of the biggest problems in international cooperation is the delay in obtaining intelligence, evidence, the suspect, and/or the return of the illicit assets. There are many causes of delay in mutual legal assistance cases. There is the availability in requested states of well-developed procedural and substantive rights of persons, the subject of foreign mutual assistance requests. For example, there were considerable delays in Switzerland in providing assistance to the Philippines (Marcos), Nigeria (Abacha), and Haiti (Duvalier) cases because of the Swiss mutual assistance process. It also took nearly five years before the Swiss authorities handed the first batch of bank documents to the government of the Philippines.[27] As a result of the delays in the Marcos case, Switzerland amended its domestic legislation so as to reduce the range of legal remedies and limit the number of parties that had appeal rights. We recommend that states streamline their mutual assistance processes so that cooperation is both timely and effective, by reducing unnecessary bureaucratic layers and redundant diplomatic niceties. This is the approach advocated by the 2005 Report of the Australian Attorney-General's Department Review on Mutual Assistance.

Delays may also be contributed by investigatory failures and the court processes in both the requesting and requested state. This is a problem for developing countries that do not have the investigatory or judicial infrastructure to supply the requested state with sufficient evidentiary material concerning the underlying predicate crime in money laundering cases. This was one of the weaknesses of the Philippine government's efforts to recover the illicit assets in the Marcos case, while in contrast in Peru in the Montesinos case (discussed later), Switzerland provided more timely assistance because of the strength of the Peruvian national investigation and amendments to its local judicial procedures. It is important that greater resources be given to developing countries for reform of their legal system, including better-funded prosecutors and courts, so that they have an increased capacity to make and act on mutual assistance requests in a timely fashion.

Costs in asset recovery cases are also a major issue. The UNCAC provides some guidance on this matter. Article 46 (28) of the UNCAC provides that the requested state should bear the ordinary cost of executing a request, but where the expenses of a substantial or extraordinary nature will be required to execute a request, the state parties shall consult as to the terms, conditions, and responsibility for the costs. Recognizing that asset recovery may entail considerable expenses, Article 57(4) authorizes the requested state to deduct reasonable expenses from the confiscated property or proceeds before its return to the requesting state.

Since the requested state bears the ordinary cost of investigation in its territory it may not have sufficient incentive to carry out a comprehensive investigation on behalf of a requesting state. This is a problem where the requested state has draconian laws restricting foreign investigations in their territory. For example, under Swiss law, it is a criminal offense to carry out an investigation or obtain information in Switzerland without authorization for the purpose of a foreign legal proceeding. The Swiss "economic espionage laws" prevents a "foreign government and their agencies from gathering non-public business and financial information in Switzerland," without the knowledge and consent of the Swiss authorities.[28] This prohibition, which protects the sovereignty of a country such as Switzerland, is endorsed by Article 4(2) of the UNCAC. Consequently, foreign governments cannot rely on their Swiss lawyers to carry out a comprehensive investigation but are very dependent on the goodwill and competence of the official Swiss investigatory procedures.

Many developing countries are not in a financial position to meet even ordinary expenses, especially in complicated and lengthy foreign requests. The UNCAC recommends that in such cases developed countries give consideration to paying for the mutual legal assistance in the requested state. The Harare Scheme on Mutual Assistance as amended in 1999 sets out specific guidelines on apportioning costs in executing mutual assistance requests, paying special attention to the needs of developing countries.

Serial Indictments: Pavlo Lazarenko

The following case study illustrates the importance of international cooperation in the prosecution of senior public officials in circumstances where the underlying crime (e.g., corruption) is committed in one state, while the money laundering occurs in another. The case of Pavlo Lazarenko has been selected because it was the first instance where a former head of government was convicted in the United States of laundering the proceeds of foreign crimes through U.S. banks.

Pavlo Ivanovich Lazarenko served as prime minister of the Ukraine from May 1996 to July 1997 and before that was governor of the regional administration in Dnipropetrovsk and head of a large energy consortium. After Lazarenko's resignation as prime minister, Switzerland in 1998 and the United States in 2000 prosecuted him for laundering corrupt monies through their financial institutions by skimming off money from transactions involving companies doing business with the government of the Ukraine.

In December 1998 Lazarenko was detained by Swiss police when he tried to enter Switzerland by car using a Panamanian passport in the name of Lopez. He was questioned by Laurent Kasper-Ansermet, a Swiss magistrate, pursuant to a request for judicial assistance from Ukraine, was released on bail, and returned to the Ukraine. In 1999 Lazarenko fled to the United States after his immunity as a member of parliament of the Ukraine was removed by his fellow parliamentarians. In June 2000 Lazarenko was convicted in Switzerland of diverting $72 million from a Ukrainian government contract, depositing $43 million of the illicit monies into Swiss banks, and then transferring most of the monies to accounts in Antigua and the Bahamas. Lazarenko was sentenced in his absence to an eighteen-month suspended prison term. The Swiss court confiscated $6.6 million from Lazarenko's Swiss bank accounts, albeit the government of Ukraine alleging that Lazarenko had embezzled about $ 880 million between 1994 and 1997, of which some $170 million had been transmitted through Switzerland.[29]

Pavlo Lazarenko's legal problems continued. He was subject to a U.S. investigation after he had been initially detained by U.S. authorities for visa irregularities. He was charged in May 2000 on fifty-three U.S. criminal charges, including money laundering and embezzlement of $114 million. Four years later, on June 4, 2004, a U.S. jury convicted Lazarenko of using his political position to extort money and then launder it through California banks. Lazarenko was found guilty on twenty-nine counts, including conspiracy to launder monies that represented the proceeds of foreign extortion, wire fraud, and transportation of stolen property. The conviction related to a $44 million loss to the Ukrainian government and the laundering of over $21 million through the American banking system, as compared to the original figure of $114 million charged in the indictment. On August 26, 2006, Lazarenko was sentenced to nine years in prison and was fined $10 million for extortion, wire fraud, and money laundering. On September 26, 2008, eight of Lazarenko's convictions relating to money laundering were affirmed, but six others relating to wire fraud and interstate transportation of stolen property were reversed on appeal. Lazarenko is to be re-sentenced in relation to the eight charges.[30]

The challenge for the U.S. prosecutors in the Lazarenko case was to "prove both that the money laundering, fraud and stolen property transfers took place in violation of American law and that the money was gained illegally under Ukrainian law in effect at the time."[31] This required significant legal assistance from the Ukrainian government in the form of expert evidence about its laws and evidence of the underlying crimes. This problem explains in part why U.S. district judge Martin Jenkins of the Northern District of California dismissed twenty-three of the forty-two charges against Lazarenko. For example, Lazarenko was indicted under the "honest services statute"[32] for using U.S. wires in a scheme to defraud the citizens of Ukraine of their intangible right to the honest services of their government officials. Judge Jenkins dismissed the honest services charges because the U.S. government failed to establish that Lazarenko had breached any similar provision of Ukrainian law.[33] Furthermore, in 2008 the U.S. Court of Appeals set aside the six wire fraud counts because the prosecution did not prove that the alleged wire transfers were conducted in furtherance of a fraudulent scheme. The Court of Appeals also dismissed the conviction for interstate transportation of stolen property because the prosecution did not establish that the money transported was "directly traceable" to the fraud or theft.

Asset Recovery and Asset Sharing

FATF Recommendation 38 provides that domestic authorities should take expeditious measures in response to foreign requests to "identify, freeze, seize and confiscate property laundered, proceeds from money laundering or predicate offences, instrumentalities used in or intended for use in the commission of these offences, or property of corresponding value." It also requires countries to enter into arrangements for coordinating seizure and confiscation proceedings, including asset sharing. Under the FATF international standards, states are encouraged to establish asset forfeiture funds and share confiscated property with the requesting state, particularly when confiscation was a result of joint investigations between the requesting and requested states. This will facilitate the tracing and recovery of illicit assets, including corrupt payments and the proceeds of corruption.

The unsatisfactory experience of developing countries in repatriating illicit assets located in developed countries resulted in a change in approach in the UNCAC. Article 51 of the UNCAC provides that the return of assets is a "fundamental principle" of the Convention, and that state parties are encouraged to give the "widest measure of co-operation and assistance in this regard." As the United Nations has optimistically argued, "the lesson that so-called 'grand corruption' can only be fought through international and concerted efforts based on genuine commitment on the part of Government has been learned" and this lesson is expressed in the UNCAC.[34]

The UNCAC differs from previous multilateral treaties, such as the Palermo Convention and bilateral mutual legal assistance treaties, under which the ownership of confiscated property belonged to the requested state where the property was located. In contrast, the UNCAC imposes mandatory obligations on requested states to return the illicit assets to the requesting states in so far as this is consistent with the principles of the Convention. There is an underlying preference under the UNCAC to return the assets to the state asserting that it is a victim of the corruption offense.

Chapter V of the UNCAC details the processes and conditions for asset recovery, including provisions dealing with direct recovery of property by way of civil and administrative actions (Article 53), mechanisms for the recovery of property through international cooperation by recognizing and/or taking action based on foreign confiscation orders (Articles 54 and 55), and implementing measures for the return and disposal of illicit assets to the requesting state (Article 57).

Article 57 imposes mandatory obligations on states to return illicit assets to the rightful legal owner. It envisages three scenarios for asset recovery, depending on the nature of the corruption offence, the strength of the evidence and claims of ownership of property, the rights of prior legitimate owners of property, as well as the entitlement of other victims of corruption offences.[35]

The first situation is where public funds are embezzled or laundered, so that the funds clearly belong to the requesting state [Article 57(3)(a)]. In such a case the requested state is obliged to return the confiscated property to the requesting state. This may be achieved by means of a confiscation order in the requested state, which may be based on a final judgment in the requesting state. The requirement of a final judgment in the requesting state may be waived. Second, in the case of proceeds of any other corruption offense under the Convention, which does not involve embezzlement but where there is an Article 55-type confiscation order, the requesting state may or may not be the owner of those funds [Article 57(3)(b)]. The requested state's obligation in such a case is to return the confiscated property to the requesting state when the requesting state "reasonably establishes its prior ownership of such confiscated property," or when the requested state "recognizes damages" to the requesting state as a basis for returning the confiscated property. This does not mean that the requested state may ignore "the rights of bona fide third parties" [Article 57(2)]; but that the Convention imposes a preference for the return of the assets to the requested state, in accordance with the "fundamental principles" of the Convention. Third, in all other cases, the requested state is obliged to give priority to returning confiscated property to the requesting state, or to its prior legitimate owners, or compensating the victims of the crime [Article 57(3)(c)].

Asset Freezing and Recovery: Vladimir Montesinos

The case of Peruvian intelligence chief Vladimir Montesinos represents the high watermark for effective international cooperation in freezing and returning illicit assets to a developing country. Montesinos was a key advisor to Peruvian President Alberto Fujimori and the de facto head of Peru's Secret Service (SIN) during the Fujimori government from 1990 to 2000. Montesinos has been described as the "Rasputin" creator and manipulator of a corruption network that touched all aspects of Peruvian society, including politicians, military, police, judiciary, and the media.[36] It is alleged that more than $2 billion was stolen during the Fujimori administration; a Peruvian congressional committee identified $782 million of illicit monies generated by more than two hundred persons during this period.[37] It took a new Peruvian government less than five years, from 1999 to 2002, to recover $175 million in illicit assets from Switzerland, the United States, and the Cayman Islands.

When a video of Montesinos bribing an opposition Congressman was televised on Peruvian TV on September 14, 2000, Montesinos' political position became untenable. President Alberto Fujimori dismissed Montesinos who disappeared in October 2000. The widespread international publicity concerning Montesinos prompted Swiss banks to carry out their own enquiries. On October 5, 2000, following the filing of five suspect transaction reports by three banks in Zurich, the Swiss authorities opened up a criminal investigation into Montesinos for suspected money laundering. The Swiss banks automatically froze $49.5 million in accounts controlled by corporations linked to Montesinos and his business associates. The timeliness of the freezing of Montesinos' funds was a direct result of the efficiency of the Swiss system of reporting suspect transactions; under Swiss law, banks that report suspect transactions are obliged to automatically freeze funds connected with those transactions.[38]

However, since the suspicious bank accounts related to arms deals dating back to 1995, questions may be asked as to why no Swiss-based bank filed a suspect report at an earlier date.

In October 2000 the Swiss authorities not only froze Montesinos' bank accounts but commenced an investigation into Montesinos based on its own money laundering law.[39] The Swiss authorities did not delay taking domestic measures until receiving a mutual assistance request from Peru. Indeed, within one month Switzerland spontaneously informed the Peruvian authorities of its investigation, requested Peru to investigate the origin of the Swiss funds, and invited Peru to make a request for legal assistance. Switzerland also made legal assistance requests to Luxembourg and the United States in pursuit of its own money laundering investigation. By December 2000 the Zurich examining magistrate had issued nineteen orders to banks, resulting in Swiss-based banks reporting twelve suspicious accounts, amounting to $22 million. The accounts were in the names of corporations that were beneficially owned by associates of Montesinos, including General Nicolas de Bari Hermoza Rios, the former chief of the joint command of the armed forces of Peru, Alberto Venero Garrido, a Peruvian arms dealer, and Victor Joy Wang, former congressional speaker and finance minister of Peru.[40]

The Swiss authorities summarized how the Montesinos-related funds were derived from corruption:

> Since 1990 Montesinos received "commissions" on arms deliveries to Peru and had this bribe money paid to his bank accounts in Luxembourg, the USA and Switzerland. Montesinos received bribes for at least 32 transactions, each worth 18 percent of the purchase price. Montesinos also collected 10.9 million US dollars in "commissions" on the purchase of three MIG29 planes, bought by the Peruvian air force from the state-owned Russian arms factory "Rosvoorouzhenie." In return, Montesinos used his position to ensure that certain arms dealers were given preference when these orders were issued.[41]

It took two years for the Swiss authorities to transfer to Peru $77.5 million from frozen Montesinos-related bank accounts in Switzerland. The relatively short time between the commencement of the Swiss investigation in October 2000 and the transfer of the funds from Switzerland to Peru in August 2002 can be explained by the high level of international cooperation between the Swiss and Peruvian authorities. This was facilitated by the enactment of significant changes in Peru's legal system in investigating and prosecuting organized crime and corruption.[42] Since much of the evidence of the underlying crimes of corruption was in Peru, it was vital that Peru find evidence to assist the Swiss money laundering investigation. However, Peru faced enormous challenges in pursuing an investigation into Montesinos because of deficiencies in its institutional and legal framework for combating corruption and organized crime. Dramatic changes in the Peruvian law enforcement system were required. In November 2000 Peru appointed a special prosecutor to investigate the labyrinth of corruption involving Peru's military and intelligence services. In December 2000 a new law was enacted giving Peruvian prosecutors exceptional powers to trace illicit assets. This was followed by a new "plea bargaining law," which allowed prosecutors to obtain information of illicit assets from more than one hundred persons, including high ranking associates of Montesinos, his personal bookkeeper, and various arms traffickers.[43] The Peruvian authorities were able to gather valuable evidence of the underlying crimes of Montesinos through the sworn statements of associates of Montesinos.[44] By June 2001 Peru had filed five legal assistance requests to Switzerland, which included details about the origins of the monies in the Swiss bank accounts and information identifying other Swiss accounts. Relying on this information, Switzerland froze an additional $43 million; in total $113 million was frozen in Switzerland.

The Swiss and Peruvian investigations were mutually reinforcing, which ultimately resulted in the repatriation of the illicit funds. By 2002 Montesinos appeared to have given up his legal fight in Switzerland. When the Zurich examining magistrate ordered on June 12, 2002, the transfer of Montesinos' assets to Peru, there was no appeal by Montesinos against that decision. This may be contrasted with cases such as Marcos and Abacha where there were lengthy appeals by the dictators and their corporate vehicles against adverse decisions by the Swiss authorities and the Swiss courts.

Voluntary cooperation in this corruption-related money laundering case played an important role in the repatriation of the illicit funds from Switzerland to Peru. An unnamed arms dealer voluntarily agreed to repatriate $7 million of his arms-trafficking illicit commissions, while former Peruvian general Nicolas de Bari Hermoza Rios, agreed to return $21 million of funds derived from bribes in connection with arms deals with Peru and the misappropriation of funds belonging to the Peruvian military.[45] Both individuals agreed to waive their claimed rights to frozen monies in return for reduced criminal sentences in Peru. There is about $33 million of funds from other account holders that still remains frozen in Zurich, and these are the subject of continuing legal disputes.

There are a number of lessons that can be drawn from the Montesinos case in relation to asset recovery. First, the Montesinos case may be judged a success on the basis that $175 million was recovered from three countries (Switzerland, the United States, and the Cayman Islands) within five years of the commencement of a Peruvian and international investigation. Second, it was the system of suspicious-based reporting, a key feature of AML international standards, that prompted official inquiries. However, Swiss-based banks only reported the suspicious transactions after international publicity of the scandal in 2000, and not when the illicit proceeds of the arms deals were generated in 1995. Third, the Swiss authorities targeted the Swiss-based institutions that facilitated the money laundering, by holding the general manager of one of the foreign banks operating in Switzerland accountable for his bank's organizational AML deficiencies in the Montesinos case. The Swiss authorities removed the general manager from his position in the bank and required a major overhaul of the bank's AML procedures.[46] Fourth, without significant changes to the law and institutional framework in Peru, the Swiss authorities would not have been able to respond to the Peruvian request in such an expeditious manner. This is a salutary lesson for developing countries that seek to recover looted assets from offshore locations.

Civil Forfeiture of Corrupt Proceeds

The term civil forfeiture refers to the permanent deprivation of illicit property without the need to obtain a criminal conviction as a prerequisite for forfeiture. Civil forfeiture takes place after a hearing before a court or other appropriate judicial body. In contrast to civil proceedings to recover assets, which may be brought by a governmental or nongovernmental party (see later), civil forfeiture is an action brought by a state to recover illicit assets under a specific statutory power.

The United Nations Expert Working Group on Mutual Legal Assistance Case Work recognized in 2001 that civil forfeiture is an effective mechanism for freezing, seizure, and confiscation of illicit assets. The Expert Working Group recommended that states should ensure that their legal mutual assistance laws "apply to requests for evidentiary assistance or confiscation order enforcement in civil forfeiture cases."

Several countries including the United States, the United Kingdom, Australia, and the Philippines have laws that permit civil forfeiture of illicit assets. The U.S. federal statute on civil forfeiture (18 U.S.C. # 981) is one of the most effective mechanisms for the recovery of corrupt proceeds arising from foreign offences.[47] Under the U.S. federal civil forfeiture provisions any property involved in a money laundering offense, or a violation of the Bank Secrecy Act, such as a currency reporting offence, may be forfeited. The action is against the property itself (in res) rather than against the defendant in person (in personam).

The U.S. federal statute on civil forfeiture does not require a concurrent criminal case in the United States against a specific defendant.[48] It may be used in circumstances where the money launderer is dead, missing, a fugitive, or cannot be located. U.S. prosecutors are not required to prove their civil forfeiture claims by relying on the criminal standard of proof: it is sufficient if it can be shown that based upon probable cause the property is subject to forfeiture. The provision permits forfeiture of property held in the name of a corporate nominee who can be shown to have been involved in money laundering, in circumstances where there is insufficient evidence to obtain a criminal conviction of that nominee. It is a necessary requirement of civil forfeiture cases that the property the subject of the forfeiture was involved in or is traceable to an offense. This requirement may not be satisfied in complex money laundering cases where the paper trail has been cleverly obscured.[49]

The U.S. civil forfeiture law has been used in numerous corruption cases to return illicit assets to developing countries. For example, in December 2007, U.S. Treasury returned $2.7 million to the Government of Nicaragua, after an "in rem" civil forfeiture action relating to crimes committed by Bryon Jerez, former Nicaraguan director of taxation under the former President Aleman. In another case, in December 2004 the U.S. Treasury returned $20 million to the government of Peru after a civil forfeiture action was brought by the U.S. Department of Justice against funds relating to corrupt acts by Victor Venero Garrido, an associate of Vladimir Montesinos during the Fujimori government.[50] In both of these cases civil forfeiture was premised on the Nicaraguan and Peruvian governments supplying critical evidence of the underlying conduct to the U.S. prosecutors.

Civil Proceedings in Common Law Countries

Taking civil proceedings in the requested state offers an alternative to criminal law based legal mutual assistance. This possibility arises because of the potential civil liability of corrupt government officials to their state employers. There are many advantages in pursuing civil remedies in asset recovery cases, rather than relying on criminal remedies. For example, in common law jurisdictions, judges may order banks that have knowingly or inadvertently participated in money laundering to disclose details about bank accounts, thereby enabling assets to be identified and traced. In civil proceedings, wrongdoers may be compelled to give a full account of what has happened to the corrupt proceeds that they allegedly received. Legal remedies, such as the doctrine of constructive trust, may result in a reckless bank being held liable for the full amount of illicit money that has been transmitted through the bank. The major disadvantage of civil proceedings is the high cost of employing private lawyers.

Article 43(1) of the UNCAC requires states to "consider assisting each other in investigations of and proceedings in civil and administrative matters relating to corruption." The Commonwealth Working Group recommends that countries explore the possibility of "using mutual legal assistance to gather evidence for use in civil proceedings brought by a victim country for the recovery of assets in corruption cases." The strategic and tactical advantages of using existing international civil procedures must be measured against relying on criminal mutual assistance treaties. There has been extensive and generally successful litigation in England, Guernsey, Jersey, and the Isle of Man, where civil proceedings have been brought against prominent PEPs. Notable examples include civil litigation in relation to assets associated with Sani Abacha, the former president of Nigeria (Ajaokuta cases), Frederick Jacobi Titus Chiluba, the former president of Zambia (Zamtrop and BK conspiracy cases), and Hutomo Manaul Putra (Tommy) Suharto, the son of the former president of Indonesia (Banque National de Paris funds litigation).

Misuse of Repatriated Corrupt Assets: Abacha

Developed countries have expressed concern that where illicit assets are returned to a developing country, it may be misused by the government. That is, concerns about corruption in the requesting state may be an obstacle in the recovering of laundered corrupt assets. In 2001 the Swiss government adopted a policy of delaying the return of illicit assets to a developing country when it perceived that there was a risk that the looted monies would be stolen or misused by the leaders of the new government. This policy has also been applied by the United States in returning illicit monies to Kazakhstan and Nicaragua.

The Swiss policy was applied in the Sani Abacha case.[51] Following the Swiss Supreme Court decision in February 2005 that the Abacha assets could be returned to Nigeria, the Swiss Federal Council in May 2005 imposed two conditions before the illicit assets could be repatriated. First, the transfer of the funds would be staggered over a period of time ostensibly because some of the assets were not liquid. The second condition was that the World Bank would monitor the Nigerian government's use of the funds for specific development projects in health, education, and infrastructure, as soon as practicable. Although initially expressing opposition to these conditions, the Nigerian government ultimately cooperated in their implementation.

In September–November 2005, $505.5 million was transferred from Switzerland to Nigeria, while $44.1 million was transferred in the first quarter of 2006. The World Bank and the Nigerian Ministry of Finance agreed to carry out a joint monitoring exercise concerning the use of the Abacha assets.[52] The field monitoring survey in 2006 involved twenty field monitors, six Nigerian government departments, and various Nigerian NGOs. The World Bank report concluded that the allocation of Abacha funds in the Nigerian budget, which occurred prior to the actual transfer of monies, had made it difficult to accurately track the use of the Abacha loot. There was no suggestion of fraud or impropriety. The problem was that there was insufficient planning of the monitoring program. The report recommended that in future monitoring arrangements and special project selection should be agreed in advance.The report noted that one of the consequences of the failure to clearly track the use of the Abacha funds was that in Nigeria there was no clear appreciation of how the Abacha loot had benefited specific development projects. This was unfortunate because it deprived Nigeria of the political, educative, and law enforcement benefits of international asset recovery. Since the recovery of illicit assets has a political dimension, the value of successful recovery should not be measured in pure monetary terms.

Sharing of Intelligence through Financial Intelligence Units

Prior to the expansion of bilateral and multilateral treaties during the late 1980s, countries often relied on informal law enforcement arrangements to fill the gap in international cooperation. The development of mutual assistance arrangements, such as the 1986 Harare Scheme within the fifty-three member countries of the Commonwealth and the UN model mutual assistance arrangements resulted in more formal arrangements. In effect, a legal infrastructure of cooperation in criminal matters based on international law was formulated. This was important in that countries allowed their legal systems to provide international assistance involving coercive measures, such as the execution of search warrants and the compulsory taking of evidence from witnesses, including bankers. Formal mechanisms of cooperation may be slow, subject to bureaucratic inertia, and seemingly inflexible in meeting the needs of a country requesting international legal assistance. Partly for this reason, the FATF, international treaties and the United Nations are increasingly recognizing the importance of informal mechanism of international cooperation, especially the exchange of intelligence between law enforcement agencies.

FATF Recommendation 40 encourages the "prompt and constructive exchange directly between counterparts, either spontaneously or upon request of information relating to both money laundering and the underlying predicates offences," such as corruption. United Nations Security Council Resolution 1373 calls upon states to "find ways of intensifying and accelerating the exchange of operational information, especially regarding actions or movements of terrorist persons or networks." Article 58 of the UNCAC require state parties to consider establishing an FIU to be "responsible for receiving, analyzing and disseminating to the competent authorities reports of suspicious transactions."

For AML purposes, the key national agency to collect, analyze, and transmit financial intelligence is the FIU, which has been established in jurisdictions under AML legislation. The international government body that provides a vehicle for cooperation between FIUs is the Egmont Group, which is headquartered in Toronto.[53] The key feature of an Egmont FIU is that it must maintain a central and national database of information on disclosure of suspicious financial transactions required by AML and counterterrorist financing laws.

In accordance with national laws, FIUs are required to quickly and securely transmit sensitive and confidential financial information to domestic and international law enforcement agencies. There are over one hundred jurisdictions that are members of the Egmont Group, including the eighteen jurisdictions (table 5.2) from the APG.

The Egmont Group has published two documents, "Principles of Information Exchange" and "Best Practice for the Exchange of Information," that provide guidelines for efficient cooperation between FIUs. The jurisdictional competence of FIUs should not be limited to money laundering but should extend to all predicate offenses for money laundering as well as terrorism financing, which would include corruption-type offenses. It is common practice for

Table 5.2 Asia Pacific Group on Money Laundering: financial intelligence units

Jurisdictions	*Name of the Financial Intelligence Unit*
Australia	Australian Transaction Reports Analysis Centre (AUSTRAC)
Canada	Financial Transactions and Reports Analysis Centre of Canada/Centre d'analyse des opérations et declarations financiers du Canada (FINTRAC/CANAFE)
Chinese Taipei	Money Laundering Prevention Centre (MLPC)
Cook Islands	Cook Islands Financial Intelligence Unit (CIFIU)
Hong Kong, China	Joint Financial Intelligence Unit (JFIU)
India	Financial Intelligence Unit-India
Indonesia	Pusat Pelaporan dan Analisis Transaksi Keuanagan/ Indonesian Financial Transaction Reports and Analysis Centre (PPATK/INTRAC)
Japan	Japan Financial Intelligence Centre (JAFIC)
Republic of Korea	Korea Financial Intelligence Unit (KoFIU)
Malaysia	Unit Perisikan Kewangan, Bank Negara Malaysia (UPWBNM)
Marshall Islands	Domestic Financial Intelligence Unit (DFIU)
New Zealand	NZ Police Financial Intelligence Unit
Niue	Niue Financial Intelligence Unit
Philippines	Anti Money Laundering Council (AMLC)
Singapore	Suspicious Transaction Reporting Office (STRO)
Thailand	Anti-Money Laundering Office (AMLO)
United States	Financial Crimes Enforcement Network (FINCEN)
Vanuatu	Financial Intelligence Unit (FIU)

some jurisdictions to require a formal agreement as a prerequisite for the exchange of financial intelligence between the domestic and the foreign FIU. Some jurisdictions do not require a memorandum of understanding, while others require a treaty before they are willing to exchange information. Since the information that is to be exchanged may include information that was obtained by compulsion, it is considered necessary in some jurisdictions that the information be subject to national data protection laws.

Whether a memorandum of understanding will provide a vehicle for the effective sharing of financial information with anticorruption agencies or investigatory bodies in other countries will depend on national laws and a deep and practical understanding of how financial intelligence may assist a foreign country in its investigations. We consider that greater attention needs to be focused on international cooperation in the dissemination of financial intelligence and that states consider modifying their laws to facilitate this exchange. An illustration of why such an approach is necessary is the Australian Wheat Board (AWB) scandal, where an Australian company paid $290 million in kickbacks to Saddam Hussein's regime allegedly in violation of United Nations sanctions.[54] The Australian Transaction Reports Analysis Centre (AUSTRAC) did not transmit to any other agency (local or foreign) financial intelligence that it had in July 2001 concerning massive transfers of money by the AWB to a Jordanian trucking company (a front for Saddam Hussein). The reason for this was that although the information was "identified as aberrant by AUSTRAC…as there was no information available to AUSTRAC (within its data source holdings) at that time to suggest that the payments were anything other than legitimate, no further action was taken. It is not unusual for large transactions by major corporations to trigger this type of statistical alert."[55] On the one hand AUSTRAC, which is regarded by its peers as a world-class model FIU, should be commended for examining the financial intelligence that it received concerning AWB and cross-checking this information against its complete data holdings. On the other hand the failure to appreciate the significance of this financial intelligence raises questions about the current ability of FIUs, such as AUSTRAC, to proactively assist in the detection of serious corruption. This is not to judge AUSTRAC with the wisdom of hindsight, but to suggest that more research is required to improve the effectiveness of AML systems. The other issue is that AUSTRAC did not have the legal authority in 2004 to transmit its financial intelligence concerning AWB to the Independent

Inquiry Committee into the United Nations Oil-for-Food program, even if it had been able to appreciate its significance for the ensuing corruption-related money laundering scandal. This reiterates the importance of national laws to facilitate international cooperation in the transmission of financial intelligence.

Conclusions

The future of international cooperation in combating corruption-related money laundering will depend on many factors, but the most important is the level of commitment and implementation of international legal instruments. The comprehensive requirements of the UNCAC will require significant levels of technical assistance to "developing and fragile countries where institutional, cultural and technological changes are not mere adjustments but occasionally near-revolutionary amendments."[56] This will require changes in domestic laws, institutions, and practices, which the international community should finance and monitor, preferably through a peer review process, as in the FATF or OECD systems. It will also be necessary for developing countries to acquire the skills, experience, and financial and technical support to gather and supply evidence of the underlying crime of corruption in relation to money laundering. If developing countries fail to provide evidence of corruption, then many developed countries will not be in a position to forfeit corrupt money in their financial institutions. The civil forfeiture case of Vladimir Montesinos is an illustration of this challenge. Similarly the prosecution of a former foreign leader, such as Pavlo Lazarenko, for crimes committed in part in the United States (money laundering) in relation to crimes committed in part in the Ukraine (corruption), required the supply of critical evidence from the Ukraine to the U.S. prosecutors.

However, the challenge of international cooperation is not only to developing countries. The reality is that the proceeds of grand corruption end up in international financial centers, such as New York, London, Zurich, and Geneva. The legal systems of these wealthy developing countries have imposed huge legal costs on developing countries that seek to recover the looted assets of their political leaders. It is incumbent on the wealthy countries to prevent the laundering of the proceeds of foreign corruption, and if this fails, to provide a much higher degree of international cooperation than has been forthcoming. Traditional doctrines, such as legal immunities, evidentiary standards, and dual criminality, will need to be addressed. The continued impact of de facto bank secrecy and commercial secrecy, which are used by international and offshore financial centers to secure profitable private banking business, and to conceal illicit crimes, should not be ignored by the wealthy countries. What is required is a dramatic change in the mindset of financial institutions in regard to money laundering in the developed world.

Finally, improved international mutual legal assistance can increase the likelihood of successful prosecution of corrupt officials and money launderers, and the recovery of looted funds, which is especially important for developing countries. In this way international cooperation will make the corrupt more accountable for their illicit acts.

CHAPTER 6

THE MARCOS KLEPTOCRACY

This chapter on Ferdinand Edralin Marcos is a practical case study of the money laundering-corruption nexus. It explains how Marcos was able to use his position as president of the Philippines to become reputedly one of the biggest thieves in history. Current estimates are that Marcos stole at least $10 billion which grew through illicit investments to a multiple of this figure. The Marcos case displays the wide variety of forms of corruption that may occur in countries controlled by authoritarian political leaders. Corruption under the Marcos regime ranged from theft of foreign and military aid to the domestic system of crony capitalism. The scale of the grand corruption of Ferdinand Marcos, his family, relatives, and cronies necessitated an extensive use of money laundering devices. The money laundering methods used by Marcos in hiding his corrupt proceeds were so sophisticated that government officials believe that less than 10 percent of his illicit assets have been recovered. Marcos's financial advisers in the Philippines and overseas utilized numerous mechanisms of secrecy to conceal and launder his illicit wealth through financial institutions, investments, and multilayered corporate shareholdings. Favored money laundering jurisdictions for Marcos included Switzerland and Liechtenstein.

Although Ferdinand Marcos was expelled in 1986, litigation concerning his illicit assets continues to this day in the Philippines, Switzerland, Liechtenstein, Singapore, and the United States. This illustrates the enormous challenge of delay in recovering corrupt assets that have been laundered domestically or internationally. There are dozens of ongoing disputes as to the ownership of the Marcos assets. For instance, in the United States, the Philippine government and the human rights victims of the Marcos regime (who are armed with a U.S. judgment of $2 billion) are competing over the U.S assets, albeit that in June 2008 the U.S. Supreme Court ruled in favor of the Philippine government's claim. Imelda Marcos, aged seventy-nine, is still facing criminal charges today that were filed against her when she was sixty-two years old. Philippine prosecutors have failed in all criminal cases brought against Imelda; in the latest case, in March 2008, Imelda was acquitted on thirty-two criminal charges relating to her Swiss bank accounts on the ground that there was no reliable witness who could testify that those accounts belonged to Imelda.

In the first section of this chapter, we examine the political roles of Ferdinand Marcos, his wife Imelda, and their children, which would render the Marcoses as PEPs under current international AML rules. The opportunities for corruption and the role of business associates of the Marcos family as PEPs are outlined. The second section provides a comprehensive analysis of the myriad varieties of corruption of the Marcos family and their cronies. We then focus on how money laundering techniques protected the illicit gains of the Marcoses from corruption, particularly how corporations and lawyers were vital to the money laundering process. We next assess the use of the civil forfeiture laws of the Philippines to recover the ill-gotten profits, especially in relation to the Swiss bank accounts of Ferdinand and Imelda Marcos. International cooperation in the recovery of the illicit wealth focuses on the United States, Switzerland, and Liechtenstein. Finally, we provide an assessment of the reasons for the failure of the criminal prosecutions of Imelda Marcos in the United States and the Philippines.

Ferdinand Marcos as a Politically Exposed Person

Ferdinand Marcos, who was born in the province of Ilocos Norte in 1917, became entangled in politics at an early age. In 1939 he was accused of murdering a political rival of his father in Commonwealth congressional elections in the Philippines. Ultimately Ferdinand Marcos, while representing himself, was acquitted of the murder charge before the Supreme Court of the Philippines. While in prison, Marcos topped the very competitive bar examinations, achieving the highest ever mark in Philippine bar history.[1] The brilliant legal skills of Marcos later became an instrument for concealing his personal corruption and laundering his illicit assets.

Ferdinand Marcos was a professional politician for almost all of his adult life. After World War II, Marcos became an assistant to the then president Manuel Roxas. From 1949 until his expulsion from the Philippines in 1986, Marcos occupied political posts in an uninterrupted fashion: congressman (1949–1959), senator (1959–1965); president of the senate (1963–1965); and president of the republic

(1965–1986). Marcos's opportunity for plundering the Filipino economy was related to the length of time that he stayed in power, his ability to use violence and legal machinations for his economic ends, and his monopolization of the traditional patron-client system in the Philippines.[2] By winning the 1969 election, Marcos became the first Philippine president to have done so a second time. Since Marcos could not run as president for more than two terms, he exploited several mysterious bombings to justify his declaration of martial law on September 21, 1972. Martial law enabled Marcos to rule the Philippines in circumstances where he used the military to crush the opposition, suppress any independent media, and subvert the judiciary and bureaucracy for his own personal ambitions.[3] Domination of executive and legislative power in the Philippines provided the legal instruments to plunder the economy. Although martial law officially ended in 1981, the authoritarian system of Marcos continued until the peaceful People's (Edsa) Revolution in February 1986.

Imelda Romualdez Marcos, the president's wife, became such a senior powerful public figure during the fourteen-year Marcos dictatorship that the Marcos regime is sometimes described as the "conjugal dictatorship."[4] Initially Imelda's political role was informal, but in 1975 the president appointed her governor of metro Manila, thereby consolidating the personal rule of the Marcoses.[5] In 1978 the president created a new Cabinet post for his wife as minister of the Philippine Ministry of Human Settlements. Imelda Marcos was chair of the Economic Support Fund Council, a Philippine government body that administered funds received from the U.S. government. Other posts included chair of the board of trustees and/or director of government corporate entities, such as the Home Development Mutual Fund, the Light Rail Transit Authority, Food Terminal Inc., National Home Mortgage Finance Corporation, and National Food Authority Council. These positions gave Imelda Marcos access to substantial government resources and the power to award contracts and concessions to favored parties. Imelda's appointment to various ambassadorial roles gave her additional opportunities for securing public monies that could be used for private spending purposes, as well as for laundering illicit monies in foreign countries.

The children of Ferdinand and Imelda Marcos may also be considered to be PEPs and the beneficiaries of corruption under the will of Ferdinand Marcos. The eldest daughter, Ma Imelda Romualdez Marcos Manotoc ("Imee"), who was born in 1955, was the cabinet representative of the Kabatang Barangay, a national youth group (1979–1986) and a member of the National Assembly (1984–1986) during her father's presidency. After returning from exile, Imee has used her legal skills to protect the Marcoses fortune and has led the Marcos family's return to political power by serving as a Congresswoman from 1998 to 2007. Ferdinand Romualdez Marcos Jnr ("Bongbong"), who was born in 1957, is the joint executor of his father's will. During his father's presidency, Bongbong was the vice governor and then the governor of his father's home province of Ilocos Norte (1980–1986). Shortly after returning from exile, Bongbong was elected to the Congress of the Philippines (1992–1995), which has been followed by positions as Governor of Ilocos Norte (1998–2007), and Congressman (2007–). Irene Marcos Araneta, who was born in 1961, is frequently described as a mere socialite, but in 2000 she was the subject of a German government/Philippine government investigation into a money laundering attempt by the Marcos family to secretly withdraw their monies from Switzerland.[6]

Identifying the Marcos's business associates or cronies as PEPs was problematic. No financial institution outside the Philippines was in a position to obtain information concerning the full extent of Marcos cronyism. Indeed, the most knowledgeable source on crony capitalism was U.S. intelligence, which gathered information about the corruption of the Marcos family and their business associates.[7] A dossier on cronyism was prepared by members of the opposition in the last years of the Marcos regime, but did not receive wide circulation until an expanded version was published in 1991 by Ricardo Manapat in his treatise *Some Are Smarter than Others: The History of Marcos Crony Capitalism*.

Based on documents found at the Malacanang Palace and the testimony of Rolando Gapud, the Philippine government alleged in April 1986 that dozens of persons were associates and/or cronies of Ferdinand and Imelda Marcos who may have been involved in concealing illicit assets.[8] The Philippine government handed a list of targeted persons to the Swiss Federal Banking Commission. The list identified members of the Marcos family, close friends such as department store owners, Bienvenido and Tantoc Tantoco, and certain ministers and technocrats, such as Geronimo Velasco. Also named in the list were fifteen Swiss and Liechtenstein lawyers, bankers, and asset managers, the more prominent of Marcos's business associates (Roberto S. Benedicto, Herminio Disini, Lucio Tan, Antonio Floriendo) and some of the key financial advisers (Jose

Yao Campos and Rolando Gapud). The list was incomplete and was skewed to information found at Malacanang Palace or sourced through Rolando Gapud.[9] The significance of the limited scope of the list is that it was unlikely that the Swiss financial institutions would have a complete picture of the extent of Marcos cronyism, and be in a position to freeze all relevant bank accounts. It has been asserted that during the Marcos dictatorship nearly "every major economic activity was controlled by the First Family, their relatives, or cronies."[10] In December 1998, Imelda Marcos claimed that "we practically own everything in the Philippines". Although Imelda Marcos's comments may be viewed as bravado, the depth of the penetration of the Philippines economy by the Marcoses should not be underestimated.

Corrupt Activities of the Marcoses

Ferdinand Marcos's corrupt activities commenced while he was a congressman and head of the Import Control Board, which allowed him to gather large bribes in return for approving import licenses.[11] As a congressman, Marcos became a millionaire largely based on his 10 percent cut from government deals.[12] When Marcos initially became president in 1965, he did not appear to be any different from previous corrupt political leaders in the Philippines. Marcos's presidential election expenses were repaid through raiding the public purse, and his relatives, friends, and business associates were rewarded with contracts, licenses, and other government favors. However, Marcos soon acquired an epic appetite for corruption so as to maintain his power and to satisfy the extravagant spending habits of his wife. What distinguished Marcos from other Filipino corrupt politicians was the scale of his corruption. He was not bound by the "socially acceptable" norms of plunder.

Ferdinand Marcos benefited from a myriad variety of corruption, including diversion of foreign economic and military aid, embezzlement of government monies, rorting of the pork barrel, theft of official gold stocks, institutionalized and private sector extortion, securing of kickbacks from private businesses, illicit takeover of private firms, and creation of monopolies for the private benefit of the Marcos family, relatives, and cronies. Under the Marcos rule, there was a seamless web of corruption stretching from government to industry. The ultimate manifestation of corruption was the system of crony capitalism.

Theft of Foreign Economic Aid and Development Assistance

Ferdinand Marcos arranged and was the beneficiary of large-scale diversion of entitlements to foreign economic assistance, including aid from the United States and Japan, as well as from international financial institutions. The United States provided $3 billion in economic and military aid to the Philippines between 1962 and 1983, while during this same period the World Bank lent $4 billion[13] U.S. development assistance included the Economic Support Fund, whereby the United States assisted the Philippine government in its foreign exchange requirements. Although the U.S. government was aware of the misuse of U.S. taxpayers' monies by Ferdinand Marcos, it continued to provide his government with funds because of the importance of the Philippines as a strategic ally during the Cold War.[14] The U.S. military bases at Clark Air Base and Subic Bay in the Philippines were the largest bases outside the United States. In 1969 U.S. senator Fulbright described the U.S. bases in the Philippines as an active incentive to theft and corruption.[15] The Philippine government received "rent" for the bases, which provided a vehicle for the Marcoses for their personal and political ambitions.

Diversion of Military Aid: Philcag Funds

The Philippine Civil Action Group (Philcag) funds is an example of how Ferdinand Marcos was able to divert U.S. military aid by relying on "national security and intelligence" as a cover story. While as a senator, Ferdinand Marcos opposed the sending of Filipino combat troops to South Vietnam. A few months after becoming president, Marcos approved the dispatch to Vietnam of Philcag, an engineering construction battalion with a security function. Ferdinand Marcos initially kept the U.S. funding of Philcag secret, but the U.S. Senate Symington hearings revealed that the U.S. government had funded Philcag with $38 million[16] A General Accounting Office investigation could not trace how the U.S. funding was deployed, and several senior U.S. public officials suspected that Ferdinand Marcos had diverted the funds for his own personal political advantage. The American ambassador to the Philippines reported that Ferdinand Marcos had admitted the he had not "felt under any obligation to use the funds... for the Philcag directly, but had actually used it for purposes, such as 'security matters.'"[17] Further, Marcos was not prepared to give details about the use of the Philcag funds because these were "too classified" to discuss even with his American allies.[18]

Diversion of Japanese Development Assistance

Since World War II, Japan has been a major financial contributor to the Philippines, initially paying substantial reparations ($550 million from 1956 to 1976) for the human and economic damages caused by its military occupation of the Philippines during the war, and subsequently through overseas development assistance. During the rule of Ferdinand Marcos, Japan provided the Philippines with $1.9 billion in assistance, in the form of tied loans for projects that benefited Japanese construction corporations.[19]

Japanese companies operating in the Philippines that received Japanese government monies were compelled to pay kickbacks to the Marcoses. In several related cases Ferdinand Marcos received approximately $53 million in kickbacks from seven Japanese corporations that were engaged in major infrastructure projects in the Philippines.[20] The Japanese corporations were financed over a twenty-year period by the Japanese government pursuant to the War Reparations Treaty with the Philippines, and by the Japanese Overseas Economic Co-operation Fund. Japanese contractors would include a 15–20 percent commission in the total bid price that was paid by the Philippine government out of Japanese government yen loans. The "commission system" was designed so that Japanese corporations could only win so-called competitive contracts by agreeing to pay kickbacks to the Marcos regime.[21] The commissions were often in the form of cash payments that were collected by intermediaries and agents of Ferdinand Marcos. Several public officials involved in the illicit commission system, including Baltazar Aquino, secretary of public highways during the Marcos administration, admitted to their role. However, the investigation into this matter was obstructed because the Japanese government refused to provide any assistance in investigating the Japanese corporations, or tracing any Marcos monies in Japan.[22] One of the reasons that Japan did not provide any legal assistance to the Philippines in 1986 was that at that time there was no law in Japan punishing the payment of bribes to public officials of foreign countries. Japanese corporations that paid bribes to Filipino government officials could only be punished under the law of the Philippines.

Embezzlement and Looting

The Marcoses used Philippine government banking institutions as "piggy banks." For instance, $27 million of Philippine National Bank (PNB) funds were diverted to the use of the Marcoses. Oscar Carino, vice president of the New York branch of the PNB, testified at Imelda Marcos's racketeering trial in the United States that Fe Roa Giminez, Imelda's social secretary, had withdrawn more than $14million in cash out of PNB, New York, and that none of the monies had been repaid.[23] U.S. prosecutors claimed that $6.6 million of PNB sourced funds financed Imelda's purchase of expensive jewelry from Cartier and Van Cleef & Arpels. In defense, the lawyers of Imelda Marcos argued that any monies that Imelda received were for official purposes, such as travel and official entertainment. Swiss documents, which were not available at Imelda Marcos's trial, corroborated the U.S. prosecutors' assertions.[24]

Imelda Marcos's extravagant spending habits have been well documented by Manapat[25] and Salonga.[26] The greed of Imelda Marcos is demonstrated by the huge array of expensive jewelry that she took with her when she fled from the Philippines in 1986; the jewelry was taken as unaccompanied baggage and was seized by U.S. Customs.[27] Imelda Marcos did not make any distinction between personal and official expenditure. Marcos believed that her expenses were justified by the fact that she was a symbol of pride of the Philippines and that the people expected her to wear expensive clothes and jewels. But Imelda's state of denial is contradicted by the steps that she took to obfuscate the source of monies for her personal expenditure. Imelda frequently dealt in cash, and sought payments for "intelligence" or "national security" purposes. Indeed, when Imelda Marcos traveled overseas on "official trips," payments would be made from the Central Bank and PNB and these would often be described as "intelligence funds."[28]

Pork Barrel, Discretionary Spending, and Theft

In the 1930s Philippines introduced a pork barrel system whereby politicians linked to the ruling party in the Commonwealth were given sizeable discretionary funds as a reward for political loyalty. The justification for the pork barrel was that it allowed politicians to fund development projects within their local area, but in practice it provided a method of buying votes and funding family, friends, and business associates. As the Philippine Centre of Investigative Journalism commented in its 1998 book *Pork and Other Perks,* it is standard operating procedure in pork barrel funded projects in the Philippines that politicians receive kickbacks, often up to 30–40 percent of the cost of a project. The kickbacks are not only used to line the private pockets of politicians but also to repay the high costs of elections and maintain the political base required to win elections.

One of the reasons that Ferdinand Marcos won an unprecedented second term as president was his astute manipulation of the pork barrel.[29] Marcos was very skilled in the patronage-style political system of the Philippines. When martial law was declared in 1972, the pork barrel for members of Congress and senators was abolished. In effect, the pork barrel was concentrated in one man: there was the "centralization of patrimonial plunder."[30] Marcos had access to huge amounts of discretionary funds that were not subject to independent auditing. Two main sources of discretionary monies were tapped: first, budgetary allocations and second, payments from government-controlled agencies. President Marcos had access to "intelligence and national security funds" and contingency funds. These funds were usually sourced through the normal budgetary procedures but when Marcos declared martial law he used his executive and legislative power to avoid any political oversight of the budgetary process. Marcos created another pork barrel source by passing a presidential decree in 1977 that established the Philippine Amusement and Gaming Corp (Pagcor), as the exclusive franchise holder of gaming in the Philippines. Under the presidential decree, Pagcor was obliged to transfer its earnings to the newly created President's Social Fund, which was known as the president's pork barrel.[31]

Yamashita Gold and Theft of Official Gold Stocks

Another source of Marcos's wealth was the purported Yamashita treasure, which General Tomoyuki Yamashita looted from several countries in South East Asia during World War II. Yamashita is alleged to have buried the treasure in secret tunnels in the Philippines while his troops were retreating from U.S. military forces.[32] In 1996 a U.S. jury in Hawaii found that Ferdinand Marcos had conspired to expropriate the Yamashita treasure from Roger Roxas, and awarded Roxas $22 billion for the conversion of "one storage area" of gold bullion, $1.45 million for the theft of a gold statue, and $ 6 million damages arising from false imprisonment and torture. In 1998 the

Hawaii Supreme Court reversed the judgment, finding that there was insufficient evidence of the value of gold bullion in the unopened boxes; the court described the jury verdict as "speculative regarding the gold's quantity and purity."[33] Although there is little mainstream scholarly support for the view that the wealth of Ferdinand Marcos was derived from the Yamashita treasure,[34] there is evidence that Ferdinand Marcos was involved in gold trading and had an obsession with gold.[35] One theory is that Ferdinand Marcos invented the Yamashita treasure story to conceal his theft of gold stocks from the Philippine Central Bank. The Philippine government in its U.S. civil racketeering complaint alleged that the Marcoses had diverted more than 8,000,000 troy ounces of gold from the official gold reserves held at the Central Bank. According to several authors, there has been no proper accounting of the gold missing from the Central Bank reserves during the Marcos rule.[36] After many years of investigations, the Philippine government's Presidential Commission on Good Government (PCGG) has recovered little if any gold accounts from Switzerland or elsewhere. Incredibly the Swiss banks have denied that they had any significant gold accounts for Ferdinand Marcos, even though their typical private bank client's investment portfolio during this period was heavily weighted in gold. In the Philippines the Central Bank has refused to allow its records to be examined by successive Philippine governments to ascertain the extent to which the Central Bank was manipulated by Ferdinand Marcos. Consequently, the full extent of his financial crimes will never be known.

Kickbacks and Crony Capitalism

The Philippines government in its U.S. civil claim accused the Marcoses of "extorting, soliciting, and accepting bribes, kickbacks, illicit gratuities, and commissions in exchange for the granting of government employment, government contracts and the legal right to do business in or with the Republic of the Philippines." The government accused the Marcoses of institutionalizing a system of kickbacks and commissions by "controlling virtually all of the valuable assets of the Philippines government." Kickbacks and illicit commissions from public works contracts under the Marcos rule were massive. For instance, shipping executive Jose Reyes testified in the U.S. racketeering criminal trial of Imelda Marcos that over a ten-year period he paid $25 million as commissions to nominees of Ferdinand

Marcos for the privilege of working in the Philippines. Reyes alleged that he made the payment in cash to one of Marcos's personal bankers at Banque Paribas in Switzerland.[37]

Corporations paid Marcos fronts or nominees kickbacks for several reasons. First, kickbacks were justified as the entry cost into a new business, such as a payment for a license, concession, or permit. Larger kickbacks might be expected when a business was granted a franchise or monopoly. Kickbacks were also paid to avoid paying income and corporate taxes, customs duties or other monies due to the Philippine government. When a corporation received a behest loan from a government-owned bank, a kickback might include a share of the loan being made.

During the Marcos regime there was an increase in the level of government intervention in the Philippines, which Marcos abused by selling or renting "privileges," particularly economic monopolies to favored families and businessmen. Marcos institutionalized this practice, which involved the extortion of, and/or the soliciting of bribes and commissions in exchange for the granting of government employment, contracts, licenses, concessions, permits, franchises, and monopolies. As Paul Hutchcroft explains, the Marcos crony system was "merely expanding on earlier patterns of patrimonial plunder," albeit that it was more centralized and on a grander scale.[38]

Ferdinand Marcos's strategy was to create new business oligarchs to replace oligarchs whom he considered a political threat. The use of extortion and illicit force to take control of assets of powerful business adversaries is illustrated by the case of Benepress Corporation.[39] Eugenio Lopez Sr and his family-owned Benepress Corporation controlled 100 percent of the shares in ABS-CBN Television, the largest broadcasting network in the Philippines, and 27 percent of Meralco Securities Corporation, the wholly owned subsidiary of the largest utility corporation in the Philippines. In 1972, not long after the declaration of martial law, Ferdinand Marcos arranged for the imprisonment of the son of Eugenio Lopez Sr on trumped-up capital charges. Marcos threatened that Lopez would only be released if the Lopez family transferred their shares to a nominee of Marcos. Eugenio Lopez Sr, who was overseas at the time that martial law was declared, returned to the Philippines where he sold and transferred his shareholding in Meralco and ABS-CBN for a pittance to Benjamin ("Kokoy") Romualdez, the brother of Imelda Marcos.

According to the Philippine government's racketeering case in the United States, the Marcoses established a criminal enterprise in the following sectors of the Philippines economy: telecommunications/media companies, banks/financial institutions, food and beverage, transportation, tourism/casinos/hotels, construction/realty, utilities, mining and oil exploration, logging, agriculture/agri-business, and commercial/industrial. In his 617-page treatise, Ricardo Manapat, one of the leading scholars on crony capitalism, documented how Ferdinand Marcos misused his power to create or encourage monopolies for fraternity brothers, close allies, and relatives of the First Family, such as Roberto Benedicto (sugar), Antonio Floriendo (bananas), Eduardo Cojuangco (coconuts). Marcos provided favorable opportunities to Glecy Tantoco (Tourist Duty Free Shops), Lucio Tan (Fortune Tobacco), and Herminio Disini (cigarette filters). Marcos-style favoritism led to the transfer of about a dozen private banks to Marcos and his associates, and the granting by the Central Bank of selective credit allocation and special privileges, such as rediscounts, foreign exchange loans, foreign exchange swaps, government deposits, and emergency loans.[40] These special privileges created new opportunities for plunder, as well as providing mechanisms for money laundering.

The mechanism for creating "quasi state monopolies" or using state power to benefit the few was the issuance of presidential decrees and orders.[41] Since Ferdinand Marcos controlled the executive and the legislature, he could enact whatever laws he wished. Marcos issued 1,941 Presidential decrees, 1,331 letters of instruction, and 896 executive orders during his rule.[42] Some of these laws were written by private parties who were the direct beneficiaries of such laws. When Marcos fell from power, none of the laws that were enacted under his regime for the benefit of the cronies were challenged or invalidated. Instead, the Philippine government sequestered 260 domestic corporations belonging to the cronies on the ground that this was a precautionary move to prevent the alleged "illicit deposits or assets of the companies being plowed back to Marcos, his relatives or cronies."[43] This has been a most controversial exercise of power that has resulted in the most intense litigation disputes that continue today.

Behest Loans and Odious Debts

A major feature of the Marcos kleptocracy was the provision by government-owned financial institutions of "behest loans" to members of the Marcos family, cronies, or political supporters of Marcos.

Behest loans are insider loans that are granted or executed on uneconomic terms and that are diverted for uses contrary to their original purposes. According to President Memorandum Order No. 61 of November 9, 1992, issued by President Ramos, a behest loan has two or more of the following characteristics: stockholders or management of the borrowing corporation are closely associated with the Marcos cronies; the borrower corporation is undercapitalized; the loan is endorsed by high government officials; the proceeds of the loan are diverted for other purposes; the loans are released at extraordinary speed; the loan is under-collateralized; the project for which financing is sought is not feasible; and corporate layering. Behest loans are inevitably nonperforming loans that cannot be collected from the debtor.

The Presidential Ad-hoc Fact Finding Committee (PAHFFC) identified 419 suspicious behest loans cases, of which 130 worth 105 billion pesos were "positively behest loans" as defined under Memorandum Order No 61. Several state-owned financial institutions, including the PNB, the Development Bank of the Philippines, the Philippine Veteran Bank, and the Government Service Insurance System, became commercially insolvent because of their substantial behest loans to cronies. The behest loans were channeled to private commercial banks and then looted.[44] In June 1992 the Commission on Audit found that 14 foreign loans worth over $1 billion had been assumed by the Philippine government, in circumstances where the loans had been contracted or guaranteed fraudulently by Marcos and/or his cronies.[45] In 2004 Senator Osmena of the Philippines estimated that 300 billion pesos of the consolidated public debt of 6 trillion pesos of the Philippines was due to Marcos behest loans.

In the Philippines the government has filed civil and criminal behest loan cases relating to the Marcos rule. Criminal prosecution is based on Sections 3(e) and (g) of the Republic Act No 3019. The Philippine government has faced significant legal hurdles in criminally prosecuting government officials in behest loan cases. There is the difficulty of proving what appears to be an "innocent business transaction" is actually a criminal act. It is necessary to establish under the statutory provisions that the "[loan] contract or transaction [is] manifestly and grossly disadvantageous" to the government, or that the loan has given a private party an "unwarranted benefit, advantage or preference through manifest partiality, evident bad faith or gross inexcusable negligence." Except in crude cases, it will be difficult to gather sufficient evidence to prosecute those public officers who have participated in these anomalous and illicit transactions. For instance, in 1998 the Philippine Supreme Court acquitted Imelda Marcos in a behest loan case on the ground that the inculpatory facts and circumstances were equally consistent with her innocence. The Court applied the presumption of innocence in the Philippine Constitution, ruling that the prosecution had failed to produce evidence sufficient to support her conviction.

After President Aquino assumed power in 1986, the president issued a declaration that the Republic of Philippines would honor all outstanding debts of the Republic. The presidential decision waived the right of the Republic to unilaterally repudiate any odious foreign loan incurred during the rule of Ferdinand Marcos. Subsequently the Supreme Court of the Philippines upheld the constitutional validity of the Aquino declaration. Nevertheless the Philippine government may challenge in the courts the validity of a loan contract on a case-by-case basis where the financial obligations have been secured by fraud or bribery.

Size of Stolen Wealth

Within a few weeks of the expulsion of the Marcos family, the Philippine government estimated that $1 billion had been stolen by Marcos and his accomplice in the twenty years of his rule. This figure was revised in April 1986 when Solicitor-General Sedfrey Ordonez estimated that the Marcoses and their associates had stolen over $5 billion. The figure of $5 billion became the official Philippine government estimate of Marcos plunder; it is found in both the 1986 Philippine government's mutual assistance request of Switzerland and the Philippine government's U.S. racketeering civil complaint against the Marcoses. The basis for calculation of the official estimate of $5 billion has never been stated, but it was largely based on documents accidentally left behind by the Marcoses at Malacanang Palace.[46] At various time senior government officials in the Philippines and the Swiss lawyers of the Philippine government have acknowledged that the $5 billion figure may be too low, and that it could be as high as $10 billion[47] What is evident is that the $5 billion estimate was not informed by a number of important sources, including the financial documents that were destroyed during the dying days of the Marcos administration; the documents that were transmitted by the Swiss authorities to the Philippines in

1991; information in the possession of the financial advisers, asset managers, bankers, trustees, and lawyers of the Marcoses and their associates in the Philippines and overseas; and information acquired through various undercover operations, including Operation Big Bird and Operation Domino.

In 1986 Operation Big Bird revealed that at least $3 billion and possibly up to $8 billion of Marcos monies were in Swiss banks and financial institutions that had assisted Ferdinand Marcos to hide his wealth over the entire duration of his presidency.[48] In 1991 Operation Domino, led by Reiner Jacobi, alleged that $13.2 billion in gold accounts had been hidden in secret precious metal accounts at one of Switzerland's leading banks.[49] The Swiss bank denied that it had any bank account of the Marcoses, including any gold accounts, but this was contradicted by a authenticated filmed admission of a senior employee of the bank that it did have Marcos accounts.[50] The Swiss Federal Banking Commission and the Swiss authorities have refused to acknowledge the existence of the filmed admission, let alone carry out a proper investigation.[51] This reflects a wider problem in estimating the size of the illicit Marcos wealth, namely the failure of the Swiss authorities to carry out an adequate investigation of the Marcos accounts,[52] and the absence of any proactive investigation in the world's international and offshore financial centers.

Money Laundering to Protect Illicit Gains from Corruption

The symbiotic relationship between corruption and money laundering is illustrated by the money laundering techniques that are discussed in the next section. The immense size, variety, and international character of the grand corruption of Ferdinand Marcos necessitated the application of money laundering techniques. For instance, where corrupt cash (yen) payments were made by Japanese contractors, Hong Kong money changers converted the yen to U.S. dollars, deposited the proceeds in international banks in Hong Kong, and wire transferred the monies to banks in other offshore locations. The staggering size of Ferdinand Marcos's graft explains in part why Marcos exploited so many money laundering vehicles. Marcos's financial advisers in the Philippines and offshore utilized every possible mechanism of secrecy to conceal and launder his illicit wealth through financial institutions, investments, and multilayer corporate shareholdings. Marcos was aware of the advantage of complex and secret money laundering tools in the hands of discreet advisers. Indeed, within eighteen months of assuming the office of president, Ferdinand and Imelda Marcos opened up their first Swiss bank accounts.

The modus operandi of receiving corrupt benefits relied on secrecy and deception, as did the laundering of the illicit proceeds. The mechanism for receiving corrupt benefits was often the first stage of the money laundering process, especially where payments were in the form of cash. The placement of illicit proceeds into banking and financial institutions in the Philippines or the smuggling of cash out of the Philippines allowed Ferdinand Marcos to conceal his corrupt activities from third parties. The second stage of money laundering, namely the layering of funds, was extensively carried out by Ferdinand Marcos (see discussion later on the role of lawyers and fiduciaries). The third stage of the money laundering, that is, the integration of the illicit proceeds into the financial system, ensured that Ferdinand Marcos like any other recipient of billions of illicit monies could protect and profit from his gains by the process of hidden investment.

The money laundering methods used by Marcos in hiding his corrupt proceeds were so sophisticated that government officials believe that less than 10 percent of his illicit assets have been recovered. During the period 1986–2007, the Philippine government recovered from the Marcos family, associates, and cronies, the sum of 86 billion pesos.[53] If this sum was translated into 2009 dollars it would amount to US$1.8 billion (at current exchange rate of 1 US$ = 47.4 Philippine peso), albeit the monies being recovered at different points of time. It is not clear whether the 86 billion pesos figure is based on the original value of the funds confiscated, or whether it also includes interest, dividends, investment income, and property value increases from the date of sequestration to the final order of forfeiture. The largest source of the funds was the original $356 million of Swiss deposits frozen in 1986, which had grown to $658 million by January 31, 2002, while being held in escrow at the Philippine National Bank.[54] Significant funds, including cash, stock, and real estate have been recovered under compromise agreements entered into between the PCGG and business cronies of Ferdinand Marcos, while large sums of assets are still subject to fiercely contested litigation in the Philippines and elsewhere.

Offshore Laundering and Illicit Capital Flight

During the Marcos era a significant portion of the Philippines borrowings from external sources was recycled out of the country through capital flight. Former president Marcos must take the lion's share of responsibility for this capital flight because of his participation in the capital flight process and the impact of his policies, including his declaration of martial law. When Ferdinand Marcos assumed the office of president of the Philippines, the external debt was less than $1 billion, while at the time of his expulsion in February 1986 the debt was approximately $28 billion. Ferdinand Marcos's legacy was that in 1986 the Philippines had the heaviest external debt burden (measured by its ratio to national income) of any country in East and South East Asia, and ranked second on the World Bank list of ten Third World debtor countries.[55] Much of the external borrowings was used in wasteful and corrupt projects in the Philippines. A key feature was that while the external debt of the Philippines was largely public—even loans to private companies in the Philippines were guaranteed by the government—the ownership of external assets was private.

Offshore money laundering of illicit monies generated in the Philippines required the transfer of monies out of the Philippines, which was for the most part in violation of the law of the Philippines. Smuggling of illicit cash to neighboring jurisdictions such as Hong Kong was a favored method of moving money offshore, especially since Hong Kong did not have a system of exchange control. Smuggled illicit cash was deposited in local bank accounts in Hong Kong, and moved by wire transfer to banks in other jurisdictions, such as Switzerland and the United States. Illicit capital flight from the Philippines was facilitated through one of the twelve banks owned by Ferdinand Marcos and his associates. Monies were sent directly from a Filipino bank to a correspondent bank in another country. Transfer of monies out of the Philippines usually required the use of false documentation to deceive the Central Bank whose permission was required under exchange control regulations.

Corporate Money Laundering

Ferdinand Marcos used both domestic and foreign corporate vehicles to benefit from corruption and to launder his ill-gotten wealth. Corporate vehicles, which included corporations, foundations, partnerships, and trusts, provide an ideal secrecy mechanism both to conceal the corrupt payment and to launder the payment and any proceeds. The evidence of domestic corporate laundering was found in documentation left behind by the Marcoses at the Malacanang Palace in February 1986. Among the documents discovered were blank deeds of assignment and stock certificates endorsed in blank, which provided prima facie evidence of ownership by Ferdinand Marcos in Filipino companies. The significance of these documents was explained by Jose Yao Campos, a former financial adviser and crony of Ferdinand Marcos, who admitted his involvement in organizing, acquiring, and managing twenty-three Filipino corporations, which were secretly held for the benefit of Ferdinand Marcos. Jose Campos stated in his affidavit dated March 21, 1986, that it was his policy to require all his business associates "to execute a Deed of Trust or Deed of Assignment (relating to the shares of a corporation) duly signed in favour of an unnamed beneficiary and to deliver the original copy thereof to the former President." Through such techniques as a deed of trust or endorsing a share certificate in blank, Ferdinand Marcos was able to secretly launder his illicit monies and acquire secret control of a significant portion of the Philippines economy.

Ferdinand Marcos's overseas interests were concealed through an intricate network of foreign corporate vehicles, including companies in Panama, Switzerland, and the Netherlands Antilles, Liechtenstein foundations, and trusts in Hong Kong. The foreign financial advisers to Ferdinand Marcos were diligent in finding new ways of hiding his illicit wealth. For example, the Marcoses Swiss bank accounts, which were originally in his own name, were replaced by Swiss bank accounts in the name of Liechtenstein foundations. Thus Ferdinand Marcos's name did not appear as the account holder. The twin advantages of a Liechtenstein foundation are that the identity of the beneficial owner is concealed in a private fiduciary agreement and the existence of a Liechtenstein foundation does not generally appear in a publicly available record.[56] The Liechtenstein foundations provided a hub of secrecy for the Marcoses Swiss accounts, the extent of which has not been fully discovered.

The civil forfeiture case filed in the Philippines against the Marcos family disclosed a pattern of money laundering in relation to the Liechtenstein foundations of the Marcoses, which held bank accounts in Switzerland. Of the sixteen Liechtenstein foundations that were documented by the Philippine government from records left by Ferdinand Marcos at Malacanang Palace only five survived. It was a critical part of the ongoing money laundering scheme that the names of the foundations were altered on a number of occasions so as to confuse any prying eyes. Another strategy was to liquidate the foundations thereby breaking the link between the original owner of the bank account and the ultimate account owner. Prior to the liquidation of the Liechtenstein foundations, the Marcos advisers would shift the bank deposits to secret Liechtenstein subsidiaries or associated companies of Swiss banks, which had overall control of the Marcos funds. In effect, these Liechtenstein companies were "cut out vehicles," a favored technique used by government intelligence agencies to conceal their financial activities. The Liechtenstein companies acted as holding vehicles for the funds. The monies would then be transferred to newly established Liechtenstein foundations that had no link to the old ones.[57]

Lawyers, Fiduciaries, and Money Laundering

In the case of Ferdinand Marcos, super-secrecy was facilitated in Switzerland by the use of lawyers and other fiduciaries in setting up Swiss bank accounts. Ordinarily a Swiss bank was required under the Swiss Due Diligence Convention to identify its customers so as to prevent the anonymous and illicit investment of assets. However, clients could conceal their identity by using lawyers who would front for their clients. The banks required the lawyers to sign Form B in which the lawyers declared that they were familiar with the beneficial owner of the account and that they were unaware of any improper business of the owner. Form B allowed lawyers and fiduciaries to vouch for their client's good standing and allowed the banks to claim that they did not know the true owner of the account.[58] Swiss financial intermediaries used this secrecy vehicle to assist President Marcos. For example, one of the documents found at the Malacanang Palace was a letter dated May 19, 1983, from a senior vice president of a major Swiss bank to President Marcos informing him that because of changes in Swiss banking law, the attorneys of his Liechtenstein foundation, who were also employees of the bank, had resigned and had been replaced by new attorneys from a prominent Geneva law firm. The advantage of this change was that "the independent lawyer (can offer)... the additional secrecy of his professional privilege."[59] This document illustrates that the Swiss advisers of Ferdinand Marcos were providing ongoing expert professional guidance as to how to avoid the increasing disclosure requirements of Swiss law.

Given that there is evidence of Ferdinand Marcos utilizing Form B, it is surprising that when the Swiss authorities disclosed to the Philippine government the Marcos accounts that had been frozen, not one of those accounts had been opened by a Swiss attorney utilizing the "super-secrecy" device of Form B. This omission gave rise to suspicion that the Swiss authorities had not disclosed the full extent of Ferdinand Marcos's bank accounts in Switzerland. It was compounded by the fact that the Swiss authorities did not interrogate the numerous attorneys in Switzerland that were employed by Ferdinand Marcos as his financial and legal advisers. This was a significant investigatory failure since it is likely that some of the Swiss attorneys were secretly fronting for the Marcos family in their financial arrangements in Switzerland. In 1991 Form B was abolished in Switzerland.

Unjust Enrichment and the Net Worth Test

An important Filipino law that has facilitated asset recovery against the Marcoses is the legal requirement that public officials and politicians, including the president, file financial disclosures. Since 1960 the Anti-Graft and Corrupt Practices Act of the Philippines has required "every public officer" on the assumption of office and annually to file "a true detailed and sworn statement of assets and liabilities, including a statement of the amounts and sources of his income, the amounts of his personal and family expenses and the amount of income taxes paid." The asset declaration of public officers includes the assets of their spouses and unmarried children under eighteen years of age living in their household.[60]

In 1965 when Ferdinand Marcos became president of the Philippines the First Couple declared their net worth as only 120,000 pesos ($7,000). This public declaration became the benchmark for an assessment of the illicit enrichment of the Marcoses during the twenty-year rule. In 1986 the Bureau of Internal Revenue analyzed the annual income tax returns of the Marcoses for the financial years 1965–1984 and calculated that the reportable income was 16.4 million pesos (US$2.4 million). The sources of income were official salaries (2.6 million pesos), legal practice (11.1 million pesos), farm income (149,700 pesos), and others (2.5 million pesos). Although Ferdinand Marcos was barred by law from practicing his legal profession during his twenty years as president, he claimed that his legal fees represented "receivables from prior years."

Ferdinand Marcos's public declaration of net worth in 1965 coupled with the annual declared income of the Marcoses provided a legal basis for asserting that they had illegally enriched themselves during their public office. Both the Philippine Supreme Court in July 2003 and the Swiss Supreme Court in December 2001 relied on the public filing of the Marcoses' declared wealth as evidence that the Marcoses' Swiss bank assets of $356 million were illicit and subject to forfeiture. Ironically by complying with the statutory requirement of financial disclosure, the Marcoses became vulnerable in their civil forfeiture litigation.

Civil Forfeiture of Ill-Gotten Wealth

In 1991, the Philippines solicitor-general Francisco Chavez filed a forfeiture petition against the illicit assets of the Marcos family, described as Civil Case No 0141. After lengthy delays caused by the Marcos lawyers, the Supreme Court in November 2003 finally ordered the forfeiture of the Swiss bank deposits in favor of the Republic of the Philippines. As on January 31, 2002, the Swiss deposits that were held in escrow at the PNB were estimated at US$658 million. This was the largest source of recovery of the ill-gotten wealth of the Marcos family.

The forfeiture proceedings in the Marcos case were taken under Republic Act 1379 and Executive Order No 14. They were "actions in rem," which meant that they did not result in the imposition of a personal criminal liability against any member of the Marcos family but merely "in the forfeiture of the properties illegally acquired in favor of the State." As civil proceedings, the Philippines government was required to show on the preponderance of evidence that the assets were ill-gotten. The petition for forfeiture was based on evidence that the Swiss bank assets of Ferdinand Marcos were disproportionate to his total government salary and other legitimate monies earned during his presidency from 1965 to 1986. The Philippine government showed that Ferdinand's Swiss banks deposits in 1986 totaled $356 million and that this could not be justified by his total legitimate earnings of $2.4 million over the twenty-one-year period and his declared wealth of $7,000 in 1965. In these circumstances, under the civil forfeiture law of the Philippines, there was a prima facie presumption of illegal provenance of assets. The burden of proving that the Swiss assets were lawfully acquired was shifted to the Marcos family.

Although Imelda Marcos has publicly denied that Ferdinand Marcos stole public assets and claimed that he was one of the wealthiest men in the Philippines, she has failed to produce any evidence that her husband had acquired his wealth through legitimate means. To do so, Imelda Marcos would risk criminal prosecution for perjury; consequently, the strategy of the lawyers of the Marcos family has been to insist on strict proof by the Philippine government of its cases, hoping that a lack of evidence will defeat the government's claims. The Supreme Court of the Philippines described the conduct of the Marcos family in its November 2003 civil forfeiture judgment:

> For twelve long years, respondent Marcoses tried to stave off this case with nothing but empty claims of "lack of knowledge or information sufficient to form a belief," or "they were not privy to the transactions," or "they could not remember (because the transactions) happened a long time ago" or that the assets "were lawfully acquired."

Despite the interminable delays in the civil forfeiture proceedings in the Philippines concerning the Marcos Swiss accounts, the case resulted in a successful recovery. This can be explained because of the lower standard of proof required in civil proceedings, and the shifting of the burden on to the Marcos family to show that the Swiss assets were legitimate. The Supreme Court expressed the view that: "Despite the absence of the authenticated translations of the Swiss decisions, the evidence on hand tilts convincingly in favor of petitioner Republic."

International Cooperation in Recovering the Illicit Marcos Wealth

The strategy of the Philippine government has been to obtain legal assistance in criminal matters from foreign governments and to launch civil litigation to trace, freeze, and recover the illicit assets of the Marcoses. The Philippine government has made mutual legal requests to governments in the United States, Switzerland, Liechtenstein, Germany, Hong Kong, and Australia. It has also filed civil claims in the United States and Singapore. However, the efforts of the Philippines government over twenty years to recover the Marcoses' illicit wealth through international cooperation have been disappointing, with the largest recovery being the $356 million frozen in Switzerland in 1986.

United States

The United States was the first country to provide assistance to the Philippines when U.S. Customs in Hawaii seized from the Marcos party documents and other evidence of the financial dealings of the Marcoses. The Honolulu papers were supplied to a U.S. Congressional subcommittee and to the Philippines government. Unfortunately, the Honolulu papers were so extensively edited by the Department of Justice, that they did not reveal anything new about the Marcos secret assets in the United States or elsewhere.[61] The redaction of the Honolulu papers was presumably done to protect the U.S. government from embarrassing disclosures, such as the alleged theft of U.S. aid monies and the payment by Marcos to the electoral campaign chests of politicians of both sides of U.S. Congress. It is not surprising that the U.S. indictment of the Marcoses did not contain any charge alleging the theft of U.S. aid monies or the diversion of U.S. tax monies to U.S. politicians, charges that would have been politically explosive and most damaging in the eyes of an American jury. The failed U.S. criminal prosecution of Imelda Marcos is discussed later; this failure was a watershed in the long and unsuccessful attempt to render the Marcoses accountable for their crimes. Senior Philippine government officials believed that if Imelda Marcos could not be convicted in a U.S. court, there was little chance that she would be convicted in the Philippines.[62]

In the United States the Philippines government used the legal system to recover the illicit Marcos assets by filing civil claims in New York, California, and Texas. The civil claims were based on allegations of violations of the RICO including the predicate crimes of mail fraud, wire fraud, and the transportation of stolen property in foreign or interstate commerce. The Philippines government successfully obtained injunctions in relation to the U.S. assets of the Marcoses, which was important in the asset recovery process. The civil cases were ultimately settled whereby the Philippine government agreed to dismiss its U.S. civil claims while the Marcoses agreed to transfer certain U.S. assets to the Philippines. This included the net recoveries from four New York buildings, which were initially estimated would fetch $400 million. Indeed, a leading U.S. investigative firm claimed that it had found nearly $1 billion of Marcos assets in the

United States. However, although the Marcoses invested more than $100 million for the purchase of leases in the New York buildings, the Philippine government recovered only $5 million, after deduction of costs.[63] In addition, the Philippine government has recovered from friends and cronies of the Marcoses assets located in the United States. For instance, under a compromise agreement dated March 5, 1987, the Philippine government granted Antonio D. Floriendo immunity from prosecution, and in return Floriendo surrendered U.S. real estate (namely, Lindenmere Estate, Long Island, New York, Olympic Towers, New York City, Makiki Heights, Honolulu, Hawaii), which generated 175 million pesos.[64]

Switzerland

Switzerland has provided the greatest amount of mutual legal assistance to the Philippines, commencing in April 1986 when the Swiss Federal Council (Cabinet) issued an emergency order freezing the assets of the Marcos family, relatives, and cronies in Switzerland. The Swiss decision was unprecedented, relying on the foreign affairs power of the Swiss Constitution, in circumstances where an agent of Ferdinand Marcos had requested Credit Suisse to transfer $213 million to an Austrian bank account.[65] The Philippine government asked the Swiss authorities to supply it with documentation of the Swiss bank accounts of Imelda and Ferdinand Marcos and to return the illicit assets. Over thirteen years a complex, lengthy, and expensive litigation battle was fought in Switzerland over these issues. The strategy of the Swiss lawyers of the Marcoses was to litigate every technical issue, a task made easier because the Swiss law (namely, the 1981 Swiss Federal Law on International Legal Assistance in Criminal Matters) was new and untested. It took more than four years before the Swiss Federal Supreme Court ruled that the Swiss authorities were entitled to transmit bank documentation to the Philippine government. Finally, in December 1997, the Swiss Court ruled that there could be "anticipatory repatriation" of the Marcos assets prior to the issuing of a final, valid, and enforceable decision of the courts in the Philippines. The assets would be transferred to the PNB and held in escrow pending a final court order in the Philippines forfeiting the assets. The Swiss Court relied on Swiss interests as justification for its decision:

> With reference to the present case of the Marcos estate—it is contrary to the interests of Switzerland, if this country turns into a haven

> for fugitive capital or criminal monies... It is the primary duty of the legislator, the banks and the banking organisations to ensure that the heads of dictatorial regimes cannot—as has happened in the present case—deposit millions of obviously criminal monies in Swiss bank accounts, if such monies nevertheless are discovered in Switzerland and their restitution requested by the aggrieved foreign state, the mutual assistance administrations and the courts are required to make a decision.

The Court was persuaded that the assets of the Marcoses were illegal, given their declared net worth and the size of their Swiss bank deposits:

> Today's state of knowledge does not allow serious doubts about the illegal provenance of the seized monies. The incompleteness of the records makes it impossible to attribute the individual assets to specific offences, and it is possible therefore that also legal assets of the Marcos families were deposited with the foundations. However, such legal assets could, as established correctly by the claimant only be minor sums compared to the total amount of the assets seized. With respect to the overwhelming majority of the assets seized the facts are sufficiently clear to allow the assumption of illegal provenance.

Although the recovery of the Marcos assets from Switzerland has been presented as an example of successful international cooperation, the Philippines government and its Swiss lawyers have expressed concern that the Swiss authorities have failed to trace and return billions of dollars of Marcos assets.[66] The criticism of the Swiss authorities is based on three propositions. First, the freezing of the Marcos bank accounts in 1986 was only the tip of the iceberg, since it related to $356 million held at two Swiss banks in the names of four Liechtenstein foundations and one Panamanian corporation. The freezing order did not capture any account held at Switzerland's largest bank, any of the private banks (with one exception), bank accounts where Form B was used by Swiss lawyers, and any substantial precious metal account.[67] Second, the Swiss legal system subverted the principles of international cooperation to maintain financial secrecy, particularly the principles of "proportionality," "speciality," and "reciprocity."[68] For instance, the Swiss authorities extensively edited the Swiss bank documentation relating to the Marcoses prior to their transmission to the Philippines, justifying this redaction process as an application of the principle of proportionality. Third, since 1990 the Swiss "competent authorities had known of money laundering committed by Marcos and the involved Swiss banks (but) did not investigate, as they could have done."[69] In 1999 the Philippine Senate Committee on Accountability of Public Officers and Investigations (Blue Ribbon Committee) commenced an inquiry into the "alleged existence of a PCGG-Swiss banker's conspiracy to hide and divide the Marcos wealth." The Senate enquiry found prima facie evidence that the Marcoses had secret accounts in Switzerland, which the Swiss authorities had refused to investigate.[70] The former solicitor-general of the Philippines, Francisco Chavez, filed a combined corruption and money laundering complaint in Switzerland concerning "anomalous and irregular" conduct by Swiss government officials, bankers, and lawyers in relation to the investigation of the Marcos bank accounts. The complaint was summarized by the deputy attorney-general of Switzerland:

> You are charging the above mentioned persons—explicitly or implicitly—of a number of illicit acts. Translated into Swiss legal terminology, these alleged acts may be summarised as money laundering; passive corruption; abuse of authority and aiding the perpetrator(s) of an offence; failure to exercise due diligence in banking operations; malfeasance and/or non-feasance in office by cantonal magistrates; and infringement of the lawyers' code of professional conduct.

The allegations of Francisco Chavez are important since they illustrate the possibility of corruption of AML agencies, public prosecutors, and the judiciary in international requests for assistance. This possibility existed even prior to the establishment of AML systems under the new international AML standards. Although the Chavez allegations were cursorily dismissed by the Swiss authorities in 1999, they were resuscitated in 2001 in a complaint filed in the United States.

Liechtenstein

Lawyers, bankers, foundations, and trust companies in Liechtenstein have played a significant role in the concealment of the illicit monies of Ferdinand Marcos and his cronies. It has been alleged that the confluence of political, economic, and legal power in Liechtenstein has resulted in a "money laundering community"[71] that has effectively resisted any cooperation with the Philippine government in tracing and recovering the assets of the Marcos family and their cronies.

After Switzerland amended its AML laws in 1990, Liechtenstein, which has stronger bank secrecy and professional secrecy laws than Switzerland, is suspected of attracting money laundering business from Switzerland. In 1991 when the Swiss Federal Banking Commission abolished Form B (see earlier), there was a flow of private banking funds from Swiss banks to Liechtenstein banks. Faced with a deadline of September 1992, all Swiss lawyers and fiduciaries who had signed Form Bs on behalf of their secret clients were required to either disclose the beneficial owner of the accounts to their bank or face closure of the accounts by the bank concerned. What happened to the suspected Marcos accounts held under Form B remains a mystery. The Swiss authorities have never explained why no new Marcos bank accounts were disclosed as a consequence of the abolition of Form B. One possible reason why Swiss lawyers and fiduciaries did not make any disclosures that they were fronting for Marcos interests was the risk of a criminal prosecution under the stolen goods law and the AML law.[72]

On January 10, 2005, the Philippine government filed a mutual assistance request with the Liechtenstein government identifying "83 Liechtenstein companies and /or foundations that continue to be involved in the administration and laundering of Marcos ill-gotten wealth."[73] The request was based on information, corporate documents, and testimony of a former Liechtenstein asset manager, supplied by one of the authors to the PCGG, and a confidential report compiled by the Swiss lawyers of the PCGG.[74] Three years later in 2008 the PCGG described the status of its request on its website in the following terms: "the petition is still pending resolution by the Liechtenstein authorities." The Liechtenstein government has not given any explanation for its failure to properly respond to this request. One of the key allegations is that prior to the 1986 freeze of the Marcos bank accounts in Switzerland, more than $400 million was transferred to a Liechtenstein company that had a secret relationship with one of Switzerland's most powerful banks.[75]

Criminal Prosecution

Criminal prosecution of the Marcoses and their accomplices have so far been a failure. Not one member of the Marcos family, any relative, friend, public official, or member of the military has spent one day in jail in relation to the massive theft, bribery, and abuse of human rights perpetuated during the rule of Ferdinand Marcos. Criminal prosecutions have so far been directed against Imelda Marcos, her relatives, and Herminio Disini. The following section tries to find an explanation as to why criminal prosecutions are problematic in the case of deposed dictators.

There are a range of unique legal and political problems in putting a deposed dictator on trial in the country where he or she has been the ruler. In legal systems of the Anglo-American tradition, criminal trials must usually be heard in the presence of the defendant. For example, under the Bill of Rights chapter of the 1987 Constitution of the Republic of the Philippines the accused is entitled to meet the witnesses face to face and no trial may take place in the absence of the accused except after arraignment, provided the accused has been duly notified and his/her failure to appear is unjustifiable. A criminal trial may require that the deposed dictator be extradited from a third country. It is contrary to international law for a deposed dictator to be returned to his/her former country after being granted political asylum. Even if there is an extradition treaty or arrangement with a third country, it is unlikely that a country of asylum or sanctuary would consent to extradition. The defendant may resist extradition by relying on well-recognized exceptions to extradition, such as the "political offence" exception, the humanitarian exception, the fair trial exception, and doctrines of immunity. The new government may oppose the return of the deposed dictator because of grave concerns about national security. For example, the government of Corazon Aquino considered that the return of the Marcoses to the Philippines would provide a rallying point to Marcos loyalists and set the stage for a coup d'etat. There is evidence to show that Marcos was conspiring in 1987 to invade the Philippines with a military force and seize power. Indeed, U.S. State Department officials, after learning of Marcos's covert schemes, confined him to Oahu Island in Hawaii.

Another possibility is to arrange for the trial to be heard in the place where the dictator is located, for example, while the Marcoses were in Hawaii. President Aquino signed an executive order authorizing the Sandiganbayan (anticorruption court) to try cases outside the territory of the Philippines. The then solicitor-general of the Philippines Francisco Chavez's request to the U.S. government that the Sandiganbayan be permitted to conduct a criminal trial of the Marcoses within the territorial jurisdiction of the United States was rejected.

The remaining option was for a criminal prosecution in the United States for U.S. offenses. Grand juries in New York and Virginia were already investigating the Marcoses. There was concern that any future trial might be heavily politicized, given that Ferdinand and Imelda Marcos had been staunch allies of the United States and they had a close personal relationship with U.S. president Ronald Reagan and his wife Nancy since 1969. The U.S. attorney-general offered a plea bargain to the Marcoses that if they pled guilty to minor offenses and surrendered certain assets, they would not serve any prison time. The Marcoses refused. Subsequently, on October 21, 1988, the Marcoses were indicted by a federal grand jury in New York for offenses under the Racketeer Influenced Corrupt Organization (RICO) Act 1979, mail and wire fraud, fraudulent misappropriation of property, and obstruction of justice. The core allegation was that Ferdinand and Imelda Marcos had used their official positions to steal more than $200 million in Philippine government funds, and had laundered those illicit funds through the purchase of works of art, jewelry, and real estate in New York. Ferdinand Marcos was too sick to attend his arraignment and on September 28, 1989, died. On March 20, 1990, Imelda Marcos was arraigned and put on trial. On July 2, 1990, Imelda Marcos and her eight codefendants (including former billionaire and arms dealer Adnan Khashoggi) were acquitted after a three-and-a-half month trial presided by Judge Keenan. The prosecution case relied on ninety-five witnesses, producing fifty-two hundred pages of court transcripts, while the defense called not a single witness in reply.[76]

A number of reasons have been suggested as to why the New York jury acquitted Imelda. A major challenge was the difficulty of linking Imelda Marcos to the criminal conduct of her husband. Jurors interviewed after the trial told some reporters that they could not hold the widow responsible for the crimes of her husband.[77] They sympathized with Imelda Marcos who was presented as a "as a loyal, naive wife—who came from a shoeless childhood of poverty and hunger—with no involvement in the business affairs of her husband."[78] The prosecutors built their case on a ton of financial documents that circumstantially suggested Imelda Marcos must have known that she was spending illicit monies. But the jury appeared to have lost interest in the stoic and humorless prosecutorial presentation. The failure by U.S. prosecutors to obtain from Switzerland banks documentation that may have implicated Mrs. Marcos in her husband's money laundering activities contributed to the unsuccessful prosecution.

The Philippines government explained Imelda's acquittal in its 1991 forfeiture complaint:

> Imelda Marcos (Imelda, for short) was acquitted in New York. There was a failure of evidence, an illusion of innocence. The American prosecutor waited for the transmittal from Switzerland of documents that would have established Imelda's direct participation in the illegal deposits in Swiss banks of money belonging to the Filipino people. The Swiss documents never came. Her defence that she had neither knowledge nor participation in the illegal dollar deposits in Swiss banks by her late husband, was consequentially sustained. Somehow, she had hypnotised herself into believing her own lies. After all, she got the American judge and jurors to believe her.

Another explanation for Imelda's acquittal is that the jurors did not understand why the trial was taking place in the United States and not the Philippines, given that the major predicate crimes were corruption and theft in the Philippines. Judge Keenan also expressed some doubt about U.S. jurisdiction but nevertheless allowed the case to proceed to a jury decision. The lack of U.S. connections and interests in the criminal prosecution were emphasized by Imelda's defense counsel, Gerry Spence. The strategy of Spence was to attack the prosecutors for overreaching; Spence accused the prosecutors of misusing the RICO statute, which had been aimed at organized crime, not at the widow of a president who had been America's ally. Spence sought to humanize his client, by showing that she was a loving wife who did not know of her husband's misdeeds. In his summation, Spence argued that Imelda Marcos "has committed no crime except the crime of loving a man for 35 years, of raising his children, of being his First Lady, of being his ardent supporter, of taking his lavish gifts."[79] Spence's theatrics were complemented by Imelda's histrionic outbursts in the courtroom.

After Imelda Marcos returned to the Philippines in 1991, the Philippine government filed more than one hundred criminal and civil cases against her. The criminal cases include twenty-six cases in the Sandiganbayan, thirty-seven in the Manila Regional Court, and sixteen in the Quezon City Regional Trial Court. The corruption charges before the Sandiganbayan have concerned offenses relating to Imelda's position as a public official, including allegations of misappropriation of public funds, criminal abuse of conflicts of interest, and involvement in behest loans. The corruption charges have been based on violations of the Anti-Graft and Corrupt Practices

Act (Republic Act No 3019). Imelda Marcos has also faced criminal charges relating to income tax evasion and estate duty evasion.

A significant problem in resolving the criminal cases against Imelda Marcos is that under the judicial system of the Philippines, excessive delays are commonplace and the judiciary is inclined to postpone hearings at the request of the defense or prosecution. Imelda Marcos's lawyers have waged a pretrial criminal litigation war by using a wide range of strategies to delay her criminal trials, for example, by filing numerous postponements. Delays in the criminal proceedings have assisted Imelda Marcos in securing acquittals in all criminal cases that she has so far faced in the Philippines. Only in relation to one matter was Mrs. Marcos convicted in 1993 by the Sandiganbayan and sentenced to prison for 18–24 years, with a minimum of 9–12 years. Imelda Marcos's motion for reconsideration of her conviction and sentence was subsequently dismissed. However, Imelda's appeal to the Supreme Court in 1998 was also initially unsuccessful but a differently reconstituted Supreme Court reheard her case afresh and acquitted her. Presently Imelda Marcos faces four outstanding criminal cases.

The challenges faced by Filipino prosecutors in securing a criminal conviction against Imelda Marcos concerning events alleged to have occurred more than two decades ago are illustrated by Imelda Marcos's trial and acquittal before the Regional Court of Manila in 2008.[80] Imelda Marcos and Roberto Benedicto (the deceased crony businessman) and the Hector Rivera (the banker) were accused in 1991 of "dollar salting" offenses. Seventeen years later Imelda Marcos and her associates faced a trial relating to thirty-two charges. Imelda Marcos was accused of failing to report foreign exchange earnings from abroad and/or failure to register her foreign banking interests with the Central Bank, offenses punishable with five years of imprisonment under section 34 of the Central Bank Act. These offenses were straightforward "exchange control offences," which involved money transfers to Switzerland from 1968 to 1976, and should have been relatively easy to prove because there was no requirement of proving "mens rea" (guilty knowledge). The offenses related to numerous foreign bank accounts. For instance, it was alleged that the Marcoses had arranged for the purchase of $50 million in Philippine-issued dollar denominated treasury notes in bearer form, through a Swiss bank (Bank Hofmann AG) for the benefit of a Liechtenstein foundation (Avertina) for which Imelda was a named beneficiary and signatory. Interest payments from these notes were paid into a secret foreign exchange account at Credit Suisse, allegedly for the benefit of Imelda and Ferdinand Marcos.

At first glance the voluminous Swiss bank documents presented by the prosecutor appeared to provide the strongest evidence of Imelda Marcos's involvement in these Swiss bank accounts. Imelda Marcos was a named beneficiary of the Avertina Foundations and her signature appeared on a number of the Swiss bank documents supplied by the Swiss authorities. However, Judge Silvino Pampilo Jr ruled that the Swiss bank documents had not been authenticated by any witness who was a party to or was present during the execution of these documents. According to this ruling, the documents could only be authenticated by Swiss bankers who had been a party or present to events occurring more than twenty-five years ago. As no Swiss banker was called by the prosecution—a number of the Marcoses' Swiss bankers are dead—the documents could not be authenticated. This is an overly technical ruling, given that the Swiss authorities had authenticated the documents in Switzerland for the purpose of proceedings in the Swiss courts. The judge also ruled that the Swiss bank documents that had been submitted by the prosecution violated the "best evidence rule" as they were not original documents. The judge stated that the government witnesses, namely the former solicitor-general Francisco Chavez, and the former assistant solicitor-general Caesario del Rosario, did not have the "authority to identify the documentary evidence that they have presented in court." This is a peculiar ruling because bank documents that are transmitted to a foreign country pursuant to a mutual assistance request are invariably copies of the original documents. Finally, the judge held that Chavez and Rosario were unqualified "handwriting experts" so that their evidence concerning Imelda's alleged signature on various Swiss bank documents was rejected. These judicial rulings on the admissibility of evidence inevitably resulted in an acquittal of Imelda Marcos. The prosecution has appealed the acquittal: one of the grounds is that the judge was biased and should have recused himself. However, whatever the outcome of the appeal, this case shows that where the prosecution relies largely on documentary evidence to establish criminality, it will face objections from the defense, which will have greater weight where the trial occurs many years after the alleged crimes. The documentary evidence rules in Anglo-American common law systems, such as in the Philippines, need to be reconsidered so that they do not impose an insuperable obstacle to criminal prosecutions. These rules were designed to ensure the reliability of documents and should not be applicable where there is no question as to the source and veracity of the documents.

Conclusions

The Marcos case study presents strong evidence that corruption and money laundering will often occur together, mutually reinforcing each other. Given the size of the Marcos corruption, it is not surprising that the corrupt proceeds were hidden by a wide variety of complex money laundering techniques. The mechanisms for receiving corrupt proceeds often involved the first stage of money laundering. Both corruption and money laundering relied on the same process of deception and secrecy.

The Marcos case provides an empirical illustration of lessons derived from the earlier chapters. First, international AML standards are required in order to combat the most serious forms of corruption. Ferdinand and Imelda Marcos were quintessential high-risk senior public figures, but were allowed to open up bank accounts in Switzerland and elsewhere without any consideration of the illicit sources of their funds. During the time of the Marcos rule there were no international AML regulations. Further, as explained in chapter 4, since the FATF definition of a PEP is limited to a foreign PEP, this would mean that if the FATF international standards had existed when Ferdinand Marcos was in power, there would be no legal requirement for banks in the Philippines to scrutinize the financial activities of the Marcos family.

Another challenge in the Marcos investigation was the absence in 1986 of any specific offense of money laundering in the Philippines and in other countries, including Switzerland and the United States. This had the consequence that U.S. prosecutors relied on the ill-suited offense of racketeering, while the Swiss authorities refused to interrogate asset managers and lawyers ostensibly on the basis that their money laundering activities were not a crime under Swiss law at that time. However, when Switzerland enacted a new money laundering offense in 1990 and implemented a comprehensive AML system, the Swiss authorities should have launched a criminal investigation into the money laundering activities of its banks. Instead, the Swiss authorities have refused to take any proactive step to trace the missing illicit Marcos monies.

The Marcos case illustrates the importance of comprehensive anticorruption preventative laws, such as annual financial disclosure requirements of public officials. Both the Philippines Supreme Court and the Swiss Supreme Court relied on the declared net worth of President Marcos and his wife to impute illegality to the substantial Swiss bank accounts. A significant weakness is the lack of effective implementation of financial disclosure laws of public officials. For example, during the Marcos rule there was no systematic monitoring of the accuracy of financial declarations of public officials. Indeed, during the presidency of Marcos, it was the general public, the opposition, and NGOs that investigated the corrupt activities of Ferdinand Marcos. In the absence of a well-resourced and independent anticorruption agency with the specific obligation to monitor the financial affairs of national senior public officials, serious cases of grand corruption are unlikely to be prevented.

CONCLUSION

SOLUTIONS AND PROSPECTS FOR THE CORRUPTION-MONEY LAUNDERING NEXUS

Corruption and money laundering have increasingly come to the top of the international policy agenda (if not the symbiotic relations between them). There is no guarantee they will stay there, however. These kinds of crime undoubtedly cause massive harm at present and with all likelihood will continue to do so in the future. But this is not sufficient to ensure that they will always enjoy the prominence they do currently. There is no necessary correlation between the quantity of human suffering attributable to a given policy problem and the political priority that problem receives. For example, diarrhea from dirty water kills millions each year, but clean drinking water does not receive the priority commensurate with its impact. The constellation of changing domestic interests, evolving intellectual fashions, coalition-building within international organizations, and serendipitous links examined in chapter 1 that brought corruption and money laundering to center stage at the international level may well shift and realign, throwing the spotlight elsewhere. Exogenous shocks or waning attention may see these concerns displaced by a new crisis or challenge. One interviewee remarked how the question of international cooperation in response to global climate change is already beginning to preoccupy policymakers in a way that tends to marginalize other issues, including corruption and money laundering. Developments such as the speedy ratification of the United Nations Convention Against Corruption (UNCAC) and the launch of the Stolen Assets Recovery initiative have generated political momentum, but this momentum could easily be dissipated when faced with the delays, complexities, and uncertainties of implementing the various high-minded declarations and commitments. All this is to say that those interested in countering the corruption-money laundering nexus face something of a window of opportunity for addressing the issues identified in the body of the book.

Rather than presenting a set-piece sequential summary of each chapter, this concluding chapter presents a list of major problems together with matching suggested solutions. This is not to suggest that the obstacles inhibiting the complementary efforts against corruption and money laundering are susceptible to quick or easy solutions. It bears emphasizing that in general they are not. But even though organizing the main conclusions of the book in this fashion may give the misleading impression of a trite to-do list on financial crime, it is hoped that this will provide a succinct, focused, and specific summary of the book's main lessons. Before doing so, however, it is necessary to return to the basic contention at the heart of this work.

Interlinked Challenges, Interlinked Solutions

The book began with the claim that corruption and money laundering are often intimately linked in a symbiotic relationship: the presence of one type of financial crime tends to bring about and reinforce the other. The significance of this relationship or nexus extends much further, however, in that these interlinked problems also have interlinked solutions. Anticorruption techniques can potentially assist in the fight against money laundering, while the spread and strengthening of anti-money laundering (AML) systems can assist in taming corruption. While the book has found that there are indeed important complementarities in these two efforts, they are probably not symmetrical. Specifically, it seems that AML systems can make a more important contribution to countering corruption than anticorruption techniques can to countering money laundering. Linking up responses to both corruption and money laundering is so far mainly a story of unrealized potential. This potential seems greater in fostering the integrity and accountability of those in public institutions and private companies than it does in lowering money laundering and the associated predicate crimes.

One logical starting point for substantiating this claim is the incredibly rapid and far-reaching spread of AML standards to at least 180 countries, juxtaposed with the long-standing and widespread existence of corrupt practices, increasingly involving cross-border financial activities. Although AML standards were at first directed at attacking the illicit drug trade, it could be expected that as the coverage of predicate offenses has been progressively expanded to cover all serious crimes, the basic pillars of the AML regime would tend to deter or detect bribery, embezzlement, and similar practices by senior public officials. But although a lack of hard evidence prevents any definite conclusions here, it seems that to date effort expended in building up AML systems has not paid dividends in deterring or detecting corruption. In a large majority of rich and poor countries alike, the powers available to the authorities to gather financial intelligence, request international cooperation, and confiscate ill-gotten gains have been greatly augmented over the last decade, but there has been no corresponding observable decline in the amount of corruption.

Working from the opposite end of the equation, one explanation for the so-far disappointing results of AML systems in this role is that the systems themselves or certain key components have been corrupted and are thus not working as they should. According to this perspective, the lack of results from the AML system in reducing corruption would be explained by the subversion of financial intelligence units (FIUs), the police, prosecutorial system, judges, private reporting entities, or some combination of these, perpetrated by those whose illicit behavior would otherwise be put at risk. There is some evidence in support of this explanation. As discussed in chapter 2, in countries such as Vanuatu, Kenya, and the United Kingdom public and private parties strongly suspected of corrupt conduct have successfully stymied the activities of accountability and oversight institutions investigating this conduct. Furthermore, standard corruption prevention measures are applied to FIUs in a relatively haphazard and partial fashion. But there is little direct evidence of corruption in AML systems distinct from the rest of the law enforcement and criminal justice system and other accountability safeguards. Of course given the secretive nature of the crime there may be important instances simply not known to any but the perpetrators. On the available evidence, however, it seems unlikely that the failure to realize the anticorruption potential of AML systems is due to these systems themselves being compromised by improper influence. This may well be because in most countries AML institutions do not at present pose much of a threat to official malfeasance, a situation that can be rectified as discussed later.

This tentative finding does not invalidate the utility of applying anticorruption measures to the AML system in general or to FIUs in particular. First, because strengthening the integrity of judges and prosecutors will tend to enhance the functioning of the criminal justice system as a whole with attendant spillover benefits, as distinct from any particular impact on fighting money laundering as such. Second, in developing countries in particular, AML systems have a relatively short track record, and cases of corruption may not yet have had time to come to light. Relatedly, once FIUs and the system of which they are a part have begun functioning in earnest and become more effective in combating financial crime, including corruption, they can be expected to become more attractive targets. It makes sense to buttress the integrity of an institution preemptively rather than wait until it has succumbed to malign outside influences and then rush to fix a compromised agency.

But the greatest possibilities for policy improvement lie in the application of components of the AML system to attacking corruption. Inherent in the policy response for countering money laundering are mechanisms for gathering large volumes of financial intelligence (e.g., Know Your Customer and Suspicious Transaction Reporting regulations), the provision of powerful legal instruments for confiscating the proceeds of crime (e.g., non-conviction based confiscation measures), and new means of international cooperation for tracing and responding to financial crime (e.g., intelligence-sharing between FIUs). Each of these could make a significant contribution to fighting corruption in rich and poor countries, all the more so when combined. So far, however, they have not, especially in the developing world. Many in developing country governments regard the AML cause as yet another expensive distraction from more important local priorities foisted upon them by domineering outsiders. The direct and indirect effects FATF's blacklisting partly explain this attitude. Probably more important is the indifference and in some cases hostility that international organizations and FATF member governments evince toward a proper appreciation of the costs of AML requirements for developing countries. But probably the most common single cause in all types of states for the failure to capitalize on the potential anticorruption benefits of AML systems is a bureaucratic disconnect between these two priorities. Anti-money laundering typologies rarely include corruption cases, meaning that reporting entities routinely fail to lodge information about corruption-related transactions. Anticorruption agencies generally do not access intelligence gathered by FIUs, either for ongoing investigations or for checking the veracity of asset registers. Erasing this gap for poor countries means that rich countries must be prepared to move away from their own preoccupations of fighting drug crime and terrorist financing, and toward the priority of corruption as the number one source of money to be laundered in the developing world. Technical assistance from international organizations needs to place a greater emphasis on linking AML and anticorruption efforts, rather than on deepening the former in isolation. The quickest way to harness the support of poorer countries for the AML regime is to demonstrate its utility in reducing corruption.

Problems and Solutions

Implementing International Agreements

The coming into force of the UNCAC and the launch of the Stolen Assets Recovery (StAR) initiative have occurred among a crescendo of regional and global efforts to counter corruption and money laundering. From almost nothing twenty-five years ago, states are now enmeshed in an overlapping web of conventions, treaties, and declarations exhorting the necessity of attacking the financial underpinnings of crime while promoting financial transparency and good governance. Existing international organizations have adopted new roles in monitoring and assisting with these commitments, while others have been purposely built from scratch. And yet for all this activity, it is hard to observe much progress in achieving these aims. In part the shortfall is due to the content of the agreements themselves. Often national sensibilities and political compromises have meant that initially strong standards have been watered down in order to gain broad acceptance, for example, in clauses of the UNCAC that some argued should have been obligatory, but ended up being optional. But a much greater problem is implementing the standards we already have, at first in the sense of pressuring governments to put into practice at home measures that they have agreed to in principle abroad. Not only the UNCAC, but regional anticorruption agreements in Africa, the Americas, and the Asia-Pacific suffer from a lack of review and implementation mechanisms.

This shortcoming stands in stark contrast to the muscular and successful approach the Financial Action Task Force (FATF) has adopted in diffusing and policing its 40+9 Recommendations. While the FATF has adopted the same sort of hortatory and outreach methods that are the stock in trade of most international organizations, its confrontational blacklisting exercise from 2000 sets it apart. Not only did this apply a great deal of political, and indirectly financial, pressure to listed states, it made many others sit up and take notice. Governments came to the realization that not only was money laundering something that they vaguely should do something about, but that there was a realistic chance they would suffer serious consequences if they did not rapidly legislate and at least try to implement a specific package of policy measures.[1] The indirect effects of the FATF's aggressive strategy also found their way into the practices of private firms, which in turn tended to reinforce the pressure to comply with international AML standards.[2] Could and should a similar blacklisting method be applied in policing international anticorruption standards?

The Non–Cooperative Countries and Territories exercise has been criticized on the grounds of double standards. The FATF tended to go much easier on its members than those in the cross-hairs of the NCCT list (e.g., on the question of regulating corporate service providers [CSPs] or immobilizing bearer shares). More broadly, it is problematic for an ad hoc club of rich and powerful states to dictate standards to others that these others have had no say in drawing up or approving (remembering that the satellite regional AML bodies cannot themselves amend the 40+9 Recommendations). The challenge for UNCAC and other agreements in this vein is different: getting countries to live up to standards they have freely committed to. Here the process of peer review pioneered and developed to its furthest extent by the OECD might be a better fit. Signatories to the OECD Anti-Bribery Convention face regular assessments by their peers. This process generates compliance pressures as government officials either feel the urge to "do the right thing" among their peers, or are cognizant of the political embarrassment that may flow from being publicly singled out as deficient or deviant. Yet the OECD is atypical in being a relatively homogenous group of high capacity states with almost half a century of close cooperation.

The implementation strategies of the FATF and the OECD Working Group on Corruption thus offer important but only partial solutions. The FATF should be much more energetic in ensuring that countries have made corruption offenses such as bribery of domestic and foreign officials a predicate offense for money laundering. Crucially, the FATF should encourage regional AML bodies to make this a priority among their members. Should any country be so unwise and unprincipled as to set itself up as a haven for the proceeds of corruption, the FATF's Recommendation 21 (applying extra scrutiny and thus constricting financial flows to, from, and through that country) would be an effective response. In the UNCAC and the Asia-Pacific the long-term goal could well be a peer review process like that of the OECD or GRECO. To build the necessary trust among members will take time, however, and intermediate steps such as self-assessment or private or informal peer reviews may be useful. The last aspect, a solution from the outside in rather than inside out, would be greater involvement of bodies such as Transparency International and the International Chamber of Commerce. Even apart from the fact that these organizations possess formidable expertise, they also make up for a major weakness common to states and international organizations: excessive politeness. Politicians and officials from almost every country in the world will rail against the evils of corruption, and then mingle on the warmest and most respectful terms with other politicians and officials whom they know are either personally corrupt or are representatives of kleptocratic regimes. NGOs are more likely to be direct and honest in naming names of individuals and countries at fault. Transparency International's reports and indices are clear and compelling examples. The power of shaming may only go so far, but it is a weak instrument indeed if the niceties of diplomatic protocol bar saying anything guilty parties don't want to hear.

Corruption-Proofing the Anti-Money Laundering System

The potential, but also the limitations, of applying corruption-prevention techniques to the AML system have been alluded to earlier, but it is worth briefly repeating some of the specific points raised earlier in the book. First and foremost is the value of asset registries, for those working in FIUs, but even more so the judiciary and senior public officials. At present declarations of income, assets, and liabilities are usually partial and inadequately enforced. To have real bite, these registries must be regularly updated, they must be cross-checked against information held by tax and AML bodies, and there must be substantial penalties for false, incomplete, and misleading declarations. Other supplementary measures to prevent corruption should be assessed with an eye to cost; particularly in developing countries, expensive "state of the art" policies and institutions should be avoided.

If grand corruption has been one of the particular concerns of the book, this is in some measure because of the intractability of the issue. The only people who can take effective action against this form of crime are those often actively involved in it, or at least receiving indirect benefits. Before Marcos lost power, there was effectively nothing those within the Philippines could do to halt his efforts to plunder the country. For corrupt officials near but not quite at the top, however, there are some possible domestic remedies. Foremost among these is to insulate the prosecutorial system against political interference. In Commonwealth countries a point of vulnerability arises from the dual role played by the attorney general: chief law officer but also member of the cabinet with a responsibility to support other cabinet colleagues. The complicity of successive British governments in hiding evidence of possible corruption by BAE illustrates what can go wrong, with current efforts by the Brown government to enable the authorities to suspend investigations on almost infinitely elastic "national security" grounds being exactly the wrong response.

For the BAE, Bank of New York, and many other scandals, the use of shell corporations to obscure the payment and receipt of bribes is a key feature. World Bank sources indicate that the use of shell companies from on- and offshore jurisdictions is one of the strongest recurring patterns in grand corruption, a finding supported in the area of corruption-related money laundering in the Asia-Pacific region.[3] The use of chains of such companies and similar corporate vehicles (e.g., trusts, partnerships, and foundations) where it is either impossible or impracticable to establish the identity of the ultimate controlling interest and beneficial owner is a standard device in complex fraud, tax evasion, money laundering, and corruption cases.[4] In general, setting up this sort of arrangement for illicit purposes requires the witting or unwitting assistance of CSPs. The situation with regards to anonymous shell companies and unregulated CSPs is better than it was a decade ago. Thanks to outside pressure, the majority of offshore financial centers have moved to require information on beneficial ownership be held in the jurisdiction, and have established a licencing regime for CSPs. However, these advances offshore have not been matched by similar moves onshore. Although it is not alone, the United States has been a conspicuously poor performer in this area, with hundreds of thousands of de facto anonymous Limited Liability Corporations being provided to nonresidents. International organizations such as the FATF and OECD have been happy to turn a blind eye to this conspicuous failing, perhaps reluctant to antagonize their single biggest source of funding. The same goes for the United Kingdom and other OECD members in licencing CSPs.

The solution here is clear: OECD members must summon the political will they have so far lacked and establish beneficial ownership and licence CSPs. These states are already committed to undertake such reforms in line with standards adopted by the OECD, FATF, and many other international organizations. Specifically, this would involve abolishing bearer shares, ensuring that information on the true, beneficial owner of companies (or the equivalent for other corporate vehicles) is kept on file, is available to authorities, and can be exchanged with foreign authorities. Licensing CSPs is eminently possible, and there are a large number of models in place offshore that onshore jurisdictions could profitably copy from.

Politically Exposed Persons

If power corrupts, then the senior public officials who wield most authority are particularly at risk. Ensuring the integrity of these politically exposed persons (PEPs) and investigating and prosecuting those abusing their office present serious complications. These individuals are by definition politically powerful, and may use this influence to prevent or subvert investigations of their corrupt conduct or related money laundering. Aside from these inherent difficulties, current measures to ameliorate this risk suffer from more specific problems. First the definition of PEPs is excessively narrow, in terms of the offices covered, but also in terms of those associated with senior political office holders. Thus corruption cases in Indonesia (Suharto) and the Philippines (Estrada) have indicated the importance that heads of religious charities and extramarital affairs can have in assisting with laundering embezzled money. Neither aspect is covered by existing PEP guidelines. Second, governments have been too quick to divest themselves of the responsibility of drawing up lists of those covered by PEP guidelines. Private firms bear the burden, but they are less interested and may be less capable than governments in determining who should be subject to enhanced scrutiny. Talking about a "risk-based approach" to dealing with PEPs should not be an excuse for public agencies to shirk their responsibilities by delegating policing and supervision functions to private firms. The most serious weakness in the current system, however, is the exclusion of domestic public officials from PEP rules. The remedies for these weaknesses are largely self-evident: an expanded PEP definition taking greater account of local and informal political arrangements, and the increased involvement of governments and international organizations in compiling PEP lists. Above all, states must close the gap and apply the same enhanced scrutiny to the finances of domestic political officials as they do to those from other countries. A large majority of the world's states have already committed to doing just this in signing up to the UNCAC. Yet with only a very few honorable exceptions, political convenience and the self-interest of those making the laws has meant that the vast majority of governments have not done what they promised to do. International organizations and even more NGOs should highlight this shortfall to generate pressure to comply.

Enhancing International Cooperation

A basic premise of this book is that the corruption-money laundering nexus has increasingly taken on an international character. As such, without deep and sustained cooperation between states, there is simply no prospect of slowing, let alone reversing, the growth in these types of crime. Perhaps more than any other reason, it is the difficulty of international cooperation that explains the success of most major instances of corruption and money laundering. The dual criminality criterion, whereby the state whose assistance is requested must have the same law on the books as the state requesting assistance, has repeatedly proved a stumbling block. Even when this factor does not by itself wreck the investigation, it adds to the time, cost, and complexity of responding to cross-border financial crime. As a result authorities may give up investigations in train, or decide not to launch them in the first place.

There are a number of partial solutions. As discussed earlier, pressure should be applied by bodies such as the FATF to make sure that countries have in fact made all corruption-related crimes predicate offenses for money laundering. Where requests for assistance involve noncoercive measures, rather than extradition, there is little justification for applying the dual criminality rule. In cases where the rule is applied, dual criminality should be applied to the conduct in question, not the wording on the statute books. Evidence from Southeast Asia suggests that even where countries do have adequate provision for Mutual Legal Assistance, these channels are rarely used. Accurately or otherwise, officials may believe that these processes are too formalistic, slow and labor-intensive to be of much use. Whether or not this is the case, there are effective and speedy substitutes for the transfer of relevant information, though these may be more useful for intelligence purposes than for material to be presented as evidence. Foremost among these are the relations between FIUs, in particular the secure website maintained by the Egmont Group. Similar ties mediated by the International Organization of Securities Commissions' Multilateral Memorandum of Understanding may provide another option.

While putting wrongdoers behind bars is an obvious priority, in the United Nations and elsewhere those countries that have fallen victim to kleptocratic regimes have sought to make the first priority the recovery of stolen assets. As the Marcos case study and others demonstrate, these instances can involve huge sums stolen from desperately poor countries. Even the touted success of asset recovery, Marcos, Abacha, Montesinos, and a few others, are incomplete. Although impossible to establish with any certainty, it seems that the majority of the funds diverted in each case is yet to be returned. But even these incomplete victories are the exception. Looted assets sent overseas are usually gone for good. The main culprit seems to be the mix of complexity, cost, and long duration in asset recovery cases, remembering that the Marcos case went on for seventeen years and has cost tens of millions of dollars in investigatory and legal fees. Once more, the responses available serve more to incrementally ease these difficulties rather than wish them away. Recent success has been recorded with the use of non-conviction based asset seizure and civil cases in common law countries. Such techniques allow for a lower standard of proof as well as resolving situations in which key suspects have fled or died. In countries that have made corruption-related crimes predicate offenses for money laundering, the AML system may provide additional options for confiscation. The UNCAC principle of returning funds to the victim country first, and then perhaps the country rendering assistance for extraordinary expenses incurred, is both fair and practical. To foster international cooperation there is a need for financial resources, but even more so the necessary expertise to be provided to poorer countries in order that they can pursue international cases, particularly those involving asset recovery. International organizations have already begun to address this priority; the StAR initiative has the potential to provide a substantial boost to these efforts. Going where international organizations too often fear to tread, NGOs can assist by naming and shaming those governments among developed and developing countries dragging their feet on international cooperation (e.g., Nigeria with respect to Charles Taylor's looting of Liberia, Britain with respect to the U.S. investigation of possible money laundering by BAE).

Balancing Means and Ends

A final, vital caveat is in order. Writings on corruption and money laundering from policymakers and scholars (including this book) tend to be understandably focused on removing obstacles to catching criminals. The priorities are effectiveness and efficiency. There is a tendency for checks and rules of procedure to be implicitly derided as slow, cumbersome, expensive, and thus in need of abolition or at least streamlining. Administrative processes are often favored over the courts, privacy is suspect as a refuge for those with something to hide, reviews and safeguards are portrayed a source of needless delay. Governments are encouraged to accrue more power to peer into citizens' financial affairs, to seize their wealth, to send them to face trial in foreign countries, and to impose prison terms, all while governments themselves are subject to fewer checks and less scrutiny. But there is an important tension in the logic of much anticorruption policy: those in authority entrusted with power are liable to misuse it, but many of the specific solutions advanced involve entrusting more power to those in authority. More fundamentally, democratic theory suggests that limits on governments are not merely annoying obstacles to efficiency, but rather vital safeguards against tyranny. These concerns are more than high-minded abstractions. Corrupt and repressive governments have themselves increasingly used the rhetoric and legal powers developed for fighting financial crime to intimidate or neutralize political opponents. Among many others, the conviction of former deputy prime minister of Malaysia Anwar Ibrahim for corruption in a highly suspect trial in 1999 after criticizing then-prime minister Mahathir's alleged use of public funds to support his family's companies represents a cautionary tale.[5]

The corruption-money laundering nexus imposes massive costs and exacts a staggering human price. Often the appropriate response does involve transferring new powers to governments. But a campaign fundamentally premised on the values of good governance and the rule of law must make sure that the means do not displace the ends.

NOTES

Introduction

1. Baker, *Capitlism's Achilles Heel.*
2. OECD, *Bribery Awareness Handbook for Tax Examiners* (Paris, 1999).
3. World Bank, *Strengthening Bank Group Engagement*, 66.
4. United Nations Office on Drugs and Crime, *UN Anti-Corruption Toolkit*, 20.

1 The Corruption-Money Laundering Nexus

1. Asian Development Bank, Anticorruption Policy, 3.
2. See the World Bank's *Literature Survey on Corruption 2000–2005*, the extensive online bibliographies maintained by the World Bank Institute and Transparency International. For a sample of academic reviews, see the special edition of *Public Administration and Development,* 2007 and also Hopkin, "States, Markets and Corruption," 574–590; Jain, "Corruption: A Review," 1–51; Doig and McIvor, "Corruption and its Control in the Developmental Context," 657–676.
3. United Nations Office on Drugs and Crime/World Bank, *Stolen Assets Recovery (StAR) Initiative.*
4. See Levi and Reuter, "Money Laundering," 325.
5. Braithwaite and Drahos, *Global Business Regulation.*
6. Bukovansky, "The Hollowness of Anti-Corruption Discourse," 186.
7. Webb, "United Nations Convention Against Corruption," 192.
8. World Bank, *Helping Countries Combat Corruption*; *World Development Report.*
9. For example, Klitgaard, *Controlling Corruption*; Rose-Ackerman, *Corruption and Government*; *Corruption: A Study in Political Economy*; Shleifer and Vishny, "Corruption," 599–617; Tanzi, Corruption, Governmental Activities, and Markets," 67.
10. IMF, "IMF Adopts Guidelines Regarding Governance Issues."
11. World Bank website.
12. World Bank, *Strengthening Bank Group Engagement*, i.

13. World Bank, *Helping Countries Combat Corruption*; *Strengthening Bank Group Engagement*.
14. Klitgaard, *Tropical Gangsters*; Filer, Dubash, and Kalit, *The Thin Green Line*; Larmour, "Conditionality, Coercion and other forms of 'Power.'"
15. Larmour, "Civilizing Techniques."
16. Lowenheim, "Examining the State: A Foucauldian Perspective on International 'Governance Indicators,'" 255–274; Larmour, "Civilizing Techniques."
17. Nye, "Corruption and Political Development."
18. For example, Alston, Eggertson, and North, *Empirical Studies in Institutional Change*.
19. Levi and Gilmore, "Terrorist Finance, Money Laundering, and the Rise and Rise of Mutual Evaluation"; Wechsler, "Follow the Money."
20. Gilmore, *Dirty Money*; Levi, "Money Laundering and Its Regulation"; Levi and Gilmore "Money Laundering Terrorist Finance"; Levi and Reuter, "Money Laundering."
21. FATF, *FATF Annual Report*.
22. FATF, *Report on Non-Co-operative Countries or Territories*.
23. FATF, *First Review to Identify Non-Co-operative Countries or Territories*.
24. FATF, *Second Review to Identify Non-Co-operative Countries or Territories*; *Third Review to Identify Non-Co-operative Countries or Territories*.
25. IMF, Monetary and Exchange Affairs Legal Department, "Report on the Outcome of the FATF Plenary Meeting."
26. Sharman and Mistry, *Considering the Consequences*.
27. Cueller, "The Tenuous Relationship"; Rider, "Law: The War on Terror"; Levi and Reuter, "Money Laundering."
28. *Economist*, May 25, 2006.
29. Sharman and Mistry, *Considering the Consequences*.
30. Sharman, "Power and Discourse in Policy Diffusion"; "The Bark is the Bite."
31. ESAAMLG, *Strategic Plan 2005–2008*, 12.
32. Reuter and Truman, *Chasing Dirty Money*, 184; Pieth and Aiolfi, *A Comparative Guide to Anti-Money Laundering*, entitle their chapter on the diffusion of these same rules "Spreading the Gospel," 12.
33. OECD, *Mid-Term Study of Phase 2 Reports*.
34. Ibid.
35. Vanuatu Ombudsman, 1998.http://www.paclii.org/vu/ombudsman/1998/8.html.,
36. Crossland, "The Ombudsman Role," 6.
37. Ibid., 7.
38. Ibid.

39. Vanuatu Ombudsman, 1997, http://www.vanuatu.usp.ac.fj/library/Online/ombudsman/Vanuatu/Digest/digest_97–16.html.
40. Author's interview, Vanuatu.
41. Transparency International, 2004.
42. http://www.mcc.gov/documents/score-fy08-vanuatu.pdf (Finance Minister Willie Jimmy is responsible for administering the $65 million grant). Author's interviews, Vanuatu, Ombudsman of Vanuatu, 2001; Transparency International, *National Integrity Systems Country Study Report Vanuatu*; Crossland, "The Ombudsman Role."
43. World Bank, *Strengthening Bank Group Engagement*, 68.
44. Reuter and Truman, *Chasing Dirty Money*, 7.
45. UNODC homepage, www.unodc.org.
46. Commonwealth Secretariat and Chatham House, *Anti-Corruption Conference*.
47. Sharman and Mistry, *Considering the Consequences*.
48. KPMG, *Global Anti-Money Laundering Survey 2007*, 8.
49. Ibid., 14.
50. Sharman and Mistry, *Considering the Consequences*.
51. KPMG, *Global Anti-Money Laundering Survey* 2007, 15.
52. Sharman and Mistry, *Considering the Consequences*.
53. Levi and Reuter, "Money Laundering."
54. Reuters and Truman, *Chasing Dirty Money*, 184.

2 International Responses to Corruption and Money Laundering

1. OECD, *Mid-Term Study of Phase 2 Reports*, 87.
2. Ibid., 87.
3. Ibid., 87–88.
4. Ibid., 88.
5. Checkel, "Why Comply?"
6. Levi and Gilmore, "Terrorist Finance, Money Laundering and the Rise and Rise of Mutual Evaluation"; Pagani, "Peer Review: A Tool for Co-operation and Change."
7. Lacey and George, "Crackdown on Money Laundering"; Webb, "United Nations Convention Against Corruption."
8. Pagani, "Peer Review: A Tool for Co-operation and Change," 4.
9. Levi and Gillmore, "Terrorist Finance, Money Laundering and the Rise and Rise of Mutual Evaluation," 347.
10. March and Olsen, *Rediscovering Institutions*.
11. Pagani, "Peer Review: A Tool for Co-operation and Change."
12. Schimmelfennig, "The Community Trap."
13. OECD, *Mid-Term Study of Phase 2 Reports*, 108.
14. OECD, *Bribery Awareness Handbook for Tax Examiners*.

15. Ibid., 6.
16. OECD, *Access for Tax Authorities to Information*.
17. OECD, *Integrity in Public Procurement*, 9.
18. Ibid.; OECD, *Bribery in Public Procurement*.
19. United Nations Office on Drugs and Crime, *UN Anti-Corruption Toolkit*, 20.
20. Ibid., 432.
21. Blum et al., "Financial Havens."
22. Webb, "United Nations Convention Against Corruption."
23. Commonwealth Secretariat and Chatham House, *Anti-Corruption Conference*, 5; Reuter and Truman, *Chasing Dirty Money*, 152; Transparency International, 2008. *Monitoring UNCAC*.
24. International Chamber of Commerce, "Business Objectives for UNCAC."
25. Webb, "United Nations Convention Against Corruption," 218.
26. United Nations Office on Drugs and Crime/World Bank, *Stolen Assets Recovery (StAR) Initiative*, 28.
27. Authors' interviews.
28. Pagani, "Peer Review a Tool for Co-operation and Change."
29. United Nations Office on Drugs and Crime/World Bank, *Stolen Assets Recovery (StAR) Initiative*, 1.
30. Ibid., 11.
31. Transparency International, *Global Corruption Report*.
32. United Nations Office on Drugs and Crime/World Bank, *Stolen Assets Recovery (StAR) Initiative*, 33.
33. Commonwealth Expert Working Group, *Asset Repatriation*.
34. United Nations Office on Drugs and Crime/World Bank, *Stolen Assets Recovery (StAR) Initiative*, 36.
35. See World Bank, *Strengthening World Bank Group Engagement*.
36. Williams, "Governance, Security and 'Development.'"
37. World Bank, *Strengthening World Bank Group Engagement*, 68.
38. Ibid, 68.
39. "Double-Edged Sword," *Economist*, September 14, 2006.
40. "Wolfowitz's New War," *Economist*, May 2, 2006.
41. Asian Development Bank/OECD, *Curbing Corruption in Public Procurement*, 58.
42. Asian Development Bank/OECD, *Mutual Legal Assistance*, 2008, 91.
43. Author's interview, International Organization of Securities Comissions, 2008.
44. Asian Development Bank/OECD, *Denying Safe Haven to the Corrupt*, 20.
45. Asian Development Bank/OECD, *Mutual Legal Assistance*, 2007, 6.
46. Takats, "A Theory of 'Crying Wolf.'"
47. OECD, *Towards a Level Playing Field*.

48. Transparency International, 2004.
49. United Nations Office on Drugs and Crime/World Bank, *Stolen Assets Recovery (StAR) Initiative*, 10–11.
50. See Kennedy, "Putting Robin Hood Out of Business," 19–26.; Sproat, "UK's Anti-Money Laundering," 169–184.
51. Authors' interview, US Justice Department, 2007.
52. ESAAMLG, *Strategic Plan 2005–2008*; GIABA, *Money Laundering in West Africa*.

3 Points of Vulnerability

1. United Nations Office on Drugs and Crime, *Legislative Guide*.
2. Asian Development Bank/OECD, *Denying Safe Haven to the Corrupt*.
3. International Chamber of Commerce, *Private Commercial Bribery*.
4. Asian Development Bank/OECD, *Mutual Legal Assistance,* 90.
5. Asia Development Bank/OECD, *Denying Safe Haven to the Corrupt*, 37.
6. Authors' interviews.
7. Larmour, *Foreign Flowers*; Commonwealth, "Developmental Impact of Anti-Money Laundering."
8. Lai, "Building Public Confidence."
9. Bhargava and Bolongaita, *Challenging Corruption in Asia*, 239; see also Larmour, "Evaluating International Action."
10. See the literature review and bibliography in McCusker, *Review of Anti-Corruption Strategies*; Asian Development Bank. 2004. *Anti-Corruption Policies in Asia*.
11. Lai, "Building Public Confidence"; Heilbrunn, *Anti-Corruption Commissions*; Doig, Watt, Williams, "Understanding the Three Dilemmas."
12. Heilbrunn, *Anti-Corruption Commissions*; Michael, "What do Donor-Sponsored Anti-Corruption Programs Teach Us," 320–345.
13. Authors' interviews, UNODC, World Bank.
14. Shah, *Performance and Accountability*.
15. Asian Development Bank/OECD, *Denying Safe Haven to the Corrupt*, 9–10.
16. Authors' interviews; Larbi, "Between Spin and Reality"; a forthcoming World Bank study, on using AML information for anticorruption purposes, may well provide more systematic evidence on this matter.
17. Authors' interview.
18. Authors' interview.
19. Authors' interviews.
20. See Chukwuemerie, "Nigeria's Money Laundering."
21. Authors' interview, 2005.

22. Commonwealth, *Judicial Colloquium*.
23. ADB/OECD, *Mutual Legal Assistance*.
24. Transparency International, *Global Corruption Report 2007*, 63.
25. See "MI6 and Blair at Odds over Saudi Deal," *Guardian*, January 16, 2007.
26. Transparency International, *Global Corruption Report 2007*, 117–118.
27. OECD, *United Kingdom: Follow-Up Report*.
28. "UK Tries to Sabotage BAE Bribes Inquiry," *Guardian*, April 24, 2007.
29. Authors' interviews.
30. "BAE's Secret Money Machine," *Guardian*, June 7, 2007.
31. See "MI6 and Blair at Odds over Saudi Deal," *Guardian*, January 16, 2007.
32. "SFO Wrong to Drop BAE Enquiry, Court Rules," *Guardian*, April 10, 2008; "Justices Side with 'Hopeless Challenge,'" *Financial Times*, April 11, 2008.
33. "BAE says U.S. is Investigating Dealings with Saudi Arabia," *International Herald Tribune*, June 26, 2007.
34. Sampson, *Arms Bazaar*, 1978.
35. "Tanzania: BAE Investigated," *Africa Research Bulletin*, January 2007.
36. *House of Lords/House of Commons Joint Committee on the Draft Corruption Bill*, 47
37. Authors' interview.
38. Government Accountability Office, *Suspicious Banking Activities*.
39. United States Senate, *Correspondent Banking*; United States Senate, *Role of US Correspondent*; "The Billion Dollar Shack," *New York Times*, December 10, 2000.
40. "Billion Dollar Shack."
41. Van Fossen, "Money Laundering, Global Financial Instability"; *Sovereignty for Sale*.
42. "Bank of New York's Bad Russian Suit," *Forbes*, May 17, 2007.
43. "U.S. Officials Say Bank of New York Transfers Involved Money in Russian Tax Cases," *New York Times*, September 15, 2000.
44. Government Accountability Office, "Company Formation."
45. FATF, *The Misuse of Corporate Vehicles*, 14.
46. Chaikin, "Impact of Swiss Principles."
47. FATF, *The Misuse of Corporate Vehicles*, 13–14.
48. Government Accountability Office, "Company Formations."
49. See http://www.gov.im/fsc/handbooks/guides/csps/welcome.xml.
50. Authors' interviews.
51. Lester, "Risk Management and the Risks Attached to Money Laundering."

4 Senior Public Officials and Politically Exposed Persons

1. See United States Senate, *Private Banking and Money Laundering.*
2. See FATF, *Report on Money Laundering Typologies*, 19.
3. Ibid., 1.
4. Basel Committee on Banking Supervision, *Customer Due Diligence For Banks.*
5. See Transparency International, *National Integrity Systems Questionnaire*, 14.
6. See GRECO, *Joint First and Second Round Evaluation Report on Turkey.*
7. See, Hong Kong Legislative Council Secretariat, *The Criminal Immunity of Head of State.*
8. Oellers-Frahm, "Italy and France."
9. See Lane, *Berlusconi's Shadow.*
10. See House of Representatives, *Nigeria's Struggle with Corruption.*
11. See Balogun, *African Leaders*, 1.
12. Authors' interviews.
13. FATF, *Report on Money Laundering Typologies*, 19.
14. See Economist, "The UN's Oil-for-Food Scandal: Rolling Up the Culprits,"
15. See Wolfsberg Group, *Wolfsberg AML Principles on Private Banking.* Basel; *Wolfsberg Statement against Corruption.*
16. European Commission, "Opinion of the Committee on the Internal Market."
17. European Banking Industry Committee, *EBIC position regarding the Council General Approach on the Proposal for a New EU Directive on Money Laundering.*
18. Wolfsberg, *Frequently Asked Questions on Politically Exposed Persons.*
19. Collins, "Indonesian Court Acquits Suharto"; Susanto, "A Peculiar Verdict."
20. FATF, *Report on Money Laundering Typologies*, 23.
21. District Attorney New York, "Brazilian Congressman Indicted."
22. Chua et al., "Can Estrada Explain His Wealth."
23. Authors' interview.
24. FATF, *Report on Money Laundering Typologies*, 20.
25. See also the 2007 survey by KMPG, which found that a majority of jurisdictions in Central and South America and the Caribbean "require banks to identify both foreign and domestic PEPs which exceeds the requirements of the US Patriot Act": *KPMG's Global Anti-Money Laundering Survey 2007*, 68.
26. OECD, "Mexico: Follow up Report on the Implementation of the Phase 2 Recommendations," 23.

27. Ibid, 23.
28. Authors' interviews.
29. See, e.g., World Check, "Politically Exposed Person." Factiva, the Dow Jones and Reuters company, that provides information on public figures and associates has noted that "Many industry figures are recommending that institutions consider screening their private clients for domestic as well as international PEPs": de Ruig, "Tracking Politically Exposed Persons."
30. Commonwealth, *Asset Repatriation,* 36.
31. Robertson, "The Importance of Senior Management," 6
32. IMF, *Country Report No. 06/72 Belgium.*
33. United States Federal Financial Institutions Examination Council. Bank Secrecy Act/Anti-Money Laundering Examination Manual.
34. See United States Treasury, *Guidance on Enhanced Scrutiny for Transactions that may involve the Proceeds of Foreign Official Corruption.*
35. See Walker, Letter from Chief Minister Frank Walker of Jersey.
36. Authors' interviews.

5 Best Practice for International Cooperation

1. Asian Development Bank/OECD, *Denying Safe Havens to the Corrupt.*
2. Asian Development Bank/OECD, *Mutual Legal Assistance.*
3. Commonwealth, *Activities of Commonwealth Working Group on Asset Repatriation.*
4. Commonwealth, Report of the Commonwealth Expert Working Group, *Asset Repatriation.*
5. Authors' interviews.
6. See UNODOC website, http://www.unodc.org.
7. Argandoña, "The United Nations Convention Against Corruption," 4.
8. OECD, *Midterm Study of Phase 2 Reports.*
9. Ibid., 105.
10. Ibid., 108.
11. Ibid., 14–18.
12. United Nations Office on Drugs and Crime, *Report of the Informal Expert Working Group.*
13. Chaikin, "Extraterritoriality," 286.
14. Ibid., for a discussion of these principles in the context of anticorruption measures.
15. Collins, *Essays in International Litigation,* 120–122.
16. Asian Development Bank/OECD, *Mutual Legal Assistance*, 38.
17. McClintock, *The United States and Peru.*
18. Düker, "The Extradition of Nationals," 165–177.

19. Chaikin, "International Extradition and Parental Child Abduction," 143.
20. United Nations Office on Drugs and Crime, "A New Extradition System."
21. AustralianAttorney-General's Department, *A New Extradition System – A Review of Australia's Extradition Law and Practice.*
22. Ibid., 24.
23. Authors' interviews.
24. Blum et al., "Financial Havens."
25. United Nations Office on Drugs and Crime, "*Legislative Guide,*" 125.
26. Chaikin, "Impact of Swiss Principles," 192–214.
27. Chaikin, "Policy and Legal Obstacles," 35.
28. Chaikin, "Impact of Swiss Principles," 195.
29. See Kostiw, "Pavlo Lazarenko," 1–6; Swissmoney Research. *Bank News of 1999–2000.*
30. See United States Department of Justice, *US v. Pavel Lazarenko* and United States v. Lazarenko, No. 06–10592 (9th Cir. 9/26/2008) (9th Cir., 2008).
31. See United States Department of Justice "*US v. Pavel Lazarenko*", and Spence, "American Prosecutors," 1185.
32. The "honest services statute" is a controversial criminal provision used in cases of public corruption. See Bookman, "Solving the Extraterritoriality Problem," 749.
33. Nichols, *United States v Lazarenko.*
34. United Nations Office on Drugs and Crime, *Legislative Guide*, 232.
35. Ibid., 264.
36. Feinstein, *National Security Archive.*
37. Townsend Commission, "Investigating Commission."
38. Chaikin, "How Effective Are Suspicious Transaction Reporting Systems?"
39. Swissmoney Research, Bank News 1999–2000.
40. See Jorge, "The Peruvian Efforts."
41. Swiss Federal Office of Justice, "Montesinos Case."
42. Jorge, "The Peruvian Efforts."
43. Ibid., 10.
44. Townsend Commission, "Investigating Commission."
45. See Samuel, "Repatriation Obligations," 58–64. See also Swiss Federal Office of Justice, "Montesinos Case."
46. Swiss Federal Banking Commission, "SFBC Orders Removal of Bank's General Manager."
47. Authors' interviews.
48. See Cassella, "The Recovery of Criminal Proceeds," 268–276; "The Case for Civil Forfeiture."

49. Winmill, "Anti-Money Laundering Law."
50. See Samuel, "Repatriation Obligations."
51. See Basel Institute of Governance, *Efforts in Switzerland to Recover Assets Looted by Sani Abacha of Nigeria.*
52. World Bank and Nigerian Federal Ministry of Finance, *Utilization of Repatriated Abacha Loot.*
53. For more detailed information about Egmont, see its website http://www.egmontgroup.org.
54. See Overington, *Kickback.*
55. Quoted in Holmes, "Cash Crop."
56. Passos, "UNCAC, Technical Assistance and Development Efforts," 282–283.

6 The Marcos Kleptocracy

1. Meimban, "The Rise and Fall of the New Society."
2. Hutchcroft, *Booty Capitalism*, 115; Salonga, *Presidential Plunder.*
3. Pimentel, *Martial Law in the Philippines.*
4. Mijares, *The Conjugal Dictatorship.*
5. Pedrosa, *The Rise and Fall of Imelda Marcos*; Ellison, *Steel Butterfly of the Philippines.*
6. Leyendecker, "Monopoly mit Marcos-Milliarden"; Cueto, "Marcos Daughter Attempted Funds Transfer."
7. Lawler, *Foreign Relations of the United States.*
8. Salonga, *Presidential Plunder,* 16–17.
9. Authors' interviews.
10. Manapat, *Some Are Smarter Than Others,* 84–87.
11. Ibid., 80–81.
12. Bonner, *Waltzing with a Dictator*
13. Boyce, *The Political Economy of Growth*, chapter 9.
14. Hamilton-Paterson, *America's Boy.*
15. Lawler, *Foreign Relations of the United States*, 416.
16. Celoza, *Ferdinand Marcos and the Philippines*, 103.
17. Lawler, *Foreign Relations of the United States*, 423.
18. Ibid., 424.
19. Tujan Jr, "Japan ODA to the Philippines."
20. Republic of the Philippines complaint, 1989.
21. Mendoza, "The Industrial Anatomy of Corruption," 43–67.
22. Seeman, "Japan's Tied Aid."
23. Wolff, "Marcos Said to Have Wept for Gift of Skyscraper from Her Husband."
24. Philippine Government, *Analysis of Swiss Bank Documents.*
25. Manapat, *Some Are Smarter Than Others*, 387–409.

26. Salonga, *Presidential Plunder*, 27.
27. Aquino, *Politics of Plunder*; *The Transnational Dynamics.*
28. Salonga, *Presidential Plunder*, 65.
29. Hedman, Sidel, and Routledge, *Philippine Politics and Society.*
30. Hutchcroft, *Booty Capitalism*, 111.
31. Mangahas and De Leon, The PAGCOR Money Machine.
32. Seagrave, *The Marcos Dynasty*; Seagrave and Seagrave, *Gold Warriors*, chapters 11–12.
33. *Roger Roxas and The Golden Budha Corporation v. Ferdinand and Imelda Marcos*, 969 P.2d 1209 (Haw. 1998).
34. But see Johnson, "The Looting of Asia."
35. Manapat, *Some Are Smarter Than Others*; Zobel, Deposition dated October 27, 1999.
36. McDougald, *The Buddha*; Henry, The Blood Bankers.
37. Wolff, "Witness Calls Commissions Routine in Marcos Dealings."
38. Hutchcroft, *Booty Capitalism*, 115.
39. McCoy, "Rent-Seeking Families," 508–512; Salonga, *Presidential Plunder*, 42–43.
40. Hutchcroft, *Booty Capitalism*, 133–140.
41. Hawes, *The Philippine State and the Marcos Regime*, 128.
42. Abinales and Amoroso, *State and Society in the Philippines.* Compare with Manapat, *Some Are Smarter Than Others*, 91, who cites a 1984 study that Marcos issued 688 presidential decrees and 283 presidential letters of instruction.
43. Aquino, *Politics of Plunder*, 114–115.
44. Hutchcroft, *Booty Capitalism*, 110–142.
45. Philippine Government, Audit Report of the Philippine Public Debt.
46. Authors' interviews.
47. Salvioni, "Recovering the Proceeds of Corruption," 79–89; Salvioni, Bericht Über Den "Restrukturierungsplan Omega."
48. Philippine Government House of Representatives. *Report on the Inquiry of Operation Big Bird.* For a different view on Operation Big Bird, see Salonga, *Presidential Plunder*, 115–133.
49. Chaikin, "Tracking the Proceeds of Organised Crime.", 19–20.
50. See Mueller, Peter. Testimony dated August 19, 1999., and Associated Press, "German Journalist Testifies against Marcoses," August 20, 1999.
51. Authors' interviews.
52. Salvioni, Bericht Über Den "Restrukturierungsplan Omega"
53. This information was taken from the website of the Presidential Commission on Good Government at www.pcgg.gov.ph. The website has been under renovation for six months.
54. See Philippine Government. *PCGG Accomplishment Report for the Year 2001.*

55. Boyce, *The Political Economy of Growth*, 279–297.
56. Ramati, *Liechtenstein's Uncertain Foundations*, 58–59.
57. Chaikin, "Tracking the Proceeds of Organised Crime," 8.
58. Chambost, *Bank Accounts*; Ramati, *Liechtenstein's Uncertain Foundations*, 31–32.
59. Chaikin, "Tracking the Proceeds of Organised Crime," 9.
60. Apostol, *The Experience of Asset Declaration*.
61. Manapat, *Some Are Smarter Than Others*, 560.
62. Authors' interviews.
63. Authors' interviews. Philippine Government. *Chronological List of Assets Recovered.*
64. Ibid.
65. Philippine Government House of Representatives. *Report on the Inquiry of Operation Big Bird*, Salonga, *Presidential Plunder*, 115–133.
66. Cueto, "Marcos Daughter Attempted Funds Transfer."
67. Authors' interviews.
68. Chaikin, "Impact of Swiss Principles," 192–214.
69. Salvioni, "Recovering the Proceeds of Corruption," 81.
70. Cueto, "$13b Marcos Account".
71. Mascolo, "An Invitation to Launder Money."
72. Salvioni, "Recovering the Proceeds of Corruption."
73. See website of the Presidential Commission on Good Government.
74. Salvioni, Bericht Über Den "Restrukturierungsplan Omega"; Swire, "Phillipines Enquiry Hears About Marcos Money In Liechtenstein."
75. Komisar, "Marcos' Missing Millions, In These Times."
76. Wolff, "Marcos Said to Have Wept for Gift Of Skyscraper"; "Marcos Was Not a Thief."
77. Wolff, "The Marcos Verdict"; Salonga, *Presidential Plunder,* 225–226.
78. United States District Court for the Southern District of New York. *A Retrospective (1990–2000).*
79. Wolff, "Marcos Was Not a Thief."
80. See Macairan, "17-year-old Trial: Imelda Cleared On 32 Counts of Dollar Salting"; Salverria, "Lawyer Contests Acquittal of Imelda Marcos."

Conclusion: Solutions and Prospects for the Corruption-Money Laundering Nexus

1. Sharman, "The Bark is the Bite."
2. Sharman, "Power and Discourse in Policy Diffusion."

3. Authors' interviews.
4. Blum et al., "Financial Havens."; OECD, *Behind the Corporate Veil*; FATF, *The Misuse of Corporate Vehicles*.
5. Human Rights Watch, *Chronology of the Case against Anwar Ibrahim*; Amnesty International, "Malaysia: Double Injustice."

Bibliography

Abinales, Patricio N. and Donna J. Amoroso. *State and Society in the Philippines.* New York: Rowman and Littlefied, 2005.

Alston, Lee. Thrainn Eggertson, and Douglass C. North (eds). *Empirical Studies in Institutional Change.* Cambridge: Cambridge University Press, 1996.

Amnesty International. "Malaysia: Double Injustice Heaped on Anwar Ibrahim." Press release, April 18, 2003. Available at http://www.amnesty.org/en/library/asset/ASA28/015/2003/en/dom-ASA280152003en.pdf.

Apostol, Pelagio S. *The Experience of Asset Declaration in the Philippines.* Quezon City, Philippines: Office of the Ombudsman, 2007. Available at http://www.oecd.org/dataoecd/5/54/39367966.pdf.

Argandoña, Antonio. "The United Nations Convention Against Corruption and its Impact on International Companies." IESE Business School Working Paper 656, 2006.

Asian Development Bank. *Anti-Corruption Policies in Asia and the Pacific.* Manila: Asian Development Bank, 2004. Available at http://www.adb.org/Documents/Books/Anti-Corruption-Policies/default.asp.

———. *Anticorruption Policy: Harmonized Definitions of Corrupt and Fraudulent Practices.* Manila: Asian Development Bank, 2006. Available at http://www.adb.org/Documents/Policies/Anticorruption/definitions-update.pdf.

Asian Development Bank/OECD. *Curbing Corruption in Public Procurement.* Manila: Asian Development Bank, 2004.

———. *Denying Safe Haven to the Corrupt and the Proceeds of Corruption.* Manila: Asian Development Bank, 2006.

———. *Mutual Legal Assistance, Extradition and Recovery of Proceeds of Corruption in Asia and the Pacific.* Final Report. Manila: Asian Development Bank, 2007.

Aquino, Belinda A. *Politics of Plunder: The Philippines Under Marcos.* National College of Public Administration and Governance, University of the Philippines, Quezon City, 1999.

———. *The Transnational Dynamics of the Marcos Plunder.* National College of Public Administration and Governance, University of the Philippines, Quezon City, 1999.

Australian Attorney-General's Department. *A New Extradition System: A Review of Australia's Extradition Law and Practice.* Canberra: 2005.

Baker, Raymond W. *Capitalism's Achilles Heel: Dirty Money and how to Renew the Free Market System*. New York: Wiley, 2005.

Balogun, Oladele Abiodun. *African Leaders and Constitutional Immunity: The Moral Question,* Ethics and Africa Conference, University of Cape Town. Cape Town: 2006. Available at http://www2.gsu.edu/~wwwphl/ethics/africa_conference/papers.html.

Basel Committee on Banking Supervision. *Customer Due Diligence for Banks*. Basel:2001.

Basel Institute of Governance. *Efforts in Switzerland to Recover Assets Looted by Sani Abacha of Nigeria*. Basel: August 2007. Available at http://www.assetrecovery.org/kc/node/52f770df-a33e-11dc-bf1b-335-d0754ba85.html.

Bhargava, Vinay and Emil P. Bolongaita (eds). *Challenging Corruption in Asia: Case Studies and a Framework for Action*. Washington DC: World Bank, 2003.

Blum, Jack A., Michael Levi, R. Thomas Naylor, and Phil Williams. "Financial Havens, Banking Secrecy and Money Laundering." Prepared for the United Nations Office for Drug Control and Crime Prevention. Washington DC: 1998.

Bonner, Raymond. *Waltzing with a Dictator*. New York: Vintage Publications, 1987.

Bookman, Pamela Karten. "Solving the Extraterritoriality Problem: Lessons from the Honest Services Statute." *Virginia Law Review* 92 (2006): 749–791.

Boyce, James K. *The Political Economy of Growth and Impoverishment in the Marcos Era*. Manila: Ateneo De Manila University Press, Manila, 1993.

Braithwaite, John and Peter Drahos. *Global Business Regulation*. Cambridge: Cambridge University Press, 2000.

Bukovansky, Mlada. "The Hollowness of Anti-Corruption Discourse." *Review of International Political Economy* 13.2 (2006): 181–209.

Cassella, Stefan D. "The Recovery of Criminal Proceeds Generated in One Nation and Found in Another." *Journal of Financial Crime* 9.3 (2002): 268–276.

——. "The Case for Civil Forfeiture: Why In Rem Proceedings Are An Essential Tool for Recovering the Proceeds of Crime." *Journal of Money Laundering Control* 11:1(2008): 8–14.

Celoza, Albert F. *Ferdinand Marcos and the Philippines: The Political Economy of Authoritarianism*. Westport CT: Praeger, 1997.

Chaikin, David. "International Extradition and Parental Child Abduction." *Bond Law Review*, 5.2 (1992): 129–151.

——. "Extraterritoriality and the Criminalization of Foreign Bribes." In *Corruption: The Enemy Within*, edited by Barry A.K. Rider, 285–301. The Hague: Kluwer, 1997.

——. "Tracking the Proceeds of Organised Crime—The Marcos Case." Paper presented at the Transnational Crime Conference, Canberra (Australian Institute of Criminology, March 9–10, 2000). Available at http://www.aic.gov.au/conferences/transnational/chaikin.pdf.

——. "Controlling Corruption by Heads of Government and Political Elites." In *Corruption and Anti-Corruption,* edited by Peter Larmour and N. Wolanin, 97–108. Canberra: Asia Pacific Press, 2001.

——. "Policy and Legal Obstacles in Recovering Dictators' Plunder." *Bond Law Review* 17.2 (2005): 27–46.

——. "Impact of Swiss Principles of Mutual Assistance on Financial and Fiscal Crimes." *Revenue Law Journal* 16 (2006): 192–214.

——. "How Effective Are Suspicious Transaction Reporting Systems?" *Journal of Money Laundering Control* (forthcoming 2009).

Chambost, Edouard. *Bank Accounts: A World Guide to Confidentiality.* New York: John Wiley & Sons, New York, 1983.

Checkel, Jeffrey T. "Why Comply? Social Learning and European Identity Change." *International Organization* 55.3 (2001): 553–588.

Chua, Yvonne T., Sheila S. Coronel, and Vinia M. Datinguinoo. *Can Estrada Explain His Wealth.* Manilla: Philippine Center for Investigative Journalism, 2000.

Chukwuemerie, Andrew I. "Nigeria's Money Laundering (Prohibition) Act 2004: A Tighter Noose." *Journal of Money Laundering Control* 9.2 (2006): 173–190.

Collins, Lawrence. *Essays in International Litigation and the Conflict of Laws.* Oxford: Clarendon Press, 1994.

Collins, Nancy-Amelia, "Indonesian Court Acquits Suharto but Finds his Charity Foundation Guilty of Graft." *Voice of America,* Jakarta, March 27, 2008.

Commonwealth. *Judicial Colloquium on Combating Corruption within the Judiciary: The Limassol Conclusions.* London: Commonwealth Secretariat, 2002.

——. *Report of the Commonwealth Working Group on Asset Repatriation.* London: Commonwealth Secretariat, 2005.

——. *Activities of Commonwealth Working Group on Asset Repatriation.* London: Commonwealth Secretariat, July 4, 2005.

——. "Developmental Impact of Anti-Money Laundering and Taxation Initiatives." Commonwealth Finance Ministers' Meeting, Colombo FM, June 17, 2006.

Commonwealth and Chatham House. *Anti-Corruption Conference: The UN Convention Against Corruption Implementation and Enforcement: Meeting the Challenges.* London: Commonwealth Secretariat and Chatham House, 2006.

Coronel, Sheila S. *Pork and Other Perks: Corruption and Governance in the Philippines.* Manila: Philippine Center for Investigative Journalism, 1998.

Crossland, K.J. "The Ombudsman Role: Vanuatu's Experiment." State, Society and Governance in Melanesia Discussion Paper 00/05. Australian National University, Canberra, Australia, 2000.

Cueller, Mariano-Florentino. "The Tenuous Relationship Between the Fight Against Money Laundering and the Disruption of Criminal Finance." Research paper 64, Stanford Law School, Stanford, 2003.

Cueto, Donna. "Marcos Daughter Attempted Funds Transfer—German, RP Gov'ts." *Philippine Daily Inquirer*, Manila, July 5, 2001.

———. "$13b Marcos Account—'I Find the Witnesses Honest and Credible,' Says Pimentel," *Philippine Daily Inquirer*, Manila, August 19, 1999.

District Attorney New York. "Brazilian Congressman Indicted in New York for Stealing Public Money." Press Release, March 8, 2007.

Doig, Alan and Stephanie McIvor. "Corruption and its Control in the Developmental Context: An Analysis and Selective Review of the Literature." *Third World Quarterly* 20.3 (1999): 657–676.

Doig, Alan, David Watt, and Robert Williams. "Why do Developing Country Anti-Corruption Commissions fail to Deal with Corruption? Understanding the Three Dilemmas of Organisational Development, Performance Expectation, and Donor and Government Cycles." *Public Administration and Development* 27 (2007): 251–259.

Düker, Arnd. "The Extradition of Nationals: Comments on the Extradition Request for Alberto Fujimori." *German Law Journal* 4.11 (2003): 165–177.

Economist. "The UN's Oil-for-Food Scandal: Rolling Up the Culprits," March 13, 2008.

Ellison, Katherine. *Imelda—Steel Butterfly of the Philippines.* New York: McGraw Hill, 1988.

ESAAMLG. Strategic Plan 2005–2008. Dar es Salaam: Eastern and Southern African Anti-Money Laundering Group, 2005.

European Banking Industry Committee. *EBIC position regarding the Council General Approach on the Proposal for a New EU Directive on Money Laundering.* Doc No 14981/2004. Brussels: January 11, 2005.

European Commission. "Opinion of the Committee on the Internal Market and Consumer Protection on the Proposal for a Directive of the European Parliament and of the Council on the Prevention of the Use of the Financial System for the Purpose of Money Laundering, Including Terrorist Financing." 2004/0137(COD). Strasbourg: European Parliament, March 18, 2005.

FATF. *FATF Annual Report 1990–91.* Paris: FATF, 1991.

———. *Report on Non-Co-operative Countries or Territories.* Paris: FATF, 2000.

———. *First Review to Identify Non-Co-operative Countries or Territories: Increasing the Worldwide Effectiveness of Anti-Money Laundering Measures.* Paris: FATF, 2000.

——. *Second Review to Identify Non-Co-operative Countries or Territories: Increasing the Worldwide Effectiveness of Anti-Money Laundering Measures.* Paris: FATF, 2001.

——. *Third Review to Identify Non-Co-operative Countries or Territories: Increasing the Worldwide Effectiveness of Anti-Money Laundering Measures.* Paris: FATF, 2002.

——. *Report on Money Laundering Typologies.* Paris: FATF, 2004.

——. *The Misuse of Corporate Vehicles, Including Trust and Corporate Service Providers.* Paris: FATF, 2006.

——. *Guidance on the Risk-Based Approach to Combating Money Laundering and Terrorist Financing.* Paris: FATF, 2007.

Feinstein, Tamara (ed). "National Security Archive Electronic Briefing Book No. 72." Peru Documentation Project. Washington DC: George Washington University, 2002. Available at: http://www.gwu.edu/~nsarchiv/NSAEBB/NSAEBB37/

FinCEN [Financial Crimes Enforcement Network]. Advisory on Shell Corporations. Washington DC: US Department of Treasury, 2007.

Filer, Colin, N.K. Dubash, and K. Kalit. *The Thin Green Line: World Bank Leverage and Forestry Policy Reform in Papua New Guinea.* Port Moresby: National Research Institute, 2000.

GIABA. *Corruption and Money Laundering in West Africa: Assessment of Problem Status and the Effectiveness of National and Regional Control Initiatives.* Dakar: Inter-Governmental Action Group against Money Laundering in West Africa, 2006.

Gilmore, William. *Dirty Money: The Evolution of Money Laundering Counter-Measures.* Strasbourg: Council of Europe, 1995.

——. *Dirty Money: The Evolution of International Measures to Counter Money-Laundering and the Financing of Terrorism.* Third edition. Strasbourg: Council of Europe, 2004.

Government Accountability Office. *Suspicious Banking Activities: Possible Money Laundering by US Corporations formed for Russian Entities.* Washington DC: Government Accountability Office, 2000.

——. "Company Formations: Minimal Ownership Information is Collected and Available." Washington DC: Government Accountability Office, 2006.

GRECO. *Joint First and Second Round Evaluation Report on Turkey.* Strasbourg: Council of Europe's Group of States Against Corruption, 2006.

Hamilton-Paterson, James. *America's Boy: the Marcoses and the Philippines,* London: Granta Books, 1998.

Hawes, Garry. *The Philippine State and the Marcos Regime: The Politics of Export.* Ithaca: Cornell University Press, 1987.

Hedman, Eva-Lotta and John T. Sidel (eds). *Philippine Politics and Society in the Twentieth Century: Colonial Legacies, Post-Colonial Trajectories.* London: Routledge, 2000.

Heilbrunn, John R. *Anti-Corruption Commissions: Panacea or Real Medicine to Fight Corruption?* Washington DC: World Bank Institute, 2004.

Henry, James S. *The Blood Bankers: Tales From the Global Underground Economy*. New York: Four Walls Eight Windows, 2003.

Holmes, Jonathan. "Cash Crop." Program Transcript, Part Two. Australian Broadcasting Corporation, Four Corners, April 17, 2006. Available at http://www.abc.net.au/4corners/content/2006/s1618113.htm.

Hong Kong Legislative Council Secretariat. *The Criminal Immunity of Head of State/Government and Whether Impeachment Proceedings Precede Criminal Prosecution*. Paper No IN10/06–07. Hong Kong Government: 2007. Available at http://www.legco.gov.hk/yr06–07/english/sec/library/0607in10-e.pdf.

Hopkin, Jonathan. "States, Markets and Corruption: A Review of Some Recent Literature." *Review of International Political Economy* 9.3 (2002): 574–590.

Human Rights Watch. *Chronology of the Case against Anwar Ibrahim* (1998). Available at: http://www.hrw.org/campaigns/malaysia98/anwar-chronology.htm.

Hutchcroft, Paul D. *Booty Capitalism: The Politics of Banking in the Philippines* Ithaca: Cornell University Press, 1998.

IMF. "IMF Adopts Guidelines Regarding Governance Issues." *IMF Survey*, August 1997, 233–234

——. "Report on the Outcome of the FATF Plenary Meeting and Proposal for the Endorsement of the Methodology for Assessing Compliance with Anti-money Laundering and Combating the Finance of Terrorism (AML/CFT) Standard." Monetary and Exchange Affairs Legal Department, Washington DC, November 8, 2002.

——. *Country Report No. 06/72Belgium: Report on the Observance of Standards and Codes—FATF Recommendations for Anti-Money Laundering and Combating the Financing of Terrorism*. Washington DC: IMF, 2006.

International Chamber of Commerce, *Private Commercial Bribery: A Comparison of National and Supranational Legal Structures*. Paris: Max Planck Institute, 2003.

——. "Business Objectives for UNCAC." Statement by the Global Business Community to the United Nations Convention against Corruption. Nusa Dua, Indonesia. January 28–February 1, 2008.

Jain, Arvind K. "Corruption: A Review." *Journal of Economic Surveys* 15.1 (2001): 1–51.

Johnson, Chalmers. "The Looting of Asia." Book review of *Gold Warriors: America's Secret Recovery of Yamashita's Gold* by Sterling Seagrave and Peggy Seagrave (November 20, 2003). Available at http://www.lrb.co.uk/v25/n22/john04_.html.

Jorge, Guillermo. "The Peruvian efforts to Recover Proceeds from Montesinos." Criminal Network of Corruption, Regional Seminar for Asia-Pacific, Bali, Indonesia, September 5–7, 2007.

Kennedy, Anthony. "Putting Robin Hood Out of Business: A Proceeds of Crime Case Study." *Journal of Money Laundering Control* 9.1 (2006): 19–26.

Klitgaard, Robert. *Tropical Gangsters: One Man's Experience with Development and Decadence in Deepest Africa*. New York: Basic Books, 1990.

——. *Controlling Corruption*. Berkeley: University of California Press, 1998.

Komisar, Lucy. "Marcos' Missing Millions." *In These Times*, Chicago, August 2, 2002. Available at http://www.inthesetimes.com/issue/26/20/feature3.shtml.

Kostiw, James. "Pavlo Lazarenko: Is the Former Ukrainian Prime Minister a Political Refugee or a Financial Criminal?" *Organized Crime and Corruption Watch*, 2.2 (Summer 2000): 1–6.

KPMG. *Global Anti-Money Laundering Survey 2004: How Banks are Facing up to the Challenge*, 2004.

——. *Global Anti-Money Laundering Survey 2007: How Banks are Facing up to the Challenge*, 2007.

Lacey, Kathleen and Barbara Crutchfield George. "Crackdown on Money Laundering: A Comparative Analysis of the Feasibility and Effectiveness of Domestic and Multilateral Policy Reforms." *Northwestern Journal of International Law and Business* 23.2 (2003): 263–352.

Lai, A. "Building Public Confidence in Anti-Corruption Efforts: The Approach of the Hong Kong Special Administrative Region of China." *Forum on Crime and Society* 2.1 (2002): 135–146.

Lane, David. *Berlusconi's Shadow*. London: Penguin Books, 2005.

Larbi, George A. "Between Spin and Reality: Examining Disclosure Practices in Three African Countries." *Public Administration and Development* 27 (2007): 205–214.

Larmour, Peter. "Conditionality, Coercion and other forms of 'Power': International Financial Institutions in the Pacific." *Public Administration and Development* 22.2 (2002): 249–260.

——. *Foreign Flowers: Institutional Transfer and Good Governance in the Pacific Islands*. Honolulu: University of Hawai'i Press, 2005.

——. "Civilizing Techniques: Transparency International and the Spread of Anti-Corruption." In *Global Standards of Market Civilization*, edited by Brett Bowdoin and Leonard Seabrooke, 97–106. London: Routledge, 2006.

——. "Evaluating International Action against Corruption in the Pacific Islands." State, Society and Governance in Melanesia. Discussion Paper 2007/01, Canberra, Australia, 2007.

Lawler, Daniel J (ed). *Foreign Relations of the United States, 1969–1977, Volume XX, Southeast Asia*. Washington DC: US Government Printing Office, 2006.

Lester, Zoe. "Risk Management and the Risks Attached to Money Laundering and Terrorist Financing." Paper presented at Money

Laundering Risk Conference, University of Sydney, Australia, July 21, 2006.

Levi, Michael. 2002. "Money Laundering and its Regulation." *Annals of the American Academy of Political and Social Sciences*, July (2002): 181–194.

Levi, Michael and Peter Reuter. "Money Laundering." *Crime and Justice* 34.2 (2006): 289–375.

Levi, Michael and William Gilmore. "Terrorist Finance, Money Laundering and the Rise and Rise of Mutual Evaluation: A New Paradigm for Crime Control?" *European Journal of Law Reform* 4.2 (2002): 337–364.

Leyendecker, Hans. "Monopoly mit Marcos-Milliarden, Wie die Tochter des Ex-Diktators Guthaben aus der Schweiz nach Düsseldorf transferieren wollte." Sueddeutsche, Germany, July 5, 2001.

Lowenheim, Oded. "Examining the State: A Foucauldian Perspective on International 'Governance Indicators.'" *Third World Quarterly* 29.2 (2008): 255–274.

Manapat, Ricardo. *Some Are Smarter Than Others: The History of Marcos' Crony Capitalism.* New York: Aletheia Publications, 1991.

Mangahas, Malou and Patricia M. De Leon. *The PAGCOR Money Machine.* Manila: Philippine Center For Investigative Journalism, 2008.

March, James G. and Johan P. Olsen. *Rediscovering Institutions: The Organizational Basis of Politics.* New York: Free Press, 1989.

Macairan, Evelyn. "17-year-old Trial: Imelda Cleared On 32 Counts of Dollar Salting." *Philippine Star*, Manila, March 11, 2008.

Mascolo, Georg. "An Invitation to Launder Money." Washington DC: Centre for Public Integrity, November 8, 1999.

McClintock, Cynthia. *The United States and Peru: Cooperation at a Cost.* London: Routledge, 2002.

McCoy, Alfred W. "Rent-Seeking Families and the Philippine State: A History of the Lopez Family." In *An Anarchy of Families: State and Family in the Philippines,* edited by Alfred W McCoy, 508–512. Manila: Ateneo de Manila University Press, 1994.

McCusker, Rob. *Review of Anti-Corruption Strategies.* Canberra: Australian Institute of Criminology, 2007.

McDougald, Charles C. *The Buddha, The Gold and the Myth: How Marcos Looted the Central Bank.* San Francisco: San Francisco Publishers, 1997.

Meimban, Adriel Obar. "The Rise and Fall of the New Society: Ferdinand Edralin Marcos 1965–1986." In *Philippine Presidents 100 Years*, edited by Rosario Mendoza Cortes, 210–249. Quezon City: Philippine Historical Association/New Day Publishers, 1999.

Mendoza, Amado Jr. "The Industrial Anatomy of Corruption: Government Procurement, Bidding and Awards of Contract" *Public Policy* 5.1 (2001): 43–67.

Michael, Bryane. "What do Donor-Sponsored Anti-Corruption Programs Teach Us about International Development in Africa?" *Social Policy and Administration* 38.4 (2004): 320–345.

Mijares, Primitivo. *The Conjugal Dictatorship of Ferdinand and Imelda Marcos.* San Francisco: Union Square Publications, 1976.

Mueller, Peter. Testimony dated August 19, 1999. Testimony given before the Senate Committee on Accountability and Public Officers and Investigations and Committee on Banks, Financial Institutions and Currencies. Manila, Republic of Philippines Senate, 1999.

Nichols, Philip M. "*United States v Lazarenko*: Filling in Gaps in Support and Regulation of Transnational Relationships" (2007). Available at: http://works.bepress.com/philip_nichols/1.

Nye, Joseph M. "Corruption and Political Development: A Cost-Benefit Analysis." *American Political Science Review* 61.2 (1967): 417–427.

OECD. *Behind the Corporate Veil: Using Corporate Entities for Illicit Purposes.* Paris: OECD, 2001.

——. *Access for Tax Authorities to Information Gathered by Anti-Money Laundering Authorities*. Paris: OECD, 2002.

——. *Mid-Term Study of Phase 2 Reports: Application of the Convention on Combating Bribery of Foreign Officials in International Business Transactions and the 1997 Recommendation on Combating Bribery in International Business Transactions*. Paris: OECD, 2006.

——. *OECD Bribery Awareness Handbook for Tax Examiners*. Paris: OECD, 2006.

——. *Tax Co-operation: Towards a Level Playing Field*. Paris: OECD, 2006.

——. *Integrity in Public Procurement: Good Practice from A to Z*. Paris: OECD, 2007.

——. *Bribery in Public Procurement: Methods, Actors, Counter-Measures*. Paris: OECD, 2007.

——. *United Kingdom: Follow-Up Report on the Implementation of Phase 2 Recommendations, Application of the Convention on Combating Bribery of Foreign Public Officials in International Transactions and the 1997 Revised Recommendation Combating Bribery in International Business Transactions.* Paris: OECD, 2007.

——. *Mexico: Follow up Report on the Implementation of the Phase 2 Recommendations, Application of the Convention on Combating Bribery of Foreign Public Officials in International Transactions and the 1997 Revised Recommendation Combating Bribery in International Business Transactions.* Paris: OECD, 2007.

Oellers-Frahm, Karin. "Italy and France: Immunity for the Prime Minister of Italy and the President of the French Republic." *International Journal of Constitutional Law* 3.1 (2005): 107–115.

Ombudsman of Vanuatu. 2001. Digested Reports of the Office of the Ombudsman of Vanuatu 1996–2000. United Nations Development Program, available at http://www.paclii.org/vu/ombudsmanreports/Vanuatu/Digest/digest_index.html.

Overington, Carole. *Kickback: Inside the Australia Wheat Board Scandal.* Sydney: Allen & Unwin, 2007.

Pagani, Fabrazio. "Peer Review: A Tool for Co-operation and Change: An Analysis of the OECD Working Method." Paper prepared by Directorate for Legal Affairs for General Secretariat, 2002.

Passos, Nikos. "UNCAC, Technical Assistance and Development Efforts." In *Recovering Stolen Assets*, edited by Mark Pieth, 281–295. Berne: Peter Lang, 2008.

Pedrosa, Carmen Navarro. *The Rise and Fall of Imelda Marcos*. Manila: Bookmark, 1987.

Philippine Government House of Representatives. *Report on the Inquiry of Operation Big Bird*. Manila: Special Committee on Public Accountability, April 29, 1991.

Philippine Government. *Audit Report of the Philippine Public Debt*. Manila: Commission on Audit, June 1992.

Philippine Government. *Analysis of Swiss Bank Documents*. Manila: Office of the Solicitor-General, Unpublished, 1992.

Philippine Government. *Chronological List of Assets Recovered*. Manila: Presidential Commission on Good Government, Unpublished, 2001.

Philippine Government. *PCGG Accomplishment Report for the Year 2001*. Manila: Presidential Commission on Good Government, Unpublished, 2002.

Pieth, Mark and Gemma Aiolfi. *A Comparative Guide to Anti-Money Laundering*. Cheltenham: Edward Elgar, 2004.

Pimentel, Aquilion Q. *Martial Law in the Philippines: My Story*. Manila: Lorraine Pimentel Borghijs, 2006.

Ramati, U.E. *Liechtenstein's Uncertain Foundations: Anatomy of a Tax Haven*. Dublin: Hazlemore Ltd, 1993.

Reuter, Peter and Edwin M. Truman. *Chasing Dirty Money: The Fight Against Money Laundering*. Washington DC: International Institute for Economics, 2004.

Rider, Barry A.K. "Law: The War on Terror and Crime and the Offshore Centres: The 'New' Perspective." In *Global Financial Crime: Terrorism, Money Laundering and Offshore Centres*, edited by Donato Masciandaro, 61–95. Aldershot: Ashgate, 2004.

Robertson, Phillip. "The Importance of Senior Management Responsibility and the Transition to a Risk-Based Approach." Speech given to the Financial Services Authority City and Financial 6th Money Laundering and Financial Crime Conference. London, United Kingdom, June 6, 2006.

Rose-Ackerman, Susan. *Corruption: A Study in Political Economy*. New York: Academic Press, 1978.

———. *Corruption and Government: Causes, Consequences and Reform*. Cambridge: Cambridge University Press, 1999.

de Ruig, Rupert. "Tracking Politically Exposed Persons: A Difficult Procedure," *RMA Journal*, September 2006.

Salonga, Jovita. *Presidential Plunder: The Question for the Marcos Ill-Gotten Wealth*. Manila: University of the Philippines, 2000.

Salverria, Leila. "Lawyer Contests Acquittal of Imelda Marcos." *Philippine Daily Inquirer*, Manila, March 27, 2008.

Salvioni, Sergio. Bericht Über Den "Restrukturierungsplan Omega" (Mit Welchem Herminio T Disini und Ferdinand E Marcos Zwischen September 1979 und August 1986 die Offshore-Struktur der Philippinischen Diktatur Reorganisiert Jaben) Und Über Die Struktur "Omega" Vom Jahr 1986 Bis Zum Jahr 2004. Unpublished, 2004.

———. "Recovering the Proceeds of Corruption: Ferdinand Marcos and the Philippines." In *Recovering Stolen Assets,* edited by Mark Pieth, 79–89. Bern: Peter Lang, 2008.

Sampson, Anthony. *The Arms Bazaar from Lebanon to Lockheed.* New York: Viking Press, 1978.

Samuel, Linda M. "Repatriation obligations under the United Nations Convention against Corruption. Case Study. Victor Alberto Venero Garrido." 125th International Training Course, Resource Material Series 65, United Nations Asia and Far East Institute for the Prevention of Crime and Treatment of Offenders, Tokyo, 58–64, March 2005.

Schimmelfennig, Frank. "The Community Trap: Liberal Norms, Rhetorical Action, and the Eastern Enlargement of the European Union." *International Organization* 55.1 (2001): 47–80.

Seagrave, Sterling. *The Marcos Dynasty.* New York: Harper Collins, 1988.

Seagrave, Sterling and Peggy Seagrave, *Gold Warriors: America's Secret Recovery of Yamashita's Gold.* New York: Verso, 2003.

Seeman, Roderick. "Japan's Tied Aid: The Marcos Connection Helps Japan's Business." *The Japan Law Letter*, July 1986.

Shah, Anwar. *Performance and Accountability in Combating Corruption.* Washington DC: World Bank, 2007.

Sharman, J.C. *Havens in a Storm: The Struggle for Global Tax Regulation.* Ithaca: Cornell University Press, 2006.

———. "Power and Discourse in Policy Diffusion: Anti-Money Laundering in Developing States." *International Studies Quarterly* 52.3 (2008), 635–656.

———. "The Bark is the Bite: International Organizations and Blacklisting." *Review of International Political Economy* 16.1 (2009), 1–24.

Sharman, J.C. and Percy S. Mistry. *Considering the Consequences: The Development Impact of International Initiatives on Taxation, Anti-Money Laundering and Combating the Financing or Terrorism.* London: Commonwealth Secretariat, 2008.

Shleifer, Andrei and Robert W. Vishny. "Corruption." *Quarterly Journal of Economics* 108.3 (1993): 599–617.

Spence, Matthew J. "American Prosecutors as Democracy Promoters: Prosecuting Corrupt Foreign Officials in U.S. Courts." *Yale Law Journal* 114 (2005): 1185–1192.

Sproat, Peter Alan. "An Evaluation of the UK's Anti-money Laundering and Asset Recovery Regime." *Crime, Law and Social Change* 47.1 (2007): 169–184.

Susanto, Elik. "A Peculiar Verdict." *Le Tempo*, Jakarta. April 1, 2008.

Swiss Federal Banking Commission. "SFBC orders removal of bank's general manager." Press Release, Swiss Federal Banking Commission, Berne. November 13, 2001.

Swiss Federal Office of Justice. "Montesinos Case: Switzerland Transfers 77 million US Dollars to Peru." Press release, Swiss Federal Office of Justice, Berne, August 20, 2002.

Swissmoney Research. *Bank News 1999–2000*. Crawley, England, 2000.

Swire, Mary. "Phillipines Enquiry Hears About Marcos Money In Liechtenstein." Hong Kong: *Tax-News.com*, May 16, 2002.

Takats, Elod. "A Theory of 'Crying Wolf': The Economics of Money Laundering Enforcement." IMF Working Paper 07/81. Washington DC, 2007.

Tanzi, Vito. "Corruption, Governmental Activities, and Markets," IMF Working Paper 94/99, 1 September 1994, Washington DC.

Townsend Commission. "Investigating Commission on the performance and the origin, movement and destiny of the financial resources of Vladimiro Montesinos Torres and their evident relationship with ex-President Alberto Fujimori." Investigation by Congresswoman Ana Elena Townsend, Government of Peru, Lima, June 25, 2002.

Transparency International. *National Integrity Systems Country Study Report Vanuatu*. Berlin: Transparency International, 2004.

——. *National Integrity Systems Questionnaire: The Gambia*. Berlin: Transparency International, 2004.

——. *Global Corruption Report*. Berlin: Transparency International, 2004.

——. *Global Corruption Report*. Berlin: Transparency International, 2007.

——. *Monitoring UNCAC. Position Paper 2008/1*. Berlin: Transparency International, 2008.

Tujan Jr, Antonio. "Japan ODA to the Philippines." In *The Reality of Aid*, edited by Antonio Tujan Jr, 137–149. Manila: Ibon Foundation, 2005.

United Nations Office on Drugs and Crime. *Report of the Informal Expert Working Group on Mutual Legal Assistance Casework Best Practice*. Vienna: UNODC, 2001.

——. *UN Anti-Corruption Toolkit*, third edition. Vienna: UNODC, 2004.

——. "A New Extradition System: A Review of Australia's Extradition Law and Practice." Submission to the Australian Federal Attorney-General's Department, 2006.

——. *Legislative Guide for the Implementation of the United Nations Convention against Corruption*. Vienna: UNODC, 2006.

United Nations Office on Drugs and Crime/World Bank. *Stolen Assets Recovery (StAR) Initiative: Challenges, Opportunities and Action Plan*. Washington DC: UNODC, 2007.

United States Department of Justice. *US v. Pavel Lazarenko*, United States Sentencing Memorandum, Response to Defendant's Sentencing Memorandum, August 18, 2006. Available at http://www.usdoj.gov/usao/can/press/press_documents/Lazarenko%20Sentencing%20Memo.pdf.

United States District Court for the Southern District of New York. *A Retrospective (1990–2000)*. The New York County Lawyers' Association Committee On The Federal Courts December 2002. Available at http://www.nycla.org/publications/fedcts.pdf.

United States Federal Financial Institutions Examination Council. Bank Secrecy Act/Anti-Money Laundering Examination Manual. Washington DC: 2006. Available at http://www.ffiec.gov/pdf/bsa_aml_examination_manual2006.pdf.

United States House of Representatives. *Nigeria's Struggle with Corruption, Hearing before the Subcommittee on Africa*, Global Human Rights and International Operations of the Committee on International Relations, 109th Congress, Second Session, Washington DC: United States House of Representatives, May 18, 2006.

United States Senate. *Private Banking and Money Laundering: A Case Study of Opportunities and Vulnerabilities*. Washington DC: United States Senate, 2000.

——. *Correspondent Banking: A Gateway for Money Laundering*. Washington DC: United States Senate, 2001.

——. *Role of US Correspondent Banking in International Money Laundering*. Washington DC: United States Senate, 2001.

United States Treasury. *US Money Laundering Threat Assessment*. Washington DC: 2005.

——. *Guidance on Enhanced Scrutiny for Transactions that may involve the Proceeds of Foreign Official Corruption*. Washington DC: January 2001. Available at http://www.occ.treas.gov/ftp/bulletin/2001–9a.pdf.

Van Fossen, Anthony. "Money Laundering, Global Financial Instability and Tax Havens in the Pacific Islands." *Contemporary Pacific* 15.2 (2003): 237–275.

——. *Sovereignty for Sale in the Pacific*. Honolulu: University of Hawai'i Press, 2009.

Walker, Frank. Letter from Chief Minister Frank Walker of Jersey to Hugh Bayley, Chair of the Africa APPG of the British House of Commons. London: April 10, 2006.

Webb, Philippa. "United Nations Convention Against Corruption: Global Achievement or Missed Opportunity?" *Journal of International Economic Law* 8.1 (2005), 191–229.

Wechsler, William F. "Follow the Money." *Foreign Affairs* 80.4 (2001): 40–57.

Williams, David. "Governance, Security and 'Development': The Case of Money Laundering." City University of London Working Paper on Transnational Politics CUTP/001, London, United Kingdom, 2008.

Winmill, Lynn B. "Anti-Money Laundering Law and Cases in the United States." APEC/National Counter Corruption Commission. Workshop. Bangkok, 2007

Wolff, Craig. "Marcos Said to Have Wept for Gift of Skyscraper from Her Husband." *New York Times*, April 10, 1990.

——. "Witness Calls Commissions Routine in Marcos Dealings." *New York Times*, April 180, 1990.

——. "Marcos Was Not a Thief, Defense Says in Summation." *New York Times*, June 27, 1990.

——. "The Marcos Verdict; Marcos Is Cleared of All Charges in Racketeering and Fraud Case." *New York Times*, July 3, 1990.

Wolfsberg Group. Wolfsberg AML Principles on Private Banking. Basel: May 2002. Available at http://www.wolfsberg-principles.com/standards.html.

——. Wolfsberg Statement against Corruption. Basel: February 2007.

——. *Frequently Asked Questions on Politically Exposed Persons*. Basel: May 2008. Available at http://www.wolfsberg-principles.com/faq.html.

World Bank. *Helping Countries Combat Corruption: The Role of the World Bank*. Washington DC: World Bank, 1997.

——. *World Development Report: The State in a Changing World*. Washington DC: World Bank, 1997.

——. *Literature Survey on Corruption 2000–2005*. Washington DC: World Bank, 2006.

——. *Utilization of the Repatriated Abacha Loot: Results of the Field Monitoring Study*. Washington DC: World Bank, 2006.

——. *Strengthening Bank Group Engagement on Governance and Anti-Corruption*. Washington DC: World Bank, 2007.

World Bank and Nigerian Federal Ministry of Finance. *Utilization of Repatriated Abacha Loot*. Abuja: December 2006. Available at http://siteresources.worldbank.org/INTNIGERIA/Resources/Abacha_Funds_Monitoring_1221.pdf.

World Check. *Politically Exposed Person: Refining the PEP Definition*. Edition II. Global Objectives Ltd: April 2008. Available at http://www.world-check.com/media/d/content_whitepaper_reference/Refining_the_PEP_Definition_-_EditionII.pdf.

Zobel, Enrique J. Deposition dated October 27, 1999. Submitted to the Senate Committee on Accountability and Public Officers and Investigations and Committee on Banks, Financial Institutions and Currencies. Manila: Republic of Philippines Senate, 1999.

Index

Abacha, General Sani, 53, 73, 92, 111, 136
  repatriation of assets from Switzerland, 134, 146–148
ADB/OECD Anti-Corruption Action for Asia and the Pacific, 33, 38, 46–48, 116–118, 120, 126
  asset recovery and asset sharing, 47, 139–148
  denying safe havens to the corrupt and proceeds of corruption, 116–117
  see also Asian Development Bank, OECD Anti-Bribery Convention
Afghanistan, 103, 120
Alamieyeseigha, Governor Diepreye, 89
Antigua, 138
anti-money laundering (AML), *see* money laundering, problems and solutions
Aquino, Baltazar, 159
Aquino, President Corazon, 92, 180
Araneta, Irene Marcos, 156
Argentina, 17, 41, 44, 51
Asia Pacific Group on Money Laundering (APG), 18–19, 40, 50
  legal status of international instruments among APG members, 120, 149
  see also Egmont Group, FATF, FATF/APG Projects Group
Asian Development Bank (ADB), 3, 4, 8, 46
  see also ADB/OECD
asset confiscation, 47, 53–54, 60, 118, 122, 132, 138, 139, 140–141, 144–145, 190, 197
  see also civil forfeiture
asset recovery and asset sharing, 136, 139–141, 175–176
asset registries, 63–65
Australia, 13, 51, 52, 60, 111, 117, 145, 174
  Australian Transaction Reports and Analysis Centre (AUSTRAC), 64, 149, 150, 151
  lack of foreign bribery convictions, 59
  legal status of international instruments, 120, 123, 149
  review of extradition and mutual legal assistance, 131, 136
Australian Wheat Board, 13, 150
  see also Australia, UN oil-for-food scandal

Bahamas, 79, 138
Bank for International Settlements, 86
Bank of New York, 61, 75–77
  see also Russia
bank secrecy, 39, 52, 134–135, 152, 171–172, 177, 179
Barbados, 29
Basel Committee on Banking Supervision, 83, 86
Belgium, 35, 84, 103
Benedicto, Roberto, 156, 164, 183

beneficial ownership, 40, 63, 79, 81, 83, 100, 101, 102, 103, 107, 109, 110, 115, 194, 195
impossible to establish in 47 states in US, 78
Marcos case, 170, 171, 179
Montesinos case, 142
study of misuse of corporate vehicles, 77–78
Berlin, Peter, 76
Berlusconi, Prime Minister Silvio, 88
blacklisting of countries, 19, 40, 50, 56, 75, 76, 192
Blair, Prime Minister Tony, 72
bogus contracts, 88
Bolanos, President Enriques, 92
Braithwaite, John, 10
Brazil, 17, 41, 55, 84, 98, 103
British Aerospace (BAE) and the Al-Yamamah Case, 37, 61, 71–74, 194, 198
British Virgin Islands, 71, 72, 79

Campos, Jose Yao, 156–157, 170
Canada, 53, 102, 120, 123, 125, 133, 149
Carino, Oscar, 160
Cayman Islands, 134, 141
Chavez, Francisco, 178, 180
Chile, 41, 80, 89–90
Chiluba, Frederick Jacobi Titus, 146
China, 13, 17, 19, 60, 64, 117, 120, 121, 129
Chirac, President Jacques, 87–88
civil forfeiture, 54, 144–145
see also asset confiscation
Cojuangco, Eduardo, 164
Commonwealth, 26, 29, 43, 46, 68, 105, 118, 132, 148
Working Group on Asset Repatriation, 118, 128, 146
Congo, 44
constitutions, 65, 87, 88, 89, 120, 129, 132, 133, 166, 176, 180
corruption
active bribery, 8, 123–125
behest loans and odious debts, 164–166
crony capitalism, 100, 153, 156, 162–166
definition and overview, 8–14
embezzlement, 1, 8, 26, 34, 85, 88, 90, 130, 133, 138, 140, 157, 160
explanation for development failures, 7
financial intelligence not used, 22
foreign bribery, 9, 10, 14, 41
grand corruption, 2, 3, 5, 7, 8, 9, 42, 51, 83, 86, 91–92, 101, 107, 115, 116, 118, 128, 139–140
illicit enrichment, 64–65, 132–134, 172–173
judicial system, 68–70, 81
kleptocracy, 42, 153–186
passive bribery, 8, 34, 178
pork barrel, 160–161
prevention, 61, 62, 63, 65–67
private sector corruption, 61, 74–75, 78
public procurement, 10
see also corruption/money laundering, problems and solutions
corruption/money laundering, 39, 83
disconnect and nexus, 21–27
similarity of crimes, 51
use of AML systems in anti-corruption, 27–30
Council of Europe
anti-corruption and anti-money laundering conventions, 118–119
GRECO, 74, 193
Cyclone Betsy, 24–27
see also Korman, Vanuatu

Davies, Governor Joshua, 89
developing countries
different perspective on corruption, 55
lack of ownership of anti-corruption and AML policies, 22

Disini, Herminio, 156, 164, 180
Duvalier, Jean-Claude, 53, 127–128, 136

economic espionage, 137
Edwards, Lucy, 76
Egmont Group, 45, 67, 78, 148–149
Estrada, President Josef (Erap), 99, 195
European Banking Industry Committee, 95
European Commission, 83, 85, 134
extradition, 128 -131
  delay and costs, 129, 131
  dual criminality, 130–131
  nationals, 129–130
  prima facie rule, 128
  see also international co-operation

FATF/APG Projects Group, 48, 149
  independence and capacity, 67–68
  points of vulnerability and solutions, 62–63
  role in international co-operation, 148–151
  study on links between corruption and money laundering, 51
  see also Egmont Group, suspicious transaction reports
Financial Action Task Force (FATF)
  40 + 9 Recommendations, 17, 18, 30, 49, 85, 125–126, 129, 132, 139
  blacklisting, 19–20
  peer assessment, 18, 19, 37
  regional-style FATF bodies, 18–19, 55
  see also APG, Egmont Group, FATF/APG
Floriendo, Antonio, 156, 164, 176
France, 35, 53, 87–88, 92, 128, 129
  see also Chirac
Fujimori, President Alberto, 130, 141, 144

Gabon, 85
Gambia, 87
Gapud, Rolando, 156–157
Garrido, Victor Alberto Venero, 142, 145
Germany, 35, 79, 121, 174
Gibraltar, 79
Giminez, Roa, 160
Goldsmith, Lord, 72
governance, 32, 42, 55
  OECD Public Governance and Management group (PUMA), 10
  World Bank and Egmont Group project on governance of FIUs, 45
Guernsey, 79, 146

Hong Kong, 24, 50, 51, 62, 65, 101, 133, 167
  legal status of international instruments, 120, 123, 149
  priority for private sector corruption, 60, 75
  role in Marcos case, 169, 170, 174
Hussein, President Saddam, 13, 150
Hutchcroft, Paul, 163

immunities, 86–90, 127–128, 138, 176
  see also international co-operation
India, 13, 17, 44, 51, 60, 64, 65, 120, 133, 149
Indonesia, 51, 53, 60–61, 96, 100, 117, 120, 121, 133, 146, 149, 195
international co-operation, 115–152, 174–184
  civil forfeiture, 144–145, 173–174
  civil proceedings, 146
  delay and costs, 135–137, 142–143, 176–177
  dual criminality, 132–134
  immunities, 127–128
  international best practice, 125–126, 149
  jurisdiction, 126–127
  mutual legal assistance, 132–137

international co-operation—*Continued*
treaties, 118
see also Abacha, asset recovery, extradition, Lazarenko, Marcos, Montesinos
International Monetary Fund (IMF), 8, 13, 18, 43, 107, 118
adopts FATF AML's standards in assessments, 20, 54
corruption causes macroeconomic failures, 11
Isle of Man, 76, 79, 80, 146
Italy, 9, 88, 91, 92

Jacobi, Reiner, 167
Japan, 60, 64, 120, 121, 129, 130, 159
Jenkins, Judge Martin, 139
Jersey (Channel Islands), 79, 98, 111, 146
Jimmy, Willie, 26
Juppé, Prime Minister Alain, 88

Kasper-Ansermet, Laurent, 138
Kazakhstan, 47, 64, 147
Keenan, Judge, 181, 182
Kenya, 44, 68, 71, 189
Khashoggi, Adnan, 181
Khomenei, Ayatollah, 96
Korea, South, 41, 51, 60, 64, 120, 123, 129, 149
Korman, Prime Minister Maxime Carlot, 24–27

Lacayo, President José Arnoldo Alemán, 92, 145
Lazarenko, Prime Minister Pavlo Ivanovich, 113, 116, 151
Swiss and US criminal proceedings, 137–139
legal mutual assistance, *see* international co-operation
Leymang, Gerald, 24
Liechtenstein, 52, 72
see also bank secrecy, Marcos
Lopez Sr, Eugenio, 163
Luxembourg, 35, 142

Macao, 117, 120, 129
Malaysia, 24, 25, 51, 60, 64, 65, 120, 133, 149, 198
Maluf, Mayor Paulo, 98
Manapat, Ricardo, 156, 160, 164
Manotoc, Imelda Romualdez Marcos (Imee), 155
Marcos, Ferdinand Edralin, 6, 92, 153–186
asset recovery, 53, 162, 168, 173–174, 175–176
corruption, 155, 158–166, 171–172
criminal prosecution, 165–166, 175–176, 179–185
crony capitalism, 153, 156–157, 162–166
international co-operation, 174–184
Liechtenstein, 153, 170–171, 174, 177, 178–179, 183
size of stolen wealth, 166–167, 168, 172–173, 177
Switzerland, 156, 162, 163, 167, 171–172, 176–178, 183, 185
United States, 153, 158–159, 160, 174, 175–176, 180–182, 185
see also money laundering, Philippines
Marcos, Imelda Romualdez, 153, 154, 165, 168, 174
criminal trials, 165–166, 175–176, 179–185
politician, 155
Marcos Jnr, Ferdinand Romualdez (Bongbong), 156
Mauritius, 29, 68
Mexico, 35, 41, 70, 84, 85, 103–104, 112
money laundering
anti-money laundering (AML) systems, 18, 19, 54, 87, 105–108
bearer shares, 59, 183, 192, 195

corporate service providers, 74–75, 77–80
definition and overview, 14–21
EU Third Money Laundering Directive, 83, 98–99, 102, 104–105
lawyers, 52–53, 72, 171–172, 178
money laundering techniques in Marcos case, 167–172
offshore, 9, 51, 169
proceeds of bribery, 34, 139
relationship to predicate offences, 14, 15, 23, 29, 148
shell banks, 76
shell corporations, 5, 14, 25, 61, 73, 75–79, 101, 194
typologies, 35, 50, 51, 80, 85, 190
vulnerabilities of AML systems to corruption, 59–81
see also APG, FATF, predicate offences, problems and solutions
Montesinos, Vladimir, 54, 113, 116, 136
Swiss and Peruvian proceedings, 141–144
see also Peru

Nauru, 75–77
Nepal, 64, 65, 117, 120
net worth, 172–173, 177, 186
New Zealand, 12, 120, 121, 123, 125, 149
Nicaragua, 70, 92, 145, 147
Niger, 29
Nigeria, 68, 73, 85, 89, 92, 111, 136, 146–147
Non Co-operative Countries and Territories, *see* blacklisting, FATF

OECD Anti-Bribery Convention, 9, 10, 14, 33–38, 41–42, 120, 123–125
demand side of corruption, 119
mid-term review, 34–35
peer review, 11, 34, 36, 37, 192
Working Group on Bribery, 10, 22
see also ADB/OECD, British Aerospace
Operation Big Bird, 167
Operation Domino, 167
Ordonez, Sedfrey, 166
Organization of American States (OAS), 10, 26, 38, 56, 119, 133
Osmena, Senator, 165

Pakistan, 47, 50, 51, 64, 85, 117, 120, 133
Pampilo Jr, Judge Silvino, 184
Panama, 52, 137, 170, 177
Papua New Guinea, 12, 64, 117
Peru, 42, 54, 113, 130, 136, 141–144, 145
see also Montesinos
Philippines, 3, 53, 54, 64, 65, 127, 133, 134, 136, 145
legal status of international instruments, 120, 121, 149
politically exposed persons, 92, 99, 100, 113
Supreme Court, 134, 154, 166, 173, 174, 183, 186
see also Estrada, Marcos
Pinochet, General Augusto, 80, 89–90
politically exposed persons (PEPs), 83 -113
business associates, 100–101
control of public assets, 95, 115, 155
corporations, 101, 169–171
family member and relatives, 98–100
identification, 92–101, 111–12
immunities, 86–90
investigatory challenges, 92, 180–181
national PEPS, 101–104
religious leaders and charities, 95–96
risks, 85–86, 91
rules and processes, 105–112
US law, 100, 103, 108–109

predicate offences, 136, 139, 175, 182, 188, 189, 192, 196, 197
  bribery of foreign officials, 11, 33
  corruption as predicate offence to money laundering, 22, 35, 39, 60
  jurisdictional competency of FIUs, 149
Previti, Cesare, 88
problems and solutions
  balancing means and ends, 198
  corruption-proofing AML systems, 193–195
  eliminating defects in politically exposed persons rules, 195–196
  enhancing international co-operation, 196–198
  implementing international agreements, 191–193
prosecutorial independence, 71, 73–74, 194
  see also British Aerospace

Ramos, President Fidel, 165
Reagan, President Ronald, 181
Riggs Bank, 80
Rios, General Nicolas de Bari Hermoza, 142, 143
Rivera, Hector, 183
Romualdez, Benjamin (Kokoy), 163
Rosario, Caesario del, 184
Roxas, Manuel, 154
Roxas, Roger, 161
Russia, 13, 17, 61, 75–77, 78, 94, 142
  see also Bank of New York

Sandiganbayan (anti-corruption court), 180, 182, 183
  see also Marcos
Saudi Arabia, 61, 71, 72, 73
senior public figures, *see* PEPs
Shah of Iran
  Pahlavi foundation, 96
Siba, Luc, 26
Singapore, 24, 25, 60, 65, 75, 117, 120, 121, 133, 134, 149, 153, 174
Solomon Islands, 103, 120
South Africa, 17, 33, 41, 51, 55, 123
Spence, Gerry, 182
Sri Lanka, 103, 117, 120
Stolen Assets Recovery (StAR) initiative, 3, 42–46, 56
  see also UNODC, World Bank
Suharto, Hutomo Manaul Putra (Tommy), 146
Suharto, President Mohamed, 53, 61, 96
suspicious transaction reports (STRs), 18, 23, 28, 39, 52, 54–60, 78, 102, 104, 144, 148
  low number in relation to bribery offences, 34–36
  see also Egmont Group, money laundering
Switzerland
  British Aerospace, 72, 73
  obstacles to international co-operation, 132, 135, 136, 137, 162
  PEPs, 83, 108
  policy on dual criminality, 132, 133, 134
  policy on repatriating illicit assets, 147
  Supreme Court, 127–128, 134, 147, 173, 176, 186
  see also Abacha, bank secrecy, Marcos

Taiwan, 19, 120, 123, 149
Tan, Lucio, 156, 164
Tantoco, Bienvenido, 156
Tantoco, Glecy, 164
  tax deductible bribes, 10, 37, 38, 60
  tax evasion, 38, 75, 76, 85, 88, 90, 104, 134, 145, 163, 172, 183, 194
  tax havens, 20, 52, 76
  tax information, 38, 53, 64, 70, 81, 134, 193

Thailand, 48, 51, 60, 64, 65, 91, 117, 120, 149
Than, Paul, 24
Timor, East, 103
Transparency International, 14, 42, 118
  Corruption Perceptions Index, 12, 107
  Bribe Payers' Index, 13
  Global Corruption Report, 69
Turkey, 87

Uduaghan, Governor Emmanuel Ewetan, 89
Ukraine, 137–139
  see also Lazarenko
United Kingdom, 48, 52, 61, 65, 69, 79, 105, 133, 134, 145, 146, 189
  dual position of Attorney-General, 73–74
  lack of foreign bribery convictions, 59
  see also British Aerospace
United Nations Convention against Corruption (UNCAC), 38–42
  anti-money laundering requirements, 28, 148, 151
  asset recovery, 41, 47, 139–141
  implementation weaknesses, 36, 41, 43, 56
  international co-operation, 116, 122, 127, 131, 132, 134–135, 136, 137, 146
  legal status, 27, 49, 120, 121
  linkage of anti-corruption and AML requirements, 39, 40
  PEPs, 84, 86, 93, 102, 104, 105, 111
  wide coverage of corruption-type offences, 8, 65, 66, 75
  see also UNODC, problems and solutions
United Nations Office on Drugs and Crime (UNODC), 17, 38–42, 63, 131
  see also StAR initiative
United Nations oil-for-food scandal, 94, 150–151
United Nations Security Council, 36, 148
United States
  asset repatriation, 54, 66, 144, 145
  Bank Secrecy Act, 80, 108–110, 145
  Financial Crimes Enforcement Network (FinCEN), 149
  flawed regulation of domestic shell corporations, 78, 194
  Foreign Corrupt Practices Act, 9–10
  implementation successes, 29, 35, 47
  lawyers not subject to STR requirement, 53
  leadership and policy influence, 7, 9, 10, 13, 14, 15, 16, 20, 54, 55, 129
  legal status of international instruments, 120, 123, 125, 149
  Patriot Act, 80, 83, 92, 94, 98
  RICO Act, 15, 160, 162, 165, 166, 175, 181, 182, 185
  senior foreign political figure, 100, 103, 104
  Supreme Court, 153, 161
  see also Bank of New York, beneficial ownership, Lazarenko, Marcos

Vanuatu, 8, 23–27, 29, 30, 64, 79, 117, 120, 149, 189
  see also Cyclone Betsy, Korman
Velasco, Geronimo, 156
Vietnam, 64, 117, 120, 158
Vithlani, Sailesh, 73

Wang, Victor Joy, 142
Wolfensohn, James, 11
  see also World Bank
Wolfowitz, Paul, 44
  see also World Bank

Wolfsberg Group, 94, 95
World Bank, 11–12, 118, 147, 158, 169
  anti-corruption programs, 32, 45–46
  corruption in borrower governments, 44, 46
  research projects on corruption and money laundering, 45–46
  role in repatriation of Abacha assets, 147
  see also governance, StAR initiative

Yamashita, General Tomoyuki, 161

Zambia, 146